Curriculum Renewal in School Foreign Language Learning

Curriculum Renewal in School Foreign Language Learning

John L. Clark

Oxford University Press

Oxford University Press
Walton Street, Oxford OX2 6DP

Oxford   New York   Toronto
Delhi Bombay Calcutta Madras Karachi
Petaling Jaya Singapore   Hong Kong   Tokyo
Nairobi   Dar es Salaam   Cape Town
Melbourne   Auckland

and associated companies in
Berlin   Ibadan

OXFORD is a trade mark of Oxford University Press

ISBN 0 19 437101 8

First published 1987
Second impression 1988

© J. L. Clark 1987

Typeset by Wyvern Typesetting Ltd, Bristol.
Printed in Hong Kong.

To Nirina, Andrew, and Mialy, without whose love and understanding nothing would have been written.

To the many modern language teachers and pupils, without whose commitment and co-operation in the two projects described in this book nothing could have been written.

Contents

viii

Acknowledgements

I am extremely grateful to Tony Howatt, who supervised me in the writing of the thesis which inspired this book. His professional guidance and friendly encouragement over the years have been invaluable.

I am deeply indebted to Judith Hamilton, who worked with me in the development of the GLAFLL project, and to Angela Scarino, who assisted me in the development of the ALL project, both of whose practical insights and creativity have permeated my thinking in many areas.

I am immensely grateful to Peter Wheeldon, Henry Widdowson, Ann Harding, Dieca Cumming, David Peat, Jean Casey, Alex Sharp, Bill Gatherer, Eric Smith, Roger Williams, David Beale, and many others who were kind enough to offer me support and advice at various moments in the writing of this book.

Last, but by no means least, I am deeply grateful to Lorna Sinclair, Margaret Thomson, Lynn Orr, and Nirina Clark who smiled their way patiently through the trials and tribulations of typing and retyping my unseemly and ever-changing scripts.

The publishers would like to thank John Steinle, Director-General of Education in South Australia and the Management Committee of the ALL Project for permission to quote from the ALL Project.

Acknowledgements are made to the following for their permission to reproduce the following material:

Centre for Information on Language Teaching and Research for the framework of Stages and Levels on page 143 and the progress card on page 148, published in *Syllabus Guidelines: Parts 1, 2, and 3*.

Acronyms and abbreviations

The following are among the more traditional acronyms and abbreviations used in this book:

EFL: English as a Foreign Language
ESL: English as a Second Language
INSET: In-service Education and Training
L1:   First Language, i.e. mother tongue
L2:   Second or Foreign Language
LOTE: Languages Other Than English

Other acronyms and abbreviations that may be less familiar are:

CCC: Central Committee on the Curriculum (Scotland)
CILT: Centre for Information on Language Teaching (London)
CSE: Certificate of Secondary Education (England)
DES: Department of Education and Science (England)
GOML: Graded Objectives in Modern Languages
H Grade: Higher Grade – a Scottish examination normally taken in the fifth year of secondary school (age 17+)
HMI: Her Majesty's Inspectorate
NFER: National Foundation for Educational Research
O Grade: Ordinary Grade – a Scottish examination normally taken in the fourth year of secondary school (age 16+)
OMLAC: Oxfordshire Modern Language Achievement Certificate
S1 up to S6: Secondary first year in Scotland (pupils aged 12) up to Secondary sixth year
SCCML: Scottish Central Committee on Modern Languages
SEB: Scottish Examination Board
SED: Scottish Education Department

Other more local acronyms and abbreviations:

ALL: Australian Language Levels
GLAFLL: Graded Levels of Achievement in Foreign Language Learning
RSGML: Regional Study Group on Modern Languages (A Lothian Region group)

Preface

> But you, who are wise, must know, that different Nations have different Conceptions of things and you will therefore not take it amiss, if our Ideas of this Kind of Education happen not to be the same as yours. We have had some Experience of it. Several of our young people were formerly brought up at the Colleges of the Northern Provinces: they were instructed in all your Sciences; but, when they came back to us, they were Bad Runners, ignorant of every means of living in the woods . . . neither fit for Hunters, Warriors, nor Counsellors, they were totally good for nothing.
>
> We are, however, not the less oblig'd by your kind Offer, tho' we decline accepting it: and, to show our Grateful Sense of it, if the Gentlemen of Virginia will send us a Dozen of their Sons, we will take Care of their Education, instruct them in all we know, and make Men of them.
>
> Response of the Indians of the Six Nations to a suggestion that they send boys to an American College in Pennsylvania, 1744.

The above quotation underlines the fact that education is required to serve the particular values of the society in which it is placed. What may be found suitable in one context may not necessarily be found appropriate in another. What is found adequate for today may be considered of little use tomorrow. This is as true of language education as it is of any other area in the school curriculum. It is the current social value placed upon foreign language learning in general, and upon certain languages in particular that will determine such things as:

— whether to include languages other than the mother tongue in the school curriculum
— which languages to include
— to whom to teach them and for how long
— what objectives to seek to achieve

Despite the obvious socio-political background to decisions about language teaching, it has become customary to view school foreign language learning from a narrow subject-specific point of view, as if its development were determined uniquely by hypotheses and practices generated by applied linguistics. The view taken in this book, however, is that a language curriculum is a function of the inter-relationships that hold between subject-specific concerns and other broader factors embracing socio-political and philosophical matters, educational value systems, theory and practice in curriculum design, teacher experiential wisdom and learner motivation. In order to understand the foreign language curriculum in any particular context it is therefore necessary to attempt to understand how all the various influences interrelate to give a particular shape to the planning and execution of the teaching/learning process.

Given the diverse and conflicting values that exist within any large social group, and given a democratic concern for the valuing of such diversity, it would seem necessary for any contemporary curriculum to attempt to embody what are agreed to be common aspirations, and yet leave space for individual interpretation within and beyond these, to accord with the individual characteristics of each teaching and learning context. The search for an ideal foreign language curriculum to apply in all circumstances and at all times is illusory. This book, on the contrary, points to the need for educational systems to seek to ensure that there is an adequate framework and process within which those concerned can work together for a continual context-sensitive renewal of interim curricular constructs, such as syllabuses, assessment schemes, resources, and teaching/learning strategies, within a broad policy for languages in education, which is itself also subject to frequent review. The need for a framework which permits constant renewal is highlighted by the fact that the act of renewal itself leads to unintended and sometimes unwelcome outcomes, which in their turn call for further renewal, in the effort to reconcile effect with intention.

I have chosen to refer to change in the curriculum by the term *curriculum renewal*, in preference to the more usual term *curriculum development*, since it indicates rather more clearly that the exercise does not often start from scratch, but from an existing state of affairs, and does not stop at the production of some new examination or some new curriculum package to be used in schools, but implies an ongoing process of refinement and re-creation.

By the term *curriculum renewal* in foreign language learning I refer to attempts to effect change in the various interrelated parts that go to make up the foreign language curriculum. These include:

– the review of principles to guide the language teaching/learning process in the light of applied linguistic theory and classroom experience

- the reworking of syllabuses embodying aims, objectives, a content
  and a broad methodology
- the review of classroom teaching/learning strategies
- the choice, adaptation and creation of resources embodying
  appropriate learning experiences
- the review of assessment designed to monitor, record, report, and
  provide feedback on learner progress
- the review of classroom schemes of work relating all of the above
  together
- the review and creation of strategies designed to assist teachers to
  evaluate classroom practices and to improve on them
- the identification of areas for research to determine possible ways
  forward in any of the above areas
- the review or devising of in-service education designed to assist
  teachers to widen their conceptual and pragmatic base in
  particular areas, and to find solutions to their own classroom
  problems

Curriculum renewal can perhaps best be likened to the creation of a
never-ending jigsaw puzzle, in which the various pieces are cut and
recut to fit together into a whole that is itself evolving to respond to
changing insights and values. A change made to the shape of one part
of the jigsaw will inevitably affect other parts. For example, a change
in what is to be assessed will normally lead to changes in classroom
practices, just as a change in the goals and content of classroom
learning implies a change in what is to be assessed. All too often,
however, attempts have been made to make changes in one part of
the curriculum jigsaw, without foreseeing that this implies changes in
other parts. Thus curriculum planners who operate from outside the
classroom have often introduced changes to school syllabuses or
assessment procedures, but have then failed to support teachers to
create the resources and to develop the necessary teaching strategies
to carry them through in the classroom. This book, therefore, points
not just to the need for an evolutionary approach to curriculum
renewal, but also to the need for coherence in the bringing about of
change.

This book is set out in two parts. Part One attempts a general
theoretical study of the various influences and constraints on
contemporary school foreign language learning. I have chosen to do
this through the framework of three broad educational value systems
suggested by Skilbeck (1982a), each of which embodies a constella-
tion of socio-political and philosophical beliefs. These permit me to

attempt to trace the interrelationships that hold between these and particular approaches to curriculum design, curriculum renewal and language teaching. A critique is then made of each value system and of the practices to which it gives rise. The conclusion is drawn that curriculum renewal in a pluralistic society should aim to integrate the best features of each of the three value systems and reconcile the apparent tensions between them in some principled way.

Part Two is an attempt to describe curriculum renewal in school foreign language learning in action through the medium of two projects – the Graded Levels of Achievement in Foreign Language Learning (GLAFLL) project, which was based in Lothian Region's schools in and around Edinburgh in Scotland, and the initial work in the Australian Language Levels (ALL) project, based in Adelaide, which is concerned with the preparation of curriculum guidelines for the teaching of all languages other than English in Australian schools. The latter is presented as a practical attempt to create a curriculum renewal process and a curriculum model which integrate the best features of each of the three value systems outlined in Part One.

PART ONE

The effects of different educational value systems

Introduction

In Part One of this book I attempt to study the way in which educational value systems embodying particular constellations of socio-political and philosophical beliefs are reflected in curriculum design, in the foreign language curriculum, and in policies for curriculum renewal. In order to do this I have adopted a conceptual framework set out by Skilbeck (1982a). He identified three broad value systems permeating the contemporary educational process. These were classical humanism, reconstructionism, and progressivism. These value systems are of course extremely broad categorizations and are not watertight compartments, but rather constellations of differently inspired principles and practices, some of which overlap.

In education, classical humanism is knowledge-oriented and is concerned with promoting intellectual and cultural values; reconstructionism is society-oriented and is concerned with the promotion of agreed social goals; progressivism is concerned with the development of individuals, and with the value of diversity. I am indebted to Skilbeck (1982a) for the broad outline of these three value systems, though I must accept the responsibility for any distortion of his original formulation in my application of them to the various areas with which this book is concerned.

In Chapter 1 classical humanism is briefly examined, since it is from classical humanist roots that recent curriculum renewal in schools has sprung. Indeed recent changes to the foreign language curriculum can perhaps best be described as the attempt to move away from classical humanist practices towards something more egalitarian on the one hand, and more learner-centred on the other. Egalitarianism is represented in reconstructionism, which is described in Chapter 2. Learner-centredness is represented in progressivism, which is examined in Chapter 3.

Within each chapter an introductory analysis is made of the broad characteristics of each value system, before examining its effects upon curriculum design, the foreign language curriculum and curriculum renewal. A critique is then made of each value system, highlighting the problems to which it gives rise.

In Chapter 4 a summary of each value system and its effects is given in tabular form, and an attempt is made to work towards some sort of reconciliation of the tensions between the various value systems, so that important and valuable features of each may be incorporated within a broader approach.

1 Classical humanism

1.1 Introduction

Classical humanism can be traced back to Plato, and to the concept of the education of an élite of guardians to govern the state.

Skilbeck's (1982a) analysis of a classical humanist approach to education indicates that it is characterized above all by the desire to promote broad intellectual capacities, such as memorization and the ability to analyse, classify, and reconstruct elements of knowledge, so that these capacities can be brought to bear on the various challenges likely to be encountered in life. Knowledge is seen as a set of revealed truths, whose underlying rules and regularities should be studied and consciously mastered. The teacher is seen as someone who possesses knowledge and whose task it is to pass it on to the learners in his/her charge. The task of the learners is to acquire knowledge and to become consciously aware of the rules underlying it, in order to control it and apply it in new contexts. There is much emphasis in the classroom on study, on conscious understanding, on reflection and awareness, and on the controlled application of knowledge. Just as knowledge is to be passed on from generation to generation, so cultural values are to be transmitted through the hidden curriculum, and through the study of works of proven moral and artistic value, whose inherent merits are then celebrated.

In the British state education system, as in many others throughout the world, classical humanism has been made to work through creating two distinct types of secondary education – a grammar or senior secondary school for the élite, who are to become the nation's guardians, and a secondary modern or junior secondary school for the masses. It has been argued that both types of school are concerned with the maintenance and promotion of two distinct, if overlapping, cultures. The élite are introduced to 'high' culture and abstract intellectual thinking, in order to promote their generalizable intellectual capacities and critical judgement, while the masses follow a more practical curriculum in tune with their less abstract life-style and their more practical vocational and leisure-time expectations (Bantock 1968).

Classical humanist concern for the maintenance of standards has usually led to the establishment of a powerful corps of national inspectors charged with the task of observing and reporting on school practices and standards in general. It has also led to the setting up of prestigious examination boards, whose task it is to create examinations that will select an appropriately sized élite and eliminate others from entry to the next level of education. In order to ensure that academic traditions and standards are maintained, the universities, as guardians of the nation's wisdom, have effectively controlled the school examination system, which in its turn has determined what has to be done in the classroom.

In brief, we can summarize classical humanism as concerned with:

– the maintenance and transmission through education of the wisdom and culture of previous generations. This has led to the creation of a two-tier system of education – one to accord with the 'higher' cultural traditions of an élite, and the other to cater for the more concrete and practical life-styles of the masses
– the development for the élite of generalizable intellectual capacities and critical faculties
– the maintenance of standards through an inspectorate and external examinations boards controlled by the universities.

1.2   Classical humanism in curriculum design

The design of a curriculum depends essentially upon the particular way in which objectives, content, and methodology are interrelated, and upon the emphasis that is placed upon each of them. Classical humanism places its emphasis on content, reconstructionism on objectives, and progressivism on methodology, thus giving rise to three very different types of curriculum. First, however, we examine the effect of classical humanism upon curriculum design.

The broad aim of a classical humanist curriculum is to promote generalizable intellectual capacities, which can be fostered through the study of the elements of knowledge and modes of thought inherent in the particular subject being studied. The chief characteristic of a classical humanist curriculum is that it is content-driven. The curriculum planner sets out to analyse what is seen as the inherent content of a subject into its constituent parts, and then sequences these from what are deemed to be the simpler elements to learn, to what are considered to be the more complex ones. The objectives are then expressed in terms of conscious control of the various elements of knowledge set out along the way. Materials are then created in the form of a course book to cover the selected content.

The teacher's task is to apply the textbook(s) in the classroom, and to follow the given sequence of learning experiences, unit by unit, in a fairly rigid manner, in order not to disrupt what is believed to be a carefully worked out grading process. Since the whole class is expected to move as a block through the various units of work in the textbook at the same pace, it is important for classes to be roughly homogeneous in achievement and in learning speed.

The methodology favoured lays considerable stress on conscious study and deliberate learning, on understanding the particular rules or principles underlying the particular knowledge elements to be learnt, and on conscious reapplication of them in new contexts. The teacher presents data designed to highlight a particular rule. These are studied and the rule extracted and explained. The learner then practises applying the rule in carefully controlled situations, before attempting to apply it in more open contexts.

Assessment in the classical humanist approach is norm-referenced. The examiner sets out to construct tests which will discriminate between higher and lower achievers, and thus create a rank order of pupils, whose performances can be compared one with another. The tests will normally be designed to assess the extent to which learners have mastered certain knowledge areas, and the extent to which they are able to apply their knowledge to new contexts. Marks will be deducted for mistakes made. The major purpose of such norm-referenced assessment is to select an appropriate number of learners for the next stage of education, and to place them in homogeneous groups within it, so that each newly constituted class can continue as a block through the next set of learning experiences, all at roughly the same pace.

Examiners aim to create tests which will produce results that reflect the normal or Gaussian curve, in which fixed quantities of a total population tested fall into prefixed percentiles or grades. Thus, if five grades are to be awarded and the population of pupils tested contains a normal distribution of achievement, it is expected that a well-constructed test will produce results that permit approximately 10% of pupils to be given a Grade A, 20% a Grade B, 40% a Grade C, 20% a Grade D, and 10% a Grade E. It is assumed that the performances of large populations will be similar from year to year.

Although several tests may be set to cover the subject matter studied (e.g. a grammar test, a translation, a reading comprehension etc), it is common for the marks to be totalled to give an aggregate mark or grade for a subject. This is then seen not only as a statement of achievement reached, but a clear indication of intellectual ability for that subject.

National external examinations are set by examination boards at or towards the end of a cycle of schooling, and certificates indicating pupil grades in various subjects are provided, in order to satisfy society's need for some principled basis on which to select people for particular vocations and/or for higher education.

In brief, classical humanism leads to a curriculum in which:

- the fundamental aim is to promote generalizable intellectual capacities
- an analysis of the content of a particular subject into its constituent elements of knowledge determines what is to be taught and learnt. This is then sequenced in what is deemed to be a logical way from the simple to the more complex
- a course book is created to cover the various elements of knowledge
- unit-by-unit objectives are seen in terms of conscious control of the various elements of knowledge set out along the way
- all learners in a class are expected to move through the course book at the same pace
- the methodology employed lays emphasis on conscious awareness of rules and patterns, and subsequent application of them in controlled and then more open contexts
- assessment is norm-referenced and concerned with the selection and placement of those who will enter the next stage of education
- reporting is seen in terms of awarding each pupil an aggregate mark or grade for each subject studied.

1.3   Classical humanism in the foreign language curriculum

The best-known approach to the foreign language curriculum to which classical humanism has given rise is the grammar-translation approach. The content to be taught and learnt is expressed in terms of the elements of phonology, grammar, and vocabulary that are seen to make up a particular language. These are sequenced from what is deemed simple to what is thought complex, and then woven into a graded series of texts created or chosen to exemplify them and the meanings they might be used to convey. Learners are required to go through these texts and master the elements of knowledge embedded within them. They are to do this through conscious understanding of the rules behind the elements, and through deliberate practice of them, one after the other. In order to promote intellectual capacities, learners are encouraged to understand the rules underlying sentence construction, to memorize paradigms and grammatical systems and subsystems, to analyse sentences into their constituent parts, to classify these, and then to resynthesize all this knowledge in translations and essay work. To this is added at higher levels the study of particular literary texts of inherent value, to promote critical and aesthetic judgement.

Languages with a high profile of literary, social, and cultural achievements are preferred to those seen as less prestigious. In this respect the aura that surrounded Latin and Greek has tended in recent times to fall upon a number of modern languages, the chief of which are English, French, and German. It is interesting to reflect that whereas in most European countries the learning of a second language has for many years been considered sufficiently intellectually and culturally stimulating for the élite, yet adequately practical and relevant to the life expectations of the masses for it to be part of the curriculum for all, in Britain it was until recently considered suitable only for the élite.

1.4 Classical humanism in curriculum renewal

The classical humanist approach towards curriculum renewal places responsibility for this largely in the hands of the universities. As guardians of the nation's wisdom, they are enabled to control the examination system, which, in its turn, controls what occurs in the classroom, not just in the upper school but in earlier years as well. The principal classical humanist strategy for effecting curriculum renewal is to change the examinations. This can only be done occasionally. Thus change tends to be slow and is characterized by periodic sudden upheavals followed by very long periods of inactivity. Change to the curriculum is brought about from outside the school.

A corps of inspectors, as guardians of the nation's educational standards, is empowered by government to evaluate classroom teaching and learning and to identify good practices. These are generally described in various policy documents, discussion documents, and reports, in the hope that these will bring about any required changes. The inspectorate also organize annual in-service courses to which heads of departments in the appropriate subject area and other 'multipliers' are invited. It is expected that those who attend the courses will spread the information obtained to the teachers in their departments.

1.5   A critique of classical humanism

Classical humanism with its socially divisive pattern of an intellectual schooling for the élite and a practical one for the masses is no longer acceptable in an age determined to promote greater social mobility and greater equality of opportunity within its education system. There is no longer a case for not providing the higher achievers with practical skills, or for not providing the average and less able with intellectual capacities that will assist them to understand the principles upon which their practical work is based. It is now generally accepted that education for all should be rooted upon intellectual, practical, and attitudinal learning, which will enable all future citizens to adapt rapidly to evolving technologies and changes in social living. The notion of education as the transmitter of immutable truths in the form of knowledge and culture to the élite, or as the promoter of immutably relevant skills among the masses, is not sensible, since the particular knowledge and skills acquired at school can no longer be expected to suffice for a lifetime.

Schools now have a duty to provide learners with the motivation and the capacity to learn beyond whatever knowledge and skills are part of the school curriculum.

The lack of concern for practical skills shown in the classical humanist curriculum for the élite has led to a foreign language curriculum whose total concern is for mastery of the various elements of grammatical knowledge and vocabulary that make up a particular language. Trim has rightly referred to this as a '*gradus ad Parnassum*' – a seemingly endless climb up a 'straight and narrow path beset with difficulties and dangers towards a distant goal which few but the truly devoted ever reach' (Trim 1978:3). The result in Britain has been that 65%–70% of school leavers abandon foreign language learning at the earliest possible opportunity, since they find themselves falling further and further behind in the arduous climb, and can find little practical relevance in their foreign language study. There is a lack of emphasis on practical everyday communication within the classical humanist foreign language curriculum. It is expected that learners will eventually be able to communicate, once they have mastered the rules of sentence construction and have acquired an adequate vocabulary.

The sort of thinking that lies behind the classical humanist approach to foreign language learning in school is exemplified by Wilkins:

> A characteristic of the general language learning course is that the learner does not claim the return on his investment in learning until that learning has been proceeding for some years. He does not expect to be able to use the language communicatively as soon as the learning effort has begun, and since he or she is often in a situation where the occasion to use the language rarely arises, it does not matter if the development of communicative ability is deferred.
>
> (Wilkins 1974a:121)

Not only has such a policy led to a massive drop-out rate among school foreign language learners in Britain, but it is also in conflict with the current methodological belief that if learners are to learn to communicate effectively, the teacher must provide opportunities for them to communicate in the classroom in the course of their learning. In the grammar-translation approach there has been little concern for the development of everyday conversational or correspondence skills, or for the use of authentic texts, such as one would expect to find in foreign magazines or newspapers relevant to the age-group concerned. There has been little to assist the would-be tourist in coming to terms with the language required for getting goods and services in relation to travel, accommodation, food and drink, and leisure pursuits. There is little to help the learner to enter into direct interpersonal contact with members of the target language speech community.

Experience has shown that despite the linguistic competence built up by high achievers in grammar-translation courses, the expected by-product – a communicative ability – has not materialized. Learners who are successful in the classical humanist foreign language classroom are often rather poor at conducting normal interpersonal conversation or correspondence, and at conducting the business of everyday life, until they have spent some time among speakers of the foreign language. When they first attempt everyday communication it is clear that not only are the verbal routines associated with normal interaction unknown to them, but the ability to encode and decode speech and negotiate personal meanings appropriate to context at normal speeds has simply not been developed. As Webbe remarked as early as 1622:

> No man can run speedily to the mark of language that is shackled and ingiv'd with grammar precepts. ˙

> (Quoted in Howatt 1984:34)

The norm-referenced form of assessment associated with classical humanism normally provides little information to teachers, pupils or parents as to *what* students can or cannot do. It indicates how a student has performed in relation to others in a group. Given the way in which grades are allocated, there will always be pupils who receive the bottom grade, irrespective of how well they have performed. Since it is frequently the same pupils who score the low grades in every test, they inevitably come to see themselves as failures. Understandably such pupils lose motivation and often become discipline problems. With strict norm-referencing there is no means by which they can taste success, since they are continually being assessed against their peers, rather than against a particular set of criteria to be achieved.

There is a tendency among teachers who adopt a classical humanist approach to confuse achievement with ability, and to assume that pupils who get the lowest grade in terms of subject achievement are automatically the poorest in terms of innate ability. The slow learner is often miscast as one lacking in ability, as is the learner whose past learning history is deficient in comparison to others in the class. This notion among teachers of an innate fixed unalterable level of ability, which dictates achievement in the classroom, leads to what Bloom (1971) has called 'a pernicious self-fulfilling prophecy', in which:

> The instructor expects a third of his students to learn well what is taught, a third to learn less well, and a third to fail or just get by. These expectations are transmitted to the students through school grading policies and practices and through the methods and materials of instruction. Students quickly learn to act in accordance with them, and the final sorting out through the grading process approximates the teacher's original expectations. A pernicious self-fulfilling prophecy has been created.

> (Bloom 1971:47)

The marks scored on various different tests covering different aspects of a subject (for example, grammar, listening comprehension, translation, etc.) are aggregated to form an overall mark or grade, yet different aspects of a subject may call upon different knowledge-bases and skills. Marks deriving from tests in these different aspects cannot sensibly be conflated into an aggregate mark or grade on anything other than an arbitrary basis designed to respond to society's requirement for a quick and easy way to judge a pupil's competence *vis-à-vis* others in the group.

The classical humanist form of curriculum renewal, which is under the control of the university and the inspectorate outside the school, has proved to be ineffective. Teachers do not often read the inspectorate's policy statements and discussion papers, and one-off annual in-service courses, to which only a handful of teachers can come, are an inadequate means to support teachers in their search for ways of improving their curricular practices. There is little dialogue between the universities and the schools whose curriculum the former largely control. Thus examination changes are often out of touch with the realities of what is required in the classroom.

In essence the classical humanist approach to education can be characterized as an élitist, 'top-down', transmissive one, in which universities and inspectors hand down the curriculum to schools, and teachers transmit it to their pupils. As a contextual solution to the particular concerns of a society which believed in selecting an élite, in order to transmit to them traditional cultural values and wisdom, and in order to promote their intellectual capacities to the full, classical humanist educational practices may have worked effectively. In an age in which such élitism has been rejected in favour of a more egalitarian view of the purposes of education on the one hand, and a more learner-centred concern on the other, classical humanism has had to give way to reconstructionism representing the more egalitarian trend, and to progressivism representing learner-centredness. Each of these is examined in the two chapters which follow.

2 Reconstructionism

2.1 Introduction

Skilbeck's (1982a) analysis of reconstructionism indicates that it is an essentially optimistic ideology which believes that man can improve himself and his environment. Reconstructionists envisage that social, economic, intellectual, and spiritual advance can all be rationally planned for. Education is seen as an important agent for bringing this about. It is seen as a means of redressing the injustices of birth and of early upbringing, and of working through consensus towards a better world in which all citizens are equally valued.

Reconstructionists tend to have great faith in the power of planning, of setting goals to be pursued, and of deliberate intervention in the education system to bring about the outcomes deemed necessary.

The egalitarian forces behind reconstructionism were opposed to the divisive nature of the classical humanist two-tier school system. This led to the establishment of comprehensive schooling, of mixed ability classes, and of a common core curriculum for all. Crosland expressed a powerful reconstructionist view when he wrote:

> Now by selecting for a superior school, children who are already well favoured by environment, we are not merely confirming, we are hardening and sharpening an existing social division. This can surely not be thought desirable. I will not argue the point in terms of equality. But I will argue it in terms of a sense of community, of social cohesion, of a nation composed of people who understand each other because they can communicate . . . We have only to consider our industrial relations and the lack of communication and mutual understanding reflected in them to see the depth of social division in Britain today . . . so long as we choose to educate our children in separate camps . . . for so long will our schools exacerbate rather than diminish our class divisions.

> (Crosland 1974)

Reconstructionists argue that human beings must be seen as persons, as purposive agents, to be valued as equals irrespective of their level of ability or achievement. Thus Daunt wrote that the ideal teacher would be:

. . . egalitarian, not in the absurd sense of believing that all talents and aptitudes are equal, but yet in a stronger sense than merely advocating equality of opportunity. He wishes to see all members of society equally valued.

(Daunt 1975)

Reconstructionists emphasize the practical aspects of education. In foreign language learning the emphasis is placed on the promotion of an ability to communicate, and thus achieve a better understanding and unity among groups and nations. It is possible to see reconstructionist values behind the Council of Europe's recent work in Modern Languages (Council of Europe 1981). In Recommendation R(82)18 the Committee of Ministers enjoins member states through their school systems:

> to encourage the teaching of at least one European language other than the national language or the vehicular language of the area concerned to pupils from the age of ten . . . with adequate time allocation and in such a way as to enable them by the end of the period of compulsory schooling, within the limits set by their individual ability, to use the language effectively for communication with other speakers of that language, both in transacting the business of everyday living and in building social and personal relations on the basis of mutual understanding of and respect for the cultural identity of others.

(Council of Europe 1982)

In brief we can characterize reconstructionism as concerned with:
- effecting social change through education planned to bring it about
- the equal valuing of all citizens
- reaching a consensus on goals to be achieved followed by rigorous planning of the means to bring them about
- comprehensive schooling with a common core curriculum and mixed-ability classes
- promoting intranational and international understanding through effective communication

2.2 Reconstructionism in curriculum design

Whereas the classical humanist curriculum was content-oriented, and was based on the structure of the subject matter to be studied, the reconstructionist curriculum is objectives-driven, and founded on the behavioural outcomes that are to be worked towards. In curriculum design reconstructionist values have given rise to what is termed the 'ends-means' approach, and in the classroom to 'mastery learning' techniques.

Tyler (1949) is generally taken to be the father of the ends-means approach. He saw curriculum development as an exercise in which particular behavioural patterns, specified as ends, could be brought about through an instructional process designed as a means towards them.

The structure of the ends-means curriculum and the steps required to elaborate it have been set out by Taba as follows:

Step 1: diagnosis of needs
Step 2: formulation of objectives
Step 3: selection of content
Step 4: organization of content
Step 5: selection of learning experiences
Step 6: organization of learning experiences
Step 7: determination of what to evaluate and of the ways of
        doing it

(Taba 1962:12)

This indicates a strictly linear view of curriculum development which is objectives-driven, starting with a diagnosis of needs and ending with a scheme for evaluating whether in the course of instruction those needs have been fulfilled.

Tyler rejected the classical humanist tradition of simply listing elements of content, since this 'does not specify what the students are expected to do with those elements'. He also argued that it was not helpful to specify highly generalized patterns of behaviour as objectives (for example, 'to develop critical thinking'), since although these were behavioural in nature, they were not specific enough to guide the choice of curriculum content. Tyler's own prescription for the setting out of educational objectives was as follows:

The most useful form for stating objectives is to express them in terms which identify both the kind of behaviour to be developed in the student and the content or area of life in which this behaviour is to operate.

(Tyler 1949:46)

The objectives, then, were to be maximally explicit, so that they would:

> guide the making of curriculum decisions on what to cover, what to emphasize, what content to select and which learning experiences to stress.
>
> (Taba 1962:197)

It became normal to advocate that all objectives should be expressed in behavioural terms. Thus Mager, for example, declared:

> Curriculum objectives must always be prespecified in terms of measurable changes in student behaviour.
>
> (Mager 1962)

In order to assist teachers to come to terms with what constituted behavioural objectives, Bloom (1956) produced a handbook outlining a taxonomy of educational objectives in the cognitive domain. These were 'designed to be a classification of the student behaviours which represent the intended outcomes of the educational process', and were set out in six categories representing an ascending order of complexity. These were knowledge, comprehension, application, analysis, synthesis, and evaluation. For each one of these Bloom produced illustrative objectives, a discussion of related testing problems, and examples of items testing objectives in the category concerned. A second handbook on objectives in the affective domain was produced by Krathwohl, Bloom, and Masia (1964), and a third handbook concerned with the psycho-motor domain was planned but never completed.

Once the behavioural ends of a particular instructional programme had been agreed upon, it was necessary to set out a series of steps designed to shape the learner's behaviour in the direction of the desired goals. The steps were to be small ones, so that learners could master them relatively easily and quickly, and then move on with a feeling of confidence in their own success. The content to be included in the various steps was to be derived directly from a study of the behavioural objectives, which were to be broken down into small elements of knowledge and part-skills. These were to be sequenced from the simple to the more complex, building up towards the global behaviour desired.

Ideally methodology in the ends-means model of curriculum design was to be determined as a result of research set up to compare one method with another, in order to determine which was the most economical and effective. Such research has usually been characterized by the setting up of a control group, which would employ a traditional method, and an experimental group, which would use a more innovative approach, in order to see which group achieved the prespecified objectives better. The methodology normally associated with reconstructionism places great emphasis on deliberate practice of part-skills and eventual rehearsal of global end-objectives. It is based on the belief that once good habits have been set up in the execution of the various part-skills of a particular behaviour, the global task will be performed without problems.

In order to determine whether the pupils were achieving the behavioural objectives set out in a particular curriculum, it soon became apparent that the classical humanist version of assessment based on norm-referencing was inadequate. Norm-referenced tests produced measurements which provided information relating an individual's performance to that of other individuals in a group, but said little or nothing directly about the performances of individual learners in relation to particular objectives. Thus the information provided by such tests did not permit one to determine whether or to what extent intended outcomes had been attained. In its place Glaser (1963) proposed a model of criterion-referenced assessment, which would 'provide explicit information as to what the individual can and cannot do', by measuring performance against a well-defined criterion, rather than against the performance of others in the group.

It was clearly important for those who were setting out to improve the quality of teaching and learning to be able to demonstrate through an evaluation of pupil performance that learning achievements were getting better. This could not be done through norm-referenced assessment, which did not enable one to see whether pupils had achieved explicit goals or standards. Criterion-referenced assessment, on the other hand, proposed a means whereby educators could specify target domains of behaviour, determine particular behavioural objectives within each, prespecify mastery levels, and then set a test or battery of tests comprising a sample of representative items from each particular target domain, in order to ascertain whether pupils had attained mastery of the objectives or not. In this form of assessment it was possible for all pupils to achieve a top grade, if their performance measured up to the criterion.

In addition to the notion of summative criterion-referenced tests designed to determine to what extent prespecified learning outcomes had been achieved at the end of a course, Scriven (1967) proposed that there should also be formative assessments conducted regularly during a course to diagnose whether students were mastering the step-by-step unit objectives, and if not, to pinpoint those areas where remedial work would have to be undertaken.

In order to introduce an element of individualization into the ends-means approach, various pupil contract schemes were created. In these, learners had to pace themselves through a predetermined set of tasks, in a predetermined way, towards prespecified learning outcomes. Thus the Dalton plan, for example, outlined in Grittner (1975), involved setting out a series of predetermined objectives, and embodying these in self-directed tasks for learners to go through. A contract was drawn up which stipulated the date by which they had to be completed. It left the individual learners free to choose which tasks to perform on any given day. This meant that the learners had to learn to budget their time to cover all the tasks in the various subjects they were studying. Learners learnt by themselves. Teachers were seen as managers rather than instructors.

Perhaps the most powerful form of reconstructionism in the classroom is mastery learning, which combines behavioural objectives, formative and summative criterion-referenced assessment, and behaviourist methodology. Mastery learning is a classroom approach which rejects the classical humanist notion of predetermined fixed levels of ability among learners, and proposes instead that a student's aptitude should not be viewed as the factor determining the level to which he can learn, but is more accurately defined as determining the amount of time he requires to learn a particular behaviour to a given level in ideal conditions (Carroll 1963). Carroll (1971) maintained that if each student was allowed the learning time he needed, and was given the instruction he required, he could achieve whatever level he wished to. Reiterating this, Bloom maintained that:

> if students are normally distributed with respect to aptitude for some subject and all students are given the same instruction . . . then achievement measured at the subject's completion will be normally distributed . . . conversely if students are normally distributed with respect to aptitude, but the kind and quality of instruction and learning time allowed are made appropriate to the characteristics and needs of each learner, the majority of students will achieve subject mastery . . . The normal curve is not sacred. It describes the outcome of a random process. Since education is a purposeful activity in which we seek to have students learn what we teach, the achievement

distribution should be very different from the normal curve if our instruction is effective. In fact, our educational efforts may be said to be unsuccessful to the extent that student achievement is normally distributed.

(Bloom 1971:49–50)

In later writings Bloom went much further than Carroll had done, maintaining that:

most students become very similar with regard to learning ability, rate of learning, and motivation for further learning when provided with favourable learning conditions.

(Bloom 1976:Preface)

and

Learning characteristics such as good-poor and fast-slow are alterable by appropriate school conditions. The research demonstrates that under appropriate conditions almost all can learn whatever the school has to teach.

(Bloom 1978:6)

Bloom proposed that the essential variables which were alterable were the pupil's past history of learning or 'cognitive entry behaviour' to each learning task, and his 'affective entry characteristics'. These, combined with the 'quality of instruction' the pupil received, determined the actual level and type of achievement reached by the pupil, his rate of learning, and the attitudes that he would emerge with regarding the subject matter, the school, and himself. Bloom recognized that variations in pre-school learning experiences meant that each pupil had a learning history that had prepared him differently from other pupils with regard to the learning to be undertaken. Bloom, therefore, proposed that in the early stages of any course it was essential to concentrate attention on those with an inadequate cognitive entry behaviour in order to remedy whatever weaknesses in their learning there might be.

Inequality of treatment may be needed at least at certain stages of the learning process if children are to attain equality of learning outcomes.

(Bloom 1976:215)

Bloom maintained that extra time spent on helping those with learning difficulties to achieve mastery in early units, and the inevitably slow start that this implied for all, would be compensated for by the fact that the learning of these initially slow pupils would tend to become as rapid as that of the initially faster learners.

Although the variation in time taken and help required never reaches a vanishing point, we have observed sets in which the variation in time and help required on the later units was only about one-third of the variation observed on the first learning task in the sequential series.

(Bloom 1976:166)

Bloom proposed that pupils should learn in mixed-ability groups and move from unit to unit together, once they had all reached the predetermined criterion for mastery on each unit. Some might achieve this in the normal time provided, others might require extra time. Formative tests of a diagnostic nature, designed to provide feedback on the state of each student's learning, were to be given towards the end of each unit, since:

the key to the success of mastery learning strategies largely lies in the extent to which students can be motivated and helped to correct their learning difficulties at the appropriate points in the learning process.

(Bloom 1976:5)

Bloom proposed various patterns of corrective remedial work for weaknesses exposed in a formative diagnostic test:

- small groups of pupils helping each other
- self-access worksheets related to particular areas of weakness
- tapes or programmed instruction units
- direct teacher assistance
- more advanced pupils helping weaker pupils

Ideally corrective work was to be done outside the regular classroom time.

Some strong claims based on case studies in particular contexts have been made for mastery learning, not least that it 'enables 75 to 90 per cent of the students to achieve the same high level as the top 25 per cent learning under typical group-based instructional methods'. (Block 1971:3). Where reconstructionist practices have been tried, it is often discovered, initially at least, that teachers find value in:

- having to make their objectives more explicit to themselves and their pupils
- keeping a more formal watch over pupil progress than they were accustomed to
- attempting to respond to feedback from assessment in a more sensitive way
- ensuring that pupils feel success in the mastery of unit-by-unit objectives.

Pupils have also shown benefits from being helped:

- to approach the learning task in a more purposeful and deliberate way than usual
- to achieve a feeling of success in every unit – an outcome often denied to the lowest achievers in conventional classes
- to compete against the criteria laid down rather than against each other, thus encouraging them to work co-operatively rather than competitively.

2.3   Reconstructionism in the foreign language curriculum

Reconstructionism in language teaching is above all concerned with bringing about a better understanding among social groups, through teaching them to communicate with each other effectively. In countries where there are, for example, two national languages and two distinct social groups associated with them, reconstructionists will tend to promote a bilingual educational policy, in which the members of both groups will each learn each other's language. Thus, in Finland for example, reconstructionists will argue that Swedish speakers should learn Finnish, and Finnish speakers should learn Swedish. In Britain, in those areas in which Welsh or Gaelic are common mother tongues, reconstructionists will tend to argue for bilingual education for all who live there. In Canada, the 'immersion' programmes, in which English speakers learn subjects through the medium of French (Swain 1974, 1978), derive from a reconstructionist aim to promote a better sense of national unity in that country. In countries where there are settled immigrant communities with distinctive languages and cultures, reconstructionists will tend to argue that it is valuable for members of the indigenous community to learn an immigrant community language. In Britain they will make a case for the teaching in school of Urdu, Punjabi, Hindi,

Chinese, Polish, Italian, Greek or Turkish, not only to those who speak these languages, but also to monolingual English speakers, in order to promote better intranational unity and understanding. This is seen as meriting the same sort of attention as the promotion of international understanding and communication across nations. Reconstructionism has had a powerful influence in recent years on the design of the foreign language curriculum. It has given rise to the audio-lingual, audio-visual/situational, topic-based, and functional-notional approaches to foreign language learning, as well as to the Graded Objectives in Modern Languages (GOML) schemes in Britain. All of these various approaches have sought to bring about an effective communicative ability in learners as their ultimate goal, but have conceptualized this ability and the way to bring it about in different ways, adopting different organizing principles in the design of the foreign language curriculum. The audio-lingual approach conceptualized a communicative ability in terms of good grammatical habits. The audio-visual/situational approach focused on the ability to understand and produce appropriate phrases related to particular situations. Topic-based approaches emphasized the ability to cope with certain topics. The functional-notional approach has focused on mastery of the formal means to interpret and express certain predetermined meanings. GOML schemes have embraced both situational and functional-notional approaches and broken language courses down into conveniently sized units called 'levels'.

Given their recent impact on foreign language learning in schools it is the functional-notional approach and the GOML schemes that will be described in the sections which follow.

2.3.1 The functional-notional approach

It was the Nuffield team working on the production of a German course for schools (*Vorwärts*), who were the first to introduce the category of what they called 'linguistic activities' into school foreign language course design. Following the suggestions of Halliday, McIntosh, and Strevens (1964), the course-writing team attempted to identify a list of likely speaker intentions (Peck 1969). These they labelled 'linguistic activities'. They were to include items such as: requesting information, expressing wishes, apologizing, telling people how to do things. These were the forerunners of Wilkins' category of communicative functions (Wilkins 1976).

The full list of syllabus categories used by the *Vorwärts* team (Schools Council 1974) embraced linguistic activities, semantic fields (a mixture of topics, situations, and what were to become Wilkins' semantico-grammatical categories, for example, 'expressions of time', 'numbers'), and grammatical categories of one sort and another, together with an alphabetical dictionary of vocabulary. This extremely rich mixture heralded the type of approach towards foreign language curriculum design adopted by the Council of Europe team in Project No. 4 (Council of Europe 1973).

The functional-notional approach proposed by the Council of Europe team derives from a reconstructionist ends-means approach to curriculum design, which lays stress on the need for course designers to follow a series of interrelated steps, leading from an analysis of communicative needs, to a definition of syllabus content, to the creation of teaching/learning materials, to assessment and to evaluation, following Taba's (1962) approach outlined earlier.

As Trim, the project leader of the Council of Europe team, described it:

> We set out to identify a number of coherent but restricted goals relevant to the communicative needs of the learner. We then attempt to work out in detail the knowledge and skills which will equip the learner to use the language for the communicative purposes defined. In the light of his characteristics and resources we have then to establish a feasible learning programme leading to the mastery of this body of knowledge and skills, and a means of testing and evaluation to provide feedback to all parties concerned as to the success of the programme.
>
> (Trim 1978:9)

The initial impetus for the Council of Europe team's work sprang from Trim's proposal that the provision of language learning in member countries of the Council of Europe might be seen in terms of an interlocking set of unit/credits. Each unit would reflect the needs of a particular group of learners. Each unit was to be 'a principled cluster of modules which together provide the basis for acquiring the communicative potential to deal with a defined language need' (Trim 1973:23). Where the needs of groups of learners overlapped, the corresponding units would have objectives and content in common, thus allowing the formation of common groups and the exchange of common materials on a wide international scale. Accreditation on similar-sized units in different countries would permit international equivalences in qualifications to be established. This would open up the possibilities for a greater exchange of ideas, resources, and personnel for language teaching, and for greater inter-European co-operation in the creation of multi-media language programmes destined for similar audiences in a number of different countries.

Trim's proposal rested upon the premise that it was possible to analyse a learner's communicative needs in advance in such a way as to guide the planning of syllabus content. Richterich was asked to devise a model to accomplish this. Communicative needs were defined as follows:

> Définir des besoins de communication consistera à décrire ce qui manque à un individu ou à un groupe d'individus pour changer par une action langagière ou autre l'état de déséquilibre dans lequel il se trouve en ce moment.

(Richterich 1973a:5)[1]

The categories devised by Richterich (1973b) for analysing needs were adopted and amplified by van Ek in *The Threshold Level* (1975), and turned into a behavioural specification for planning learning objectives. This drew upon the sociolinguistic hypotheses of Hymes, from whom the Council of Europe team took the notion that: 'there are rules of use without which the rules of grammar would be useless' (Hymes 1971:278).

Hymes had maintained that there were rules and regularities governing the relationship between the actual linguistic form of a message and other constituent components of speech events. These latter he listed as the roles and relationships of the participants, the physical setting, the psychological scene, the topic, the purpose, the attitudinal key, the channel of communication, the code of language variety, the norms of interaction, the physical distance, the norms of interpretation, and the genre. According to Hymes (1971:279) the rules of appropriacy linking forms to contextual features were not simply to be grafted on to grammatical competence, but were to be acquired simultaneously with it. Drawing on Hymes' work, van Ek (1975) drew up a behavioural specification for setting out learning objectives at a 'threshold level' of language competence based on:

- the *situations* in which an adult learner might wish to use the foreign language. This covered social roles, psychological roles, settings, and topics;
- the *language activities* the adult learner might wish to engage in. This meant describing what learners would be likely to have to do in the four skills of listening, speaking, reading, and writing;

— the *degree of skill* which the adult learner was expected to attain in the various activities.

Mastery at the 'threshold level' was deemed to have been achieved, if the learner could understand and make himself understood 'without obliging the native-speaker to exert himself unduly' (van Ek 1975). In order to turn such a behavioural specification into a statement of language content, Wilkins proposed that it would be necessary:

> to abandon the conventional grammatical syllabus which attempts to teach the entire grammatical system without regard to its application to specific language needs and to the fact that not all parts of the system are equally important to all learners.

> (Wilkins 1973:131)

Instead he proposed a notional or semantic approach which would reflect the behavioural needs of learners, would take the communicative facts of language into account from the beginning, without losing sight of grammatical and situational factors, and would attempt to set out what the learner might want to *do* and to *say* through language.

> The whole basis for a notional approach to language teaching derives from the conviction that what people want to do through language is more important than mastery of the language as an unapplied system.

> (Wilkins 1976:42)

In order to set out what people might want to do and to say through language, Wilkins drew upon Austin's (1962) speech act theory. This suggested that in addition to conceptual meaning all utterances have an illocutionary value which embodies the speaker's intention. Sometimes we express our intention directly, (for example, 'I congratulate you'), but more often, as Searle (1975) pointed out, we tend to do this indirectly, for example, when we use a question about someone's ability ('Can you speak a little louder') to serve as a request for action. Indirect speech acts tend to predominate in normal everyday adult conversation in English. This highlights the fact that we do not use an interrogative form, for example, uniquely to ask for information, or a declarative form simply for giving information. There is no simple one-to-one relationship between particular forms and the illocutionary values that should be attached to them. Values must be interpreted in the light of the context in which the forms occur.

Despite this problem, Wilkins felt that there were enough regularities in form-function relationships to make it worthwhile attempting to predetermine the language content to be taught in semantic rather than purely grammatical terms. He called such a syllabus a 'notional' one, and suggested that it might be set out in two basic parts – one covering 'functions or functional meanings, i.e. the social purpose of the utterance' (Austin's illocutionary value), while the other would cover the 'concepts or conceptual meanings' that were to be referred to (Wilkins 1976:23–4).

It was this proposal that van Ek was to adopt in *The Threshold Level* (van Ek 1975), in which the meanings to be covered and the forms associated with them were set out in terms of functions, general notions, and specific notions assembled under topic areas.

For Wilkins (1976) syllabus design was to involve the selection and sequencing of language content designed to provide the learner with a growing capacity to express meanings:

> In a notional approach the aim is to ensure that the learner knows how different types of meaning are expressed, so that he can then adapt and combine the different elements of this knowledge according to the requirements of a particular act of communication.
>
> (Wilkins 1976)

Any act of adapting and combining elements clearly involves grammar, and Wilkins himself was at pains to point this out:

> It is taken here to be almost axiomatic that the acquisition of the grammatical system of a language remains a most important element in language learning.
>
> (Wilkins 1976)

Wilkins was, therefore, not proposing to do away with grammar. The basic units of organization were to be semantic, however, since:

- it was meanings and not forms that the learners would have to be able to understand and express;
- setting out the meanings that a learner would wish to learn to convey would guide the teacher in the determination of which parts of the total grammatical system should be taught.

In answer to the criticism that semantic categories would give rise to heterogeneous unsystematic exponents, Wilkins claimed:

> It is perfectly feasible to meet the need for systematicity by
> focusing on some part of the grammatical system within an
> environment that is not controlled linguistically.
>
> (Wilkins 1981:100)

In fact this represents little departure from what was done before,
except in so far as the sequence of grammar that emerges from a
semantic approach might be rather different to the one derived from
a structural approach.

For beginners, the exponents to be taught were to be chosen on the
basis of maximum usefulness and of learnability. An unmarked form
that could be used for the same function in a wide range of situations
would be taught earlier than a more contextually marked one. Forms
that could fulfil a number of different functions would be preferred
to those with a narrower coverage. Some forms could be unpackaged
into their constituent parts, which could be used to generate further
sentences, while others, whose grammar was complex or opaque,
would simply have to be learnt as fixed locutions, until learners were
able to take them apart.

As they progressed, learners were to be recycled through the same
semantic categories at different levels, with a wider range of
exponents being offered at each succeeding level to reflect a richer
potential of semantic nuances.

As far as can be ascertained, the methodology implicit in the
functional-notional approach, as set out by Wilkins and van Ek, is
essentially behaviouristic in character. It would seem to involve
learners in the deliberate learning and gradual mastery of an
ever-growing set of language forms realizing particular meanings in
particular situations. These were to be embodied in activities that
depended heavily on the sort of role-play in the classroom in which
learners simulated various social and transactional activities,
following the conventions of members of the speech community
whose language was being learned.

Assessment was to be based on criterion-referenced principles.
Tests which sampled the content of *The Threshold Level* were
devised (Groot and Harrison 1982), and mastery scores worked out.
Wilkins also set out proposals for definitions of language proficiency
in the various skills at various levels of learning (Appendix C in Trim
1978). These followed the pattern of other similar scales, for
example the FSI language proficiency ratings (Wilds 1975). These
were to be used to guide the assessment of a learner's global
performance in the different skills.

In brief, the functional-notional approach as set out by the Council of Europe team in their various writings, was a strict embodiment of the reconstructionist ends-means approach to curriculum design.

2.3.2 The Graded Objectives in Modern Languages (GOML) schemes in Britain

Like the functional-notional approach, GOML schemes, which sprang up in Britain in many Local Education Authorities in the late 1970s and early 1980s (Harding, Page, and Rowell 1980, and Page 1983), also embodied reconstructionist values and an ends-means approach to curriculum design. The two earliest GOML schemes were in Oxfordshire (Downes 1978, Oxfordshire Modern Language Advisory Committee 1978, Gordon 1980) and in York (Buckby 1976, Clarke 1980). These were overtly situational in approach, while others such as those in Lothian (Clark 1979b) and West Sussex (Garner 1981) derived their impetus more directly from the Council of Europe's functional-notional proposals.

Primarily, however, all GOML schemes arose from a desire to come to terms with the wide differences in achievement in foreign language learning manifested by school learners, and with the high drop-out rate among them. All GOML schemes past and present, whatever their differences of approach, share the common objective of wishing to break down the classical humanist *gradus ad Parnassum* into smaller units or levels set out in some sort of sequence from the bottom upwards. Through this they aim to provide appropriate and attainable transitional and end objectives for the whole range of pupils in school, some of whom may opt out at the end of a short compulsory period of foreign language learning, while others may continue or even take up a second foreign language.

The notion of a graded approach to foreign language learning is not a new one. It can be traced back at least to Comenius (1592–1670), who wrote of the child growing towards wisdom through a gradual 'unfolding of the objective world to the senses' (Comenius, quoted in Howatt 1984:42). Comenius had envisaged a four-stage education in a language, symbolized as a journey through the Temple from the outer porch to the inner sanctum. The pupil would progress through:

- the *Vestibulum* (the porch), in which a basic vocabulary sufficient for simple conversations would be provided;
- the *Janua* (the gates), in which there would be a textbook

composed of graded texts of intrinsic value for expanding linguistic knowledge;
- the *Palatium* (the great court), in which there would be a concentration on the use of language in context, and on style;
- the *Thesaurus* (the inner sanctum), in which comparisons and translations between languages would be made.

Comenius believed that a foreign language should be learnt solely for communicative purposes, and that study should not last for more than a year and a half.

> The complete and detailed knowledge of a language, no matter which it be, is quite unnecessary, and it is absurd and useless on the part of anyone to try and attain it.
>
> (Comenius, quoted in Howatt 1984:43)

Following the move to comprehensive education and to foreign language learning for all in Britain, Perren had called for an approach based on 'levels':

> Each level needs its own useful surrender value, and determining exactly what this shall be calls for a great deal of careful experiment in many schools by many teachers . . . It would indeed be capricious to put Modern Languages in the curriculum for all as a mere gesture, without specifying realistic goals . . .
>
> (Perren 1972:11)

All GOML schemes have shared Perren's vision of a series of 'levels', explicitly defined in some way, each with its own surrender value. The early GOML schemes were based on the notion of a graded series of levels, each expressed in the form of externally defined syllabuses (Harding and Honnor 1974) and graded external tests (Davidson 1973, Page 1973, Harding and Page 1974, Buckby 1976, Clark 1977). As a model, reference was made to the graded syllabuses and examinations produced by the Associated Board of the Royal Schools of Music for instrumental performers. The analogy between the learning of a musical instrument and the learning of a foreign language seemed a particularly fruitful one. The musician practises notes, progressions, scales and arpeggios, and tackles simple pieces contrived to suit his capacity at the time. Gradually these pieces increase in complexity and in the demands made on the musicianship of the performer. Thus the musician practises deliberately, plays pieces tailored to his current ability, acquires musicianship, develops a deliberate control over his playing, and over time becomes increasingly aware of the nature and value of music. School foreign language learners seemed also to have to practise deliberately, carry out communicative tasks adapted to their level, acquire a feel for the language, develop deliberate syntactic and stylistic control, and over time develop an awareness of the nature and function of language.

The examinations of the Associated Board of the Royal Schools of Music contained set pieces, theory, and sight-reading. The Oxfordshire and York schemes for foreign language learning were, however, to neglect the theory and the sight-reading aspects, and to concentrate solely upon the set pieces. The Lothian GLAFLL scheme, which is described in detail in Part 2 of this book, reintroduced 'sight-reading' in the form of a concern for unrehearsed performance, and 'theory' in the sense that there was an overt concern that pupils acquire some awareness about the grammatical and other rule-governed aspects of foreign language learning (Clark 1979b, 1980).

The only other existing foreign language curriculum model which set out to break foreign language learning down into 'units' or 'levels', and to retain the notion of a surrender value for each, was the Council of Europe's one (Council of Europe 1973). It is therefore not surprising to find that over the years GOML groups have drawn more and more heavily on Council of Europe documents (particularly the early Lothian and West Sussex schemes – see Clark 1979b, Garner 1981). It is also noted that the Council of Europe's network of projects in the school sector was in turn influenced to some extent by GOML work (Bergentoft 1981, Harding 1983).

It was not possible, however, at school level to accept the Council of Europe's original claim that the 'threshold level' represented 'a minimum level of foreign language competence . . . below which no further levels could be usefully distinguished'. Nor was it accepted that in school circumstances it could be seen as a 'short-term objective requiring no more than an average learning period of 8–9 months' (van Ek 1975). In contrast to the Council of Europe's original formulation, all GOML schemes have seen fit to:

- set out a number of levels below the 'threshold level';
- relate one level to the next in a sequential way, while retaining the principle that each one should form a free-standing unit with its own surrender value.

The early levels in both the OMLAC and the York schemes were based on the notion of the pupil as a potential tourist. Thus the syllabus and tests were set out in terms of tourist-related social and transactional tasks in various predictable situations (OMLAC 1978, Clarke 1980). Both schemes adopted a somewhat impoverished instructional view of learning. Their aim was to reduce the 'input' to be learnt to the sort of level expected as 'output' from the learner, and thus to concentrate on a thorough mastery of a highly restricted content. The distinction between the levels was seen largely in terms of the quantity of predictable phrases and vocabulary that the learners were expected to produce and to understand in the various situations given.

OMLAC also envisaged differentiation between the levels on a psychological basis. At Level 1 'the pupil is on a family visit with parents who do not speak the language, and the pupil acts as interpreter'; while at Level 2 'the pupil is going to France to stay with a French pen-friend' (OMLAC 1978). This concept was elaborated further by Harding and Naylor (1979) on the basis that a pupil's education in general could be seen to reflect a 'distancing process from the self to the outside world'. Their plan for school foreign language learning, however, reflected mother-tongue development, forgetting that the pupils they were dealing with were already adolescents. This led them to propose, for example, that the reading of any fiction should be postponed till Level 4, and the need to draw inferences or make value judgements till Level 5.

The methodology adopted in GOML schemes has been a behaviouristic one relying on the careful building up and practice of forms related to particular functions, and on the rehearsal through role-play of the various situations set out in the defined content syllabuses.

Graded tests were created in each scheme to reflect the syllabuses at each level. Indeed in the York scheme the tests preceded the syllabuses. The tests have tended to sample the situations and the discrete functions of the syllabuses in such a direct way that it has been easy for pupils to rehearse for them and to obtain high levels of success in them.

Before attempting to criticize the effects of reconstructionist values on the contemporary foreign language curriculum, I turn now to examine briefly its effect on the way in which curriculum renewal is brought about.

2.4   Reconstructionism in curriculum renewal

Reconstructionism in curriculum renewal is characterized by a 'Research, Development, and Diffusion' approach. This has been outlined by Havelock *et al.* (1973). It generally involves the setting up of a central committee of selected 'experts' to develop a new curriculum product. The committee conducts initial research into what is required, produces draft materials, obtains feedback from classroom teachers who use the draft materials in a number of designated pilot areas chosen to be representative of a range of contexts, and finally revises the materials for publication. Schon (1971:81) has called this form of innovation the 'centre-periphery' model, which rests on three premises:

- the innovation to be diffused exists, fully realized in its essentials prior to its diffusion
- diffusion is the movement of an innovation from a centre out to its ultimate users
- directed diffusion is a centrally managed process of dissemination, training, and provision of resources and incentives.

(Schon 1971:81)

The centre itself may be responsible for supporting and training the eventual users of the product, or in larger educational contexts it may be the role of a primary centre to train those in secondary centres to provide training for users in their area. Schon refers to this second version as a 'proliferation of centres' (Schon 1971). In this way, as outlined by Havelock *et al.* (1973), curriculum renewal in the Research, Development, and Diffusion model proceeds in a logical way from research to development, and to adoption by schools. It is a top-down approach to curriculum renewal, effected from outside the classroom, as are, for example, the recent GCSE proposals in England, and the Standard Grade and Action Plan proposals in Scotland.

2.5   A critique of reconstructionism

From a democratic viewpoint reconstructionism can be criticized, because within it the teacher and the learner become servants of the curriculum, which has been determined in advance outside the particular classroom in which the teaching and learning are to take place. The teacher's task is reduced to that of bringing about certain prespecified behavioural changes in all pupils in a predetermined stereotypical manner. Neither teachers nor pupils are considered as individuals with the need to teach and learn in mutually responsive ways towards ends that they themselves have agreed upon. There is no notion of a plurality of values or of individually determined outcomes.

From an epistemological viewpoint it is argued that in those areas of the curriculum that depend upon knowledge and understanding, rather than upon the training of particular skills, any attempt to specify predetermined objectives and target levels of performance will set arbitrary limits to performance, and will suggest to the learner that knowledge is a closed set of truths, rather than a series of hypotheses borne of our current perceptions, serving transient contemporary purposes (Stenhouse 1975). Like classical humanism, reconstructionism tends to conceptualize knowledge as something external to the learner, to be fed in, rather than as something that grows within in response to the need to impose a pattern upon the world. Learners are active agents transmuting input through imposing the patterns of their existing mental schemata upon it. The reconstructionist causative view of teaching appears to ignore the evidence for an 'inbuilt syllabus', or stages of development, where mastery of certain knowledge or skill areas would seem to unfold in a sequence not directly related to the teaching one.

Mastery learning would appear to be deeply flawed in so far as it fails to take into account that acquisition is not linear, and that it does not occur on an all-at-once basis simply as a result of teaching or immediate remedial re-teaching. As Prabhu remarks:

> We take in several items, more or less at once; some of them only momentarily, superficially, others a little more, maybe one of them such that it is retained for a while. Thus the learner has at one time several things at several degrees of imperfection, and some of them mislearnt. These things are encountered again and some of them are learnt a little more and some of them which had been mislearnt modified and so on. Therefore the model is not one thing thoroughly at a time but several things at a time at several degrees of thoroughness.
>
> (Prabhu 1980b:21)

On this view a cyclical gradualist approach with less concern for immediate mastery might pay more dividends. As Parkinson *et al.* point out, it is at least worth speculating upon the possibility that:

One class using mastery learning might be brought to complete mastery of three units . . . whilst a parallel class using traditional methods might have attained partial mastery of ten, and learned more worthwhile things outside the basic course.

(Parkinson *et al*. 1981)

In so far as it sees teaching as able to cause immediate internalization of correct behaviour at will, the reconstructionist approach would seem to be based, in part at least, on a fallacy.

Many of the higher order outcomes of educational experiences that we aspire to are notoriously difficult to set out as explicit behavioural objectives, for example those concerned with artistic or creative pursuits, with critical or reflective ones, or with areas to do with awareness or with learner responsibility. Yet, if we exclude these from our list of objectives, because they cannot easily be made explicit, we are in danger of losing the all important shape of the wood through an over-concentration on some of the more easily discernible trees. Some contemporary foreign language courses, for example, have been trivialized into a total diet of tourist objectives such as finding the way, buying tickets, getting ice-creams, and other such restricted concerns, since such objectives are easily listed. It can be argued that it is neither possible nor indeed helpful to predetermine the outcomes of all learning experiences. Teachers can, through experience, tell what will make a good lesson. They do not always need predetermined objectives. Stenhouse (1970) points to the futility of attempting to specify what predetermined behavioural outcomes should be attained from the study of a work of literature such as Hamlet, and asserts somewhat provocatively:

Education as induction into knowledge is successful to the extent that it makes the behavioural outcomes of the students unpredictable.

(Stenhouse 1970)

Most reconstructionist approaches involve an initial analysis of learners' needs as the basis upon which the curriculum will be founded. This is certainly true of the Council of Europe's approach to the foreign language curriculum, which was to be based on 'goals relevant to the communicative needs of the learner' (Trim 1978). The term 'needs', however, is an extremely slippery one, and in trying to come to terms with it, it is helpful to refer to the German language, which makes a useful distinction between *Bedarf* (objective needs, not necessarily felt by the individual), and *Bedürfnisse* (subjective needs internally felt by the individual). There is unfortunately no such distinction encoded in English. There is also, along very much the same lines, a distinction between 'things done in the best *interests* of the pupils', and 'things done in accordance with pupil *interests*'. Reconstructionist curricula are more likely to be concerned with *Bedarf* and the 'best *interests* of pupils', while pupils may be more motivated by some appeal to their 'felt needs' (*Bedürfnisse*) and to their own individual *interests*. Dearden (1972) rightly warns:

> The two notions of needs and interests offer glorious opportunities for seeming both to have one's cake and eat it, for, by sliding about between the ambiguities of meaning, curricular recommendations can be made to seem to satisfy everybody.
>
> (Dearden *et al.* 1972:54)

There is little doubt that the interpretations placed upon the initial needs analysis approach adopted by the Council of Europe did indeed slide about between the concepts of *Bedarf* and *Bedürfnisse*, and often failed to make the distinction. That it is important to do so is obvious when one realizes that learner motivation is harnessed by *Bedürfnisse*, but may not be by *Bedarf*.

From the outset, however, Richterich (1973a, 1973b, 1978) showed an awareness of the tension between the desire to predetermine a rational curriculum based on the learners' socially predictable communicative needs (*Bedarf*), and the wish to cater sensitively and flexibly for each individual's changing *Bedürfnisse*. Richterich was also aware that there was something fundamentally odd about trying to forecast communicative needs, since the essence of much communication is that it is unpredictable.

> A fundamental contradiction may be seen . . . between the desire to define precise needs and aims and the fact that the use of a language as a means of communication and of controlling social situations requires a capacity to react appropriately to things which cannot be accurately foreseen or defined . . .
>
> Whereas what is really needed is an ephemeral educational theory fully meeting the needs of individuals, production requirements may well impose an educational theory which corresponds only to the general and theoretical needs of a few broad categories of people . . . Nuances, differentiation and a

certain degree of individualisation will have to be introduced
when it comes to creating specific units.

(Richterich 1973b:32)

Porcher captured the essential problem of a needs-based curriculum
for school foreign language learners when he wrote:

Pour un apprenant scolaire l'avenir adulte est toujours
incertain, aléatoire et même seulement potentiel. Cet apprenant
ne peut donc avoir qu'une conscience floue de ses besoins
langagiers.

(Porcher 1980:45)[2]

It is interesting to note that in more recent years Richterich and his
Council of Europe colleagues have moved away from the strategy of
trying to encapsulate learners' needs in a rigidly predetermined
syllabus towards a two-stage strategy. The first stage is concerned to
provide initial data about the learners and their aspirations, based on
simple and rapid techniques of analysis. Where the learners form a
reasonably homogeneous group in terms of the purposes for which
they are learning the foreign language, these data can be used to
provide some sort of initial stereotype of *Bedarf*. The second stage in
the strategy involves ongoing classroom negotiation to ensure that
the teaching that the learners receive is in line with their evolving
Bedürfnisse. This is intended to ensure a matching of teacher and
learner interests. It allows for individual differences to be catered for,
and for any change in needs to be incorporated into the teacher's
provision of learning experiences. On this view the predetermined
syllabus remains one source of reference, but is no longer viewed as
dictating what should happen all the time.

A serious flaw in the particular way in which the Council of
Europe team conceptualized communicative needs was the fact that
they assumed a total identity of concerns between what native
speakers might need and what foreign language learners would need.
As Holec (1980) emphasized, however, where learners suffer from
limited tools of vocabulary and syntax, and have insufficiently
diversified interactive and illocutionary options for their purposes,
what they need most are strategies to make up for such deficiencies.
Thus any initial specification reflecting learners' rather than native
speakers' needs should include some concern for the transfer from
mother-tongue experience of compensatory communicative
strategies, such as the use of enlightened guessing, gesture, para-
phrasing, or the creation of likely neologisms. Indeed Canale and

Swain (1980, updated by Canale 1983) identified four components of communicative competence, of which one was compensatory or strategic competence. The other three were based on contemporary applied linguistic hypotheses, and comprised linguistic competence, sociolinguistic competence (contextual appropriacy), and discourse competence (the ability to create coherent discourse). The Council of Europe's curriculum model accounts for the latter three to some extent, but fails to take strategic competence into account, since it seems to be operating from the erroneous principle that it is only through accumulating native-speaker language norms that a learner can learn to communicate in a foreign language.

Reconstructionist approaches all seem to imply that learners have to learn to recreate the exact speech patterns of the target language community. Learners tend to be asked to learn stereotypical language. They act out particular roles, but do not often seem to create what they say and do. In real life, however, the roles that we adopt are functions of the interactions we engage in, rather than static possessions. The language we use originates from deep roots in our personality, rather than from a predetermined script. If we do not have practice at making the necessary links between the deeper processes of our cognitive and affective make-up and whatever language tokens are available to us, we may never learn how to mould the foreign language to our own ends. As Di Pietro puts it:

> The textbook which provides only samples of stereotypical
> exchanges among people in its dialogues will never allow
> learners to develop the verbal strategies which go with being a
> person in a new language . . . To be somebody in another
> language, you must know how to speak not only in
> accordance with your own age group, your own sex-
> membership, but also with regard to your personal
> psychological disposition towards others.
>
> (Di Pietro 1976:53)

Burstall *et al.* (1974) found evidence to support this in their research into Primary French:

> There is some evidence that dependence on rote learning may
> actually inhibit any natural inclination towards a less rigid
> form of conversation.
>
> (Burstall *et al.* 1974)

To learn to be somebody in a foreign language one needs practice, not just in role-play in the sense of acting out someone else's script, but in role-making and role-negotiating of a sort that involves the inner self, whether this is done through behaving as oneself, or as some other adopted but well-internalized persona as proposed in 'suggestopaedia' (Lozanov 1978).

Studies of cross-cultural interference have shown how difficult it can sometimes be to learn to move outside one's own cultural patterns. In order to conform to another culture's conventions, one may have to learn to manage interactions in a different way, to avoid topics one is used to discussing, to use other forms of address, and to encode one's speech acts in quite different ways. If one employs one's own cultural patterns in another speech community one may appear either dull of mind or deliberately rude. Alarmingly it is often in the most common interpersonal speech events such as greetings, apologies, compliments, and requests that such cultural differences are crucial. It is psychologically difficult for British learners to speak in the direct way Germans do, or for Germans to adopt the attenuated circumlocutions that the British use. It can be argued that in classroom circumstances it may be more important to concentrate on linguistic competence, discourse competence, and strategic competence, than to spend too much time on strict sociolinguistic appropriacy in the absence of target language native speakers. Contrary to what Hymes suggests, it may indeed be possible in foreign language learning to add a sociolinguistic dimension to the other competencies later when in direct contact with members of the other speech community.

It is often difficult to know what use is to be made of the various syllabus categories set out in reconstructionist approaches to the foreign language curriculum. From a theoretical point of view many critics have pointed out that categories such as situations, topics, functions, and notions are of dubious value. They conform neither to any particular theory of language acquisition (Paulston 1981), nor to any theory of language use (Corder undated). The content of the categories can be said to be 'plucked out of the air' (Brumfit 1981a), can be 'specified to infinity', and is 'repetitive across lists' (Hill 1977). As Richterich (1973) observed:

On se prend parfois à rêver à des catalogues raisonnés et exhaustifs auxquels on pourrait simplement se référer pour préparer un matériel pédagogique et déterminer des stratégies d'apprentissage adéquates, mais on déchante rapidement devant l'infinité des besoins et des facteurs dont ils dépendent,

et l'on est réduit à se satisfaire d'approximations dont
l'efficacité et l'utilité peuvent souvent paraître douteuses.

(Richterich 1973a:3)[3]

The problem that the course writer or language teacher inevitably
faces is neatly summed up by Monippally:

> The categories we create for descriptive and referential purposes
> are so convenient and so indispensable that the temptation to
> accord them ontological status is great. But they are nothing but
> conceptual artefacts.

(Monippally 1983:Chapter 4)

Syllabus definition inevitably reduces the dynamic and creative
character of language to a static inventory of parts, whether these are
expressed in the form of activities, situations, functions, notions, or
structures. It is necessary always for course writers and teachers to
find a means of bringing the static parts to life again in their provision
of learning experiences in the form of coherent discourse, so that
through time learners can develop their capacity for the negotiation
of personal meanings, if indeed they are to learn to communicate
rather than merely to display the language forms that have been
assigned to a particular behavioural, conceptual, or grammatical
category.

We do not consciously select particular functions and notions to
embody in language any more than we choose to display particular
grammatical categories. We communicate, and if it is found useful
we can look at the product of our efforts and discuss what has
occurred by examining the exponents and attempting to relate them
to particular functions and notions, or to grammatical and lexical
categories. But this is an after-the-event way of breaking up the flux
and flow of a particular discourse, rather than a means of
predetermining what one may wish to say. This does not deny that
the teacher and pupil may need to focus on particular elements of
rhetorical, semantic, and grammatical content that arise in discourse. It seems important to insist, however, that such focuses
should arise out of language in use rather than precede them, so that
learners are enabled to discover rules of use, form-meaning
relationships, and formal rules and systems against the backcloth of
real contextualized discourse.

Since the grammatical system provides the learner with the most
economical, systematizable, and generative layer of language in use,
Brumfit has argued that:

The simplest proposal is to use the grammatical system as the
core of the syllabus in a ladder-like series of stages, and to be
prepared to relate all other essential material to this series.
Thus notional, functional, and situational specifications can be
conceived of as a spiral round a basically grammatical core.

(Brumfit 1980:5)

Brumfit maintains that a focus on grammar need not divert the
learners' attention away from the meaning of what they are exposed
to, provided, of course, that the course writer succeeds in embedding
the particular pattern(s) to be focused upon into a communicative
framework in a natural way. There is little doubt that it is easier to
find pedagogical logic, and even some psychological reality, behind
the sequencing of grammar, provided it is set in a communicative
framework, than behind the sequencing of any of the other
organizational categories proposed so far (topics or themes,
situations, functions, or notions). There is no obvious reason, for
example, why one might wish to teach the topic of 'sport' before
'travel', or the situation 'in the restaurant' before 'at the cinema', or
the function 'asking for permission' before 'expressing a wish'.

The problem posed by situational, topic-based, or functional-
notional approaches that are not based on grammatical progression
is that they seem to place a great burden on the learners' capacity to
memorize data and to find system for themselves. In school foreign
language learning where both exposure to the language and learner
motivation may be restricted, this is too large a burden for most
learners to take on.

We conclude this discussion about descriptive categories with the
reflection that in recent years the urge to produce ever better
analytical tools, through which to categorize language, has obscured
the essential fact that for the learner the categories matter less than
the verisimilitude, interest, level of challenge, and apparent relevance
of the talk and texts to which they give rise. Learners do not come
into direct contact with a teaching syllabus in order to learn. They
encounter and create texts, and it is the quality and inherent value of
these texts that matters, rather than the particular linguistic,
semantic, rhetorical, or situational features that may have led to their
choice or creation.

Teachers do not find long lists of objectives, or syllabus content
derived from them, of much use to them in their choice of learning
experiences, as Popham for one has belatedly concluded (Popham
1983). There is a certain irony in the fact that the Council of Europe

team set out to reject the 'systematic taxonomic division of language as subject-matter in favour of an analysis of learning situations' (Trim 1979). What they ended up by doing was to turn syllabus design from a cottage craft concerned with one or two taxonomic divisions into a multi-dimensional and thoroughly self-indulgent industry in which more and more ways of dividing up the subject matter were devised, but no advance in how to teach it was achieved. The end product in the various Threshold Levels resembles a thesaurus, a phrase book, a grammar book, and a lexicon all combined, whose categories and exponents might indeed be established with a particular audience in mind, but which do not help teachers to determine how the teaching and learning are to take place, a point to which we shall return in a moment.

The 'ends-means' approach is based upon the assumption that learning tasks should be broken down into their component parts. Welford, however, has shown that this may well not be the best way to approach the teaching of complex skills:

> Where the whole task is a closely co-ordinated activity such as aiming a rifle or simulated flying of an aircraft, the evidence suggests that it is better to tackle the task as a whole. Any attempt to divide it up tends to destroy the proper co-ordination of action and subordination of individual actions to the requirements of the whole . . . and this outweighs any advantage there might be in mastering different portions of the task separately.
>
> (Welford 1968:291)

This suggests that in order to learn to perform a particular communicative task, it may be better to attempt it as a whole, gradually approximating more and more closely towards some native-speaker ideal, rather than to focus sequentially on particular functions or notions or grammatical features likely to be involved.

Evidence from pupil contract schemes seems to indicate that many students do not like an inflexible individualized learning mode designed to lead them to various predetermined goals by their own efforts.

> It's a system under which the teachers do nothing and the pupils have to find everything out for themselves. At best that's what it looks like to me . . . The Dalton thing is a washout. No one can understand a thing . . . There is no way of working in the lab because of the noise. It's the same every

day. At the end of the month you have to hand in your tasks
and nothing is finished . . . Damn that Dalton Plan.

(Ognyov 1928, quoted in Grittner 1975:326)

It would appear that the refusal to allow the teacher to negotiate with
learners, to respond to their needs of the moment, to cater for the
cognitive needs of weaker pupils by providing them with the extra
back-up of concepts and guiding methodological principles, and
direct instruction when necessary, made these contract schemes just
as inflexible as the classical humanist teacher-directed classrooms
they sought to replace.

It can be argued that mastery learning which sets out to bring
about an equalization of achievement, implies inequality of opportunity, since the high-flyers are to be held back until the lower
achievers catch up with them. Leaving aside the question as to
whether such a notion is not simply wishful thinking, it can be argued
that contriving an equalization of achievement is every bit as
unacceptable a form of 'pernicious self-fulfilling prophecy' as the one
Bloom (1971) was aiming to avoid. Bloom's is an approach that
assumes equality of innate ability, and insists that the task of
education is to readjust the inequalities of early nurture. Teacher
experience, however, would indicate that this is not achievable in
practice.

All students do not learn a foreign language – or anything else
in the curriculum equally. Incontrovertible evidence of this
fact, albeit circumstantial evidence, is provided by hundreds of
thousands of teachers worldwide in whose classrooms student
achievement runs the gamut from zero mastery to full mastery
of the material to be learned.

(Altman 1979:5)

Many educational pscholoolgists would reject Bloom's view that the
cognitive differences between children are entirely due to environment, rather than being in part at least innate.

Equality of innate ability is not a fact of nature, and any
educational system founded on such beliefs is doomed to
failure; equality in the sense of being permitted to develop
whatever abilities one is born with to the highest degree is
quite another matter. A democratic society is almost by
definition dedicated to such ends.

(Eysenck 1972)

An unfortunate corollary to the decision to predetermine a mastery level, and to test at regular intervals to ensure that it is being achieved, is that there is a risk of creating anxiety among the pupils, particularly among those who repeatedly find themselves in the 'remedial' group after the test. Much of the current American 'humanistic' concern springs from a reaction against the anxiety that is brought about by adopting mastery-learning techniques.

The most important concern of mastery learning would seem to be the desire to promote a feeling of success in the learner. A feeling of success, however, is not necessarily determined by the teacher's view of what constitutes mastery, and is more a question of the pupil's own perceptions of what he/she wishes and is able to do. It seems more sensible to plan for differentiation in what constitutes success and mastery rather than to set common criteria arbitrarily. On this view a mastery level is a matter to be negotiated between teacher and pupil on the basis of what the pupil can achieve, aspires to, and wishes to commit himself to. As Altman noted:

> Some learners would willingly and happily settle for a lower evaluation of their efforts, for example a Grade B or a C instead of an A, if the lower evaluation assured the commitment of less of their time and energy.

> (Altman 1979:12)

Although it was never clear how the Council of Europe team envisaged that their taxonomies of objectives were to be used in the teaching/learning process, it would seem that it was some sort of mastery learning approach that they envisaged. Wilkins, for example, had written:

> When objectives have been defined, the most important single methodological principle is to ensure that the linguistic and learning experience is planned so as to be completely representative of components of those objectives . . . The quantity of each activity in the classroom should reflect its place in the overall objectives.

> (Wilkins 1974b:59–60)

This would seem to imply the deliberate learning of predetermined language forms and a rehearsal of situations, which, as Widdowson (1983) points out, is closer to training than to education. Learning a language involves more than being able to recognize and reproduce language tokens or behaviours attached to particular syllabus categories. As Brumfit puts it:

We are not teaching a limited set of behaviours but a capacity to produce those behaviours.

(Brumfit 1980:2)

Learners have to be helped to generalize from whatever particular instances they may be exposed to. They must learn to exploit whatever language resource they possess for the personal interpretation and expression of meaning. This is dependent not just upon being able to adopt shared conventions of communicative competence, but also upon a creative capacity to bend the socially accepted norms to their own personal ends in order to negotiate meanings with others.

Where reconstructionism can be said to be at its weakest is in its assumption that if one can describe the *product* of learning in sufficient detail, this will guide one in the choice of learning experiences to bring it about. Describing the hoped-for products of learning, whether in terms of behavioural activities, or the ability to express certain functional/notional meanings, or the knowledge of particular native-speaker forms, or indeed combinations of all of these, does not tell the teacher or learner how they are to get to these final products. Describing what a flower in bloom looks like in all its detailed glory tells one little about how it gets to this state. In order to encourage a seed's growth, although it may be of interest to have a picture of what it should eventually look like, what we really need is some idea of how to go about gardening, some notion of what will help or hinder growth, and an indication as to how to react to the particular way our plant is developing. What language teachers really need, rather than descriptions of expected outcomes, or impressionistic etchings of what proficiency *might* look like as one moves through hypothetical points or levels on a developmental continuum, are principles of procedure as to how to promote language development and communicative proficiency through providing appropriate classroom learning experiences and feedback.

In criterion-referenced assessment the criteria upon which levels of performance and pass/fail distinctions are made are often assumed to be absolute. They are however plucked out of the air on the basis of intuition, which is frequently shown on closer examination to be wrongly conceived. As Gronlund warns:

There is little empirical evidence to support any given level of mastery in classroom instruction. The best we can do is to arbitrarily set a standard and then adjust it up and down as experience dictates.

(Gronland 1973:12)

In other words the criteria we set should be related to the norms of performance and to classroom reality, and not simply to some neat and tidy intuitive ideal. In the elaboration of proficiency scales there is no objective way of determining how many levels there should be, or the size of the increments in the performance continuum. This is highlighted by the fact that B. J. Carroll (1980:134) sets out nine levels, Wilkins (in Trim 1978:71–8) seven, and the FSI (Wilds 1975:36–8) five, each purporting to lead from zero ability to native-speaker-like proficiency. All of these scales suffer from the limitations pointed out by Trim (1978:6). They tend to employ impressionistic and relational terms, to which no precise meaning can be attached (for example, 'adequate' or 'intelligible'). They also tend to over-discriminate at the lower end and under-differentiate at higher levels. More worryingly, as Clark (1984) points out, they tend to assume that learners develop in all aspects of communicative proficiency in roughly the same way along a predetermined path, whereas in reality one learner may develop fluency to a high level but remain relatively inaccurate, while another may do the reverse, and yet in terms of global proficiency an assessor may wish to give them the same overall grade. It might be suggested that it is better to attempt to chart progress in each of the sub-components of communicative proficiency separately. A learner might then be scored at Level 3 with respect to strategic competence, while remaining at Level 1 for example, in sociolinguistic competence. This sort of scoring, however, is extremely complex, and given the number of important sub-components of communicative proficiency for which a score would have to be given, it is quite impractical in the school setting. There is little doubt that at present the intentions behind criterion-referencing can be said to have gone well beyond the capacity of existing assessment techniques to fulfil them. The descriptions of expected learner performance at each grade of the new Scottish Standard Grade and English GCSE exams, for example, remain at best gross averagings out of important individual variations, and at worst fictional distortions of reality. We must guard against giving them any ontological status, and treat them rather as the abstract artefacts that they are, however much impressive evidence may be collected as to the reliability with which trained teachers can allocate learners to the various grades or levels described. Unless extreme caution is used, they may well lead teachers to mould pupils to the descriptions, rather than encourage them to exercise their judgement and provide descriptive information that would reflect their pupils' performances more accurately.

Research and evaluation based on reconstructionist values have been criticized for their lack of concern for individual differences in different contexts. Reconstructionism assumes that what works in one context will automatically work in another. The emphasis on outcomes of learning rather than on the process has also been criticized. Reconstructionist research and evaluation seem concerned solely with determining whether initial objectives have been achieved, ignoring human variables, and unexpected outcomes. The terms 'agricultural-botany paradigm' (Parlett and Hamilton 1972) and 'factory-farming approach' (Monippally 1983) have been used to describe this approach.

> Students rather like plant-crops are given pretests (the seedlings are weighed or measured) and then submitted to different experiences (treatment conditions). Subsequently . . . their attainment (growth or yield) is measured to indicate the relative efficiency of the methods (fertilisers) used.
>
> (Parlett and Hamilton 1972:7)

The reconstructionist or Research, Development, and Diffusion form of curriculum renewal can also be criticized for its concern with products rather than with the renewal process. It tends to assume that all classrooms are the same, and that a stereotypical product in the form of some curriculum package created from outside the classroom will be appropriate to all teaching-learning contexts.

The sort of in-service training associated with the Research, Development, and Diffusion form of curriculum renewal tends to be a 'top-down' affair in which teachers are informed about a new innovation and trained to adopt it. It is the common fate of externally imposed curriculum packages, however, that various internal constraints are allowed to reduce their effectiveness. Thus, such things as the timetable, class sizes, insufficient resources etc. may well frustrate the exercise. It is rare for teachers to feel much commitment to any curriculum in whose making they have not been involved. The reconstructionist 'top-down' approach does not normally provide teachers with a sense of belonging to what is to be done. This lack of commitment is reflected in the classroom. It is also common for teachers to remove all the innovatory parts from 'top-down' packages in order to make them conform to their own existing practices, rather than to attempt to work within the spirit of the whole (Brown, McIntyre *et al.* 1976).

The conclusion must be drawn that over and above any form of *training* for the adoption of Research, Development, and Diffusion packages, there needs to be some form of in-service *education*, designed to assist teachers over time to make the package their own, by amending it to their own classroom requirements. An externally imposed curriculum package should be viewed not as a panacea, but as an enlightened hypothesis, whose various aspects have to be tested against the realities of the particular classroom in which they are to be used.

In the same way as it is not so much a syllabus or a textbook that determines the effectiveness of a curriculum, as the actual teaching and learning process that it gives rise to, so it is not so much a curriculum package that determines the effectivess of curriculum renewal as the process of change that derives from it. Reconstructionism is more concerned with syllabuses and plans and curricular products than it is with the teaching, learning, and renewal processes. It thereby lays itself open to the charge that it is more concerned with appearance than essence, and with intention rather than reality.

Notes

1 Defining communicative needs means setting out what is required by an individual or a group of individuals to change through linguistic or other activity their current deficient state.

2 For a school learner the adult future is always uncertain, unpredictable and only potential. Such a learner can only have a vague notion of his language needs.

3 Sometimes one dreams of rational and finite categories to which one could refer in order to prepare pedagogical material and select appropriate learning strategies, but one soon abandons this because of the infinite number of needs and of factors upon which they depend. One is reduced to having to be satisfied with approximations whose usefulness and adequacy often appear to be in doubt.

3 Progressivism

3.1 Introduction

Progressivism looks to Rousseau for its inspiration and to Piaget among others for its pragmatic support.

It makes for a learner-centred approach to education, which attempts to promote the pupil's development, as an individual with intellectual and emotional needs, and as a social being. The learner is seen as a whole person and not just as a disembodied intellect or as a skilled performer.

Progressivists tend to see education as a means of providing children with learning experiences from which they can learn by their own efforts. Learning is envisaged as a continuum which can be broken up into several broad developmental stages. For progressivists, 'growth' through experience is the key concept.

Transmitting a cultural heritage is made subservient to following the developing rhythms of the individual child. There is sometimes, therefore, a tendency towards a somewhat goal-free style of learning, though it must be admitted that the education Rousseau proposed for Emile (Boyd 1956), far from being haphazard, was a thoroughly structured affair, with the pupil's spontaneity harnessed to a well worked-out developmental programme.

For progressivists, education is not seen as a process for the transmission of a set of closed truths, but as a way of enabling learners to learn how to learn by their own efforts. Teachers are not instructors but creators of an environment in which learners learn and learn how to learn.

> The only man who is educated is the man who has learned how to learn; the man who has learned how to adapt and change; the man who has learned that no knowledge is secure, that only the process of seeking knowledge gives a basis for security.

> (Rogers 1969)

Knowledge is not seen as a set of fixed facts, but as a creative problem-solving capacity that depends upon an ability to retrieve appropriate schemata from a mental store, to utilize whatever can be automatically brought to bear upon a situation, and to bend existing

conceptual structures to the creation of novel concepts that offer a
working solution to the particular problem in hand.

For progressivists, knowledge is never static.

> The dependence of knowledge on a conceptual structure means
> that any body of knowledge is likely to be of only temporary
> significance. For the knowledge which develops from the use
> of a given concept usually discloses new complexities of the
> subject matter which call forth new concepts. These new
> concepts in turn give rise to new bodies of inquiry and,
> therefore, to new and more complete bodies of knowledge
> stated in new terms.
>
> (Schwab 1964:13)

Education for progressivists, therefore, is concerned with developing
an open, speculative view of knowledge, based on an understanding
of the transient nature of our current conceptual structures. Learning
involves the perception and internalization of ever 'better' schemata,
which appear to describe and explain phenomena for us better than
those in our current mental store. This is not achieved simply by
replacing one set of schemata by another, as one would replace plugs
in a car, but by gradually building on existing conceptual structures
through the assimilation of new perceptions and the adapting of
what exists to accommodate these. There is no implication that
newer schemata are in any objective sense 'better'. They may still be
incomplete or inadequate conceptualizations. What matters is that
they work for us at the time.

Learners are seen as active participants shaping their own
learning, with the teacher cast in the role of guide or facilitator. Thus
progressivists lay great stress on the need for learning by doing,
rather than by being taught. Gide, reflecting on the inadequacy of his
own formal education, wrote:

> J'ai passé trois années de voyage à oublier tout ce que j'avais
> appris par la tête. Cette désinstruction fut lente et difficile,
> mais elle me fut plus utile que toutes les instructions imposées
> par les hommes, et vraiment le commencement d'une
> éducation.
>
> (Gide 1897. In 1947:19)[1]

Progressivists are more concerned with learning processes and
methodology than with predetermining objectives.

A further aspect of progressivism is its view of the school or the classroom as a self-contained community, responsible for creating its own subculture and interaction networks among its various participants. Thus one of the major roles of education is to promote healthy personal relationships and a sense of group responsibility.

> The first principle of human nature is mutuality . . . A person
> is always one term in a relation of persons . . . For this reason
> the first priority in education is learning to live in personal
> relation to other people. Any kind of teaching involves
> establishing a personal relationship between teacher and
> pupil, and the success or failure of the teaching depends very
> largely on the character and quality of this relation.
>
> (MacMurray – date untraced)

In foreign language learning the progressivist approach is generally represented by those who see progress or growth in terms of interlanguage development. Language learning is seen as an implicit intuitive developmental process for which human beings have a natural capacity, rather than as the product of the deliberate study and practice of knowledge elements and skills towards predetermined objectives.

In brief, we can summarize progressivism as being concerned with:

— individual growth from within through interaction with a favourable environment
— learning through experience
— a speculative view of knowledge
— natural learning processes and stages of development
— sensitivity to the interests, rhythms, and styles of learning of individual learners
— the learner as a whole person
— the social nature of the learner and the development of healthy relationships with others in the classroom community
— the promotion of learner responsibility and of learning how to learn

3.2 Progressivism in curriculum design

Progressivism in curriculum design is represented by the process approach. Unlike the classical humanist approach, which emphasizes content, and the reconstructionist approach, which emphasizes objectives, the progressivist approach emphasizes methodology and the need for principles to govern the teaching/learning process.

I take as my example of a 'process' approach to curriculum design the one proposed by Stenhouse (1975:84–97), since this appears to have considerable affinity with some of the foreign language curriculum models recently proposed. For Stenhouse a 'process' approach is built upon the notion of 'principles of procedure' which guide the teaching/learning process, and a light 'syllabus specification' to assist teachers to set the process in motion.

As an example of what he meant by 'principles of procedure' Stenhouse (1975:92) set out those established for the project *Man: A Course of Study*.

- to initiate and develop in youngsters a process of question-posing
- to teach a research methodology where children can look for information . . .
- to help youngsters develop the ability to use a variety of first-hand sources as evidence from which to develop hypotheses and draw conclusions
- to conduct classroom discussions in which youngsters learn to listen to others as well as to express their own views
- . . . to give sanction and support to open-ended discussions where definitive answers to many questions are not found
- to encourage children to reflect on their own experiences
- to create a new role for the teacher, in which he becomes a resource rather than an authority.

(Hanley *et al.* 1970)

These principles are clearly designed to bring about a classroom where inquiry, activity, discussion, reflection, and open-ended personal interpretations feature, rather than predetermined objectives, content, and mastery levels.

Stenhouse goes on to propose that having established the principles of procedure that will govern a particular process, it is necessary to provide only a very light syllabus specification to assist teachers to create their own scheme of work adapted to their own context. He is at pains to point out that a specification should not take the form of a monolithic predetermined package to be implemented unthinkingly. It is offered 'as a starting point for experiment' to be modified in the light of experience (Stenhouse 1975).

The basic building blocks for such a provisional specification were to be an indication of content and of activities. Stenhouse leans to Peters' (1966) classical humanist view that education should be concerned with inherently valuable knowledge, with its nature and its significance, rather than with the predilections of pupils, the demands of society, or the values of politicians. Thus content and activities were to be selected for 'the standards immanent within them, rather than because of what they lead to' (Peters 1966).

Stenhouse cites Raths' (1971) criteria for the selection of activities. These can be summarized as indicating that they will be of maximum value where they engage learners actively in inquiry, in making informed choices, in taking risks, in carrying out tasks which can be accomplished at several levels, in co-operating with others, and in transferring the knowledge or skills acquired to new settings.

The active engagement of the learner is also a feature of the progressivist form of assessment, which involves teachers and students negotiating assignments for students to complete, and agreeing the process activities by which they are to complete them. Students are encouraged to describe and evaluate the process they undergo, and to reflect upon whether the learning or 'doing' strategies adopted were effective, and to consider their reactions to them. Thus assessment covers not only cognitive aspects of learning, but also invites learners to express how they feel about what they have been doing. As a result of reflecting upon their learning experiences, they are expected to learn how to go about their learning tasks better, in other words to learn how to learn. There is an emphasis on peer-evaluation and self-evaluation. Students are encouraged to examine and evaluate their completed assignments with the help of a peer or the teacher, in order to see how they might be improved.

Ideally any report on student progress in a progressivist approach would be the result of teachers and students coming to some agreement as to what should be said in terms of the assignments completed and the process undergone. Such a report would be an individual statement of a student's achievements and how they had been attained. There would be no attempt to relate these achievements to those of others, as in norm-referenced assessment, or to any stereotypical predetermined levels of performance, as in criterion-referenced assessment.

The process approach lays emphasis on the individuality of each teaching and learning context. Thus the process approach to evaluation, as outlined by Parlett and Hamilton (1972) draws attention to the fact that curricula and methods inevitably take on different shapes, as they are interpreted by teachers and learners in different learning milieux. They were sceptical of research which attempted to test the general value of one curriculum or one teaching method against another on the basis of the products achieved, for three interrelated reasons:

- There is an assumption in such work that it is the curriculum or the methodology that causes the learning. It is clear, however, that even if a correlation can be established between one particular teaching method and one particular learning product, there is no necessary implication that the relationship is a causal one.
- There are many other important contextual variables at work that are simply ignored.
- It is normally assumed that the findings from such work can be generalized, from the particular contexts in which they have operated, to all contexts, irrespective of changes in the learning milieu.

Parlett and Hamilton emphasized instead the importance of attempting to portray the process of innovation as it unfolded, rather than judging its outcomes in terms of an initial specification of objectives. They aimed, through various techniques, to illuminate the various constraints, adaptations to an initial curriculum specification, and achievements, as well as the attitudes and reactions of those involved. They proposed a model of 'illuminative evaluation', based on three stages — observation, further inquiry, and attempts to explain what had actually occurred.

> Within this three-stage framework an information profile is assembled using data collected from four areas: observation, interviews, questionnaires and tests, documentary and background sources.
>
> (Parlett and Hamilton 1972:15)

Other progressivists, such as Adelman (1976) and Elliott (1976), have emphasized the importance of helping teachers to develop skills and strategies that will allow them to evaluate and improve their own classroom performance. According to them the ideal model of evaluation would be one in which the teachers learnt to evaluate themselves. Teachers would be encouraged to observe, study, and reflect upon their classroom practices. In addition they would listen to what their pupils had to say about their lessons and would encourage them to keep diaries noting their impressions. Elliott advocated:

gathering accounts of a teaching situation from three quite different points of view, namely those of the teacher, his students, and a participant-observer ... By comparing his own account with accounts from the two other standpoints, a person at one point of the triangle has an opportunity to test and perhaps revise it on the basis of more sufficient data.

(Elliott 1976:22)

The progressivist concern for learners becoming responsible for their own learning is thus paralleled by a similar concern for teachers becoming responsible for improving their own curriculum in the classroom.

3.3 Progressivism in the foreign language curriculum

Process approaches to the foreign language curriculum tend to concentrate on creating the right environment for individual internal interlanguage development to proceed smoothly. There is less stress on syllabus definition and more emphasis on the need for a set of methodological principles of procedure designed to set the language learning process in motion. There is also a concern for individual differences among learners and for developing strategies to respond to them and to promote each learner's sense of involvement and responsibility in his/her own learning.

The principles of procedure within process approaches to the foreign language curriculum spring from psycholinguistic studies of language acquisition allied to sociolinguistic studies of the creation and processing of discourse, rather than from an analysis of language or of learners' communicative needs. We shall examine several proposed process approaches to the foreign language curriculum. These cover suggestions for a pre-production phase to language learning, the procedural syllabus, the 'deep-end' approach, and the 'medium of instruction' or 'immersion' approach. We shall then examine ways in which individuals may vary in their learning, and consider strategies that have been proposed to respond to these. Before examining concrete examples of process approaches to school foreign language learning, however, it seems sensible to attempt to outline the sort of applied linguistic hypotheses that underlie them.

From the psycholinguistic evidence available it would seem that language acquisition is a subconscious process leading to the build-up of an internal store of implicit knowledge. This appears to follow a common developmental sequence, in which learners of a particular foreign language, largely irrespective of mother tongue, progress, fossilize, or regress along the same developmental continuum, albeit at different rates (Bailey, Madden, and Krashen 1974, Hyltenstam 1977, Corder 1981).

> Interlanguage, like child language, is a continuum of more or less smooth change, and we can locate learners, like infants, along the continuum of change or development.
>
> (Corder 1978:74)

Having already acquired an L1, foreign language learners are aware of the intentionality of language use and of the functions that language serves. They are thus primed to seek out propositional meaning and illocutionary value with all the faculties and experience that they can bring to bear on the matter. Thus, when interpreting real talk or text, foreign language beginners will tend to devote most if not all of their attention to processing the essential semantic units. The more or less redundant grammatical features will simply not be attended to. It would seem that it is the reduced language intake to which this gives rise, rather than any attempt consciously to simplify native-speaker syntax, that leads to the simple interlanguage forms that learners tend to produce (Ellis 1983). As they become more familiar with the forms of the language being learnt, so learners become more able to pay attention to redundant markers, as well as to the more important semantic ones. It has been suggested that whereas the mastery of those aspects of the grammar of a language which are semantic in nature tends to follow a particular order, the mastery of the more redundant features depends upon individual motivation. For those wishing to integrate fully into the speech community whose language is being learnt, there is obviously a need for a high level of morphological as well as syntactic accuracy. For those who wish merely to build a limited communicative bridge to that community, there is less need for morphological accuracy. Classroom foreign language learners are likely to be of the latter variety, but may have their lack of integrative motivation replaced to some extent by an extrinsic exam-passing motivation in which accuracy may play a major role.

Evidence would seem to show that acquisition is not a linear cumulative process but a gradual developmental one, in which many knowledge elements are all growing at once, at different rates, and at different levels of perfection. Most knowledge is not immediately accommodated on first presentation. A gestation period, in which further exposure to the same knowledge elements occurs in different contexts, is normally necessary before data can be fully incorporated into the implicit knowledge store. What the learner is able to take in from the data to which he is exposed is determined by the state of his internal grammar.

> We can only teach someone something if he already possesses the necessary conceptual framework to accommodate the new information.
>
> (Corder 1978:82)

The question as to whether to focus at all on grammatical or other formal matters is one which divides progressivists.

One of the protagonists for the view that focusing on form is unlikely to lead to improvement in spontaneous communicative performance is Krashen. Krashen (1981, 1982) borrows Palmer's (1921) notion of the distinction between 'spontaneous capacities' for learning, and 'studial capacities'. These Krashen calls 'acquisition' and 'learning', but goes further than Palmer and creates a theory around the notion that acquisition and learning are separate processes, and that the mental representations derived through each are in some way stored and accessed separately. He suggests that the acquisition process feeds an implicit store of knowledge, to which access is usually unconscious and immediate, and that the deliberate learning process feeds an explicit store of knowledge, to which access seems to require more conscious effort and more time.

Krashen claims that in everyday oral communication our utterances are initiated by our implicit knowledge, because we do not normally have time to call upon our explicit knowledge. The role of the latter is restricted to that of monitoring our utterances, either before or after production. He maintains that we can only make use of our explicit knowledge as a monitor if:

- we are given sufficient time to do so
- we focus on the form of what we say
- we know the rule we wish to apply.

Krashen's acquisition-learning distinction seems to provide an explanation for the well-known phenomenon of the foreign language learner who has consciously learnt the rule of how to produce a particular structure, yet produces an interlanguage *error* in spontaneous communication. It seems also to provide an explanation for the fact that learners who are able to perform structures correctly in a drill situation, may get them wrong in real communication (Clark 1969, Dakin 1973). By stating that both conscious understanding of rules and deliberate practice through drills and exercises form part of the learning process, but not of acquisition, and by restricting the role of explicit knowledge to that of a monitor, Krashen appears able to explain the failure of both the grammar-translation and the behaviourist audiolingual/audio-visual approach to bring about spontaneous use of language. It must be pointed out, however, that since conscious understanding of rules involves cognitive activity, while drills may not, it seems less than useful to associate them both with an apparently identical mental process.

Krashen claims that the evidence indicates that there is no interplay between that which has been learnt and that which has been acquired. He concludes that a deliberate focus on form in the classroom, whether in the input to which the learner is exposed, or in the feedback on learning provided by the teacher, will not lead to any improvement in implicit knowledge. According to Krashen the classroom should therefore concentrate on acquisition-promoting activities.

Krashen's position is a powerful echo of the position taken by Newmark and Reibel (1968), who claimed that since language learning was an intuitive process a formal emphasis on grammar was neither a necessary nor a sufficient condition for successful language learning.

> That it is not necessary is demonstrated by the native speaker's success without it; that it is not sufficient is demonstrated by the typical classroom student's lack of success with it.
>
> (Newmark and Reibel 1968)

On this view, any form of strict structural control over input data, either in the selection or the grading of it, can be rejected. Corder too writes:

> There is . . . no good reason to suppose that whatever 'logic' structural grading has is related to the internal logic of a learner's programme or built-in syllabus.
>
> (Corder 1978:82)

Instead of being based on structural concerns, grading for these progressivists is to be achieved through the sort of sensitive raising and lowering of the rhetorical level of talk and of text that native-speaker interlocutors manifest when interacting with learners, or that mothers and other caretakers show when talking to young children.

Other progressivists, however, believe that if teachers were to follow the sequence of structural development revealed in studies of natural (largely untutored) language learning, they would have a principled means of determining what forms to focus on at which time (for example Valdman 1980). This notion is rejected, however, by those who believe like Newmark and Reibel that nothing at all is to be gained from focusing on grammatical form.

Other progressivists adopt a more pragmatic viewpoint. While they would reject any attempt to control input on formal grounds alone, they would nevertheless encourage learners to develop their own more conscious awareness of system, through reflecting on the rules that seem to lie behind form-meaning relationships, and behind the creation of discourse within the various communicative texts encountered or created in the classroom. Such progressivists believe that foreign language learners beyond the age of about eight have conscious system-building needs as well as communicative needs, and that the teacher should respond to them.

Studies of how discourse is created and processed have shown that it is necessary to appeal beyond the formal features of the text to internalized areas of knowledge and experience that we gradually build in to our mental schemata, through the process of living and interacting with others. Our interpretation of discourse is assisted by such things as our understanding of the context in which the utterance is produced, the presuppositions we share with other interlocutors, our knowledge of the world, and our experience of previous similar discourse.

Information-processing theory sees the human being as a complex mechanism struggling to impose organization on information derived through the senses. 'Bottom-up' data-driven processing permits us to attend to perceptions, organize them, and then extract meaning from them. 'Top-down' conceptually-driven processing enables us to obtain a rapid expectation of what is likely to occur on the basis of previous experience, and to match this against the incoming sensory data. We do not have to process all the bottom-up information available to us through our senses, since we use the top-down contextual clues and expectations based on past experiences and general knowledge to avoid having to process the whole input. New information is thus derived as a result of expectations produced by top-down processing eventually merging with the data derived from bottom-up processes. Where tasks encountered present novel problems with little relationship to existing schemata and with few contextual clues, effective bottom-up processing becomes very important. Where tasks present familiar problems, top-down processing may provide rapid solutions. Since our attention is limited, we find interpretation difficult when processing demands exceed our capacity. It is important, therefore, that we build up a series of relatively automatic processes requiring very little of our attention, so that we can release our energy for the concerns which require more deliberate bottom-up processing.

Human beings are not simple input-output mechanisms, as Miller, Gallanter, and Pribram (1960) have attempted to show in their view of how cognition is translated into action. They suggest that we make plans – hierarchical processes that control the order in which a sequence of operations is performed. The operations are constantly monitored by the execution of various tests which provide feedback as to how the realization of the plan is proceeding. Any deficiencies between an original intention and ongoing performance are repaired through self-monitoring, or the original intention may be changed or abandoned *en route*.

> Humans are not automatons, smoothly and automatically encoding and decoding whatever messages they wish. The system is full of bugs, and its capabilities frequently fall short of the demands placed upon it.
>
> (Morrison and Low 1983:247)

In this view, developing the self-monitoring capacity becomes an important element in effective information processing.

There is no complete agreement about the form in which experience is stored in the memory, but it is generally presumed to be systematically organized, with numerous cross-references, so that it can be easily accessed for the interpretation of incoming data and the projection of future possibilities. There is also no complete agreement about how experience reaches the long-term memory, but Craik and Lockhart (1972), among others, emphasize that retention is a function of depth of processing. This is brought about by the learner finding or deliberately making the incoming data meaningful, so that it can be passed to the existing material in the long-term memory. It would appear that incoming sensory data are taken into the short-term perceptual memory, where messages reverberate and fade unless we take deliberate steps to make them meaningful and to process them in some way into the long-term store. Miller (1956) revealed that we can only retain seven (plus or minus two) discrete bits of information at any one time in the short-term memory. In order to increase this, a relation between items has to be discovered or imposed by the processor, thus forming a 'chunk'. Further chunking permits yet further quantities of information to be retained. Since short-term memory is largely a perceptual store, limited to some two seconds' retention, it is important to shift information into the long-term memory store as quickly as possible. This can be effected by the use of 'elaborative rehearsal strategies' (Norman 1976). These embrace various mnemonic techniques, such as finding sound or meaning association between items, or between items and the context in which they occur. They seem to involve the creation of some superordinate pattern combining the relevant discrete elements. Thus the learner is always looking for ever more complete systems to make sense of the discrete phenomena to which he is exposed. These are then passed through to the existing schemata in the mind, and have to be adapted to conform to them before they can be accommodated.

The lesson to be learnt from the depth-of-processing hypothesis is that utterances that are devoid of illocutionary value, and therefore of any pragmatic meaning, are unlikely to be processed properly. Many classroom 'sentences', made up to exhibit structures or vocabulary, have propositional meaning but no illocutionary value. They are unlikely to reach the long-term store, since the learner will not find them worth processing at all. Utterances which contain no new information are unlikely to achieve depth of processing.

> Information can be received only when there is doubt; and doubt implies the existence of alternatives where choice, selection or discrimination is called for.
>
> (Cherry 1956)

Much traditional classroom interaction is focused on form rather than on new information of any sort. Teachers ask questions to which they know the answers, and pupils provide answers which are seldom, if ever, judged in terms of their truth or information value. It is not surprising, therefore, that little of what occurs is retained.

While processing involves a matching of incoming data with existing schemata, creation involves converting multidimensional simultaneous personal experiences into unidimensional linear discourse. To express experience in discourse, therefore, involves a substantial effort of mental reorganization of information. We have to negotiate between our mental representations and the language resource we possess to express them. Where our language resource proves to be deficient, we have to adopt other communicative strategies in order to get over the difficulties.

Although we may be largely unconscious of it in conversation with others, we spend much of our time attempting to ensure a satisfactory meeting of minds with our interlocutors. We have to verify continually that we are all operating within the same framework of reference in terms of knowledge of the world, interpretation of the particular situation, use of the conventions of gesture, intonation, facial expressions, and of forms employed to convey particular meanings. In Widdowson's words, we have to work for 'a reciprocity of perspectives for the conveyance of information and intention' (Widdowson 1984). The more distant from our own culture the target language and the psychological world of its speakers are, the more difficult it will be to achieve this reciprocity of perspectives. Learning to communicate effectively is thus to a large extent a question of learning to decentre from one's own perspective to embrace the perspective of one's interlocutor(s). Grice (1975) suggests that on the whole we make things as easy as we can for each other in our conversations by conforming as best we can to certain maxims:

— to say only that which is necessary
— to say what we believe
— to be relevant
— to be clear and brief

Thus we co-operate with each other in a joint negotiation of meaning, which we hope, leads to effective communication.

While some proponents of a process approach to foreign language learning put more weight on principles that derive from their desire to promote acquisition, others place more emphasis on the development of the capacity to create and process discourse and negotiate meanings, while yet others, such as Breen, Candlin, and Waters see both concerns as inevitably intertwined.

Rather than encourage learners to learn language in order to communicate, we may encourage learners to communicate in order to develop their own learning ... We would be justified in doing so if we consider that the same abilities which underlie the communicative process also underlie the learning process.

(Breen, Candlin, and Waters 1979:4)

In brief, the following are the sort of principles of procedure underlying a process approach to foreign language learning that seem to emerge from the various concerns above:

- The learner must participate in meaningful interaction in the target language, so that information-processing mechanisms can be involved at some depth. For this to occur there must be some sort of information gap.
- The language used by the teacher-interlocutor should be adapted rhetorically to the learner's level through sensitive 'caretaker' strategies that promote top-down processing based on knowledge of the context, and bottom-up processing through such techniques as:
  - a slow rate of speech (clearer articulation, fewer contractions, longer pauses, exaggerated intonation), comprehensible vocabulary (less slang, fewer idiomatic turns of phrase, avoidance of pro-forms through repetition of names for people and things)
  - extra definition and explanation strategies (repetition, use of gesture)
  - a simplified syntax (short units set out conceptually rather than in subordinate clauses or embeddings, simple propositions giving a clear topic focus)
  - discourse-facilitating techniques (giving a possible answer within the question, yes/no questions, confirmation checks, clarification requests, and techniques for building in redundancy) (cf. Terrell 1980, Krashen 1981, and Ellis 1981).

It has become customary in process approaches to conceptualize learning experiences in terms of problem-solving tasks and activities, in which the learner is actively engaged in the interpretation and expression of meaning in order to create an appropriate solution (Birkbickler 1977). Such tasks and activities have formed the basis for the light syllabus specifications associated with the process approach.

In many communicative tasks there are often several ways of achieving a solution, and therefore divergent rather than convergent thinking is fostered.

The teacher is encouraged to set tasks with the appropriate level of contextual support, and leave pupils to find their own solution. Subsequently, through discussion, they are to be helped to become aware of what they have done, and of how else they might have done it. The key to good teaching in this approach lies in the teacher's ability to decentre to the pupil's level and viewpoint, and to structure tasks in such a way as to harness the learner's existing knowledge and experience, and to create an atmosphere and a purposeful context in which learners are willing to take risks and invest themselves in the solution of the various problems posed.

Having outlined the sort of principles of procedure and learning experiences that underlie the process approach, we move to an examination of some concrete proposals and practices.

3.3.1 Proposals for a pre-production phase

It has frequently been observed that in natural language acquisition in a foreign language environment, learners will listen for quite a long time before venturing to say very much beyond necessary routines (Ervin-Tripp 1978, Savignon 1981). A similar picture has emerged in some classroom foreign language learning. In a discussion of her experiences as a teacher in a Glasgow school, where the foreign language was used for normal classroom interaction, McGregor (1982) noted that in the first year of learning pupils made little creative use of what they were exposed to. They would merely regurgitate lesson material in question and answer work, and would reuse phrases in paired role-play. They would also reuse whole routines that had been consistently associated with classroom management activities. It was not until the second year that they showed signs of a generative capacity to transfer some of these routines and patterns to new situations, to unpackage phrases, and to create novel combinations.

Too early insistence on beginner speech seems to lead to task overload and to a fallback on L1 grammar (Krashen 1981). In the early phases, Terrell (1977) has advocated that students be allowed to respond in L1 first, or in L1 or L2 as the spirit moves them for quite some time. L2 responses are to be encouraged only when a learner's 'self-image and ease in the classroom is such that a response in the second language will not produce anxiety' (Terrell 1977:333).

Asher (1969), noting the high drop-out rate, low standards, and negative attitudes among two-year American school learners, concluded that what was required was a more limited objective restricted to listening fluency. He found that by getting beginners to listen to simple commands and carry them out physically, (Total

Physical Response or TPR method), acquisition was more effective than with those who listened without response, or with those who responded verbally. Those who responded physically also learnt better than those who were asked to translate into L1 what they had heard. Asher, Kusudo, and De la Torre (1974) found that the aural comprehension skills of those taught by TPR were far in advance of a control group who had received normal college instruction. In addition to this, they were shown to be able to adapt their aurally acquired competence very quickly to the skills of speaking and reading, in which they also out-performed the control group. On the basis of Asher's and other similar findings, it has been suggested that the initial activities in which beginners are involved should involve listening, and that there should be a delayed start to speaking (Postovsky 1974, Olmsted–Gary 1975, Nord 1980, Gary and Gary 1981, Richards 1983). It has also been suggested that it is a knowledge of vocabulary (rather than syntax) that is of most use to the beginner.

The sort of activities that have been suggested for a pre-production phase in foreign language learning, which might form the basis of a light syllabus specification, are indicated below. All involve a great deal of teacher-talk:

— commands and instructions which pupils carry out physically (Asher 1969). This can be extended to the notion of pupils acting as robots, or be done in the form of a game (for example 'O'Grady says'), or be turned into a gymnastics or aerobics session, or be converted into a cooking lesson, or an origami or model-making one
— routine classroom management talk
— descriptions of objects, people, or diagrams for pupils to draw
— description, as above, requiring some minimal response from pupils, such as choosing an appropriate picture from among several alternatives, naming a person described, putting pictures in order, or matching them
— story-telling, with pictures to assist understanding. Stories known in the mother tongue can be told in the foreign language. Students can process meaning by latching onto a few cognate words
— information related to a map or grid involving pupils in a minimal response or a mark at an appropriate spot
— simple games which involve the pupils in little or no speech (for example, Bingo)

As Krashen and Terrell (1983:78) point out with respect to a number of the activities outlined above, there is little 'real communication' involved. They are merely designed to:

- provide comprehensible input
- maintain focus on the message
- help lower affective filters

3.3.2   The procedural syllabus

The earliest language course to be based on problem-solving tasks that we have discovered is *Concept Seven-Nine* (Wight, Norris, and Worsley 1972), which was designed to enable ESL learners to use whatever language resource they already had in tasks designed to link conceptual and language development. To do this the authors devised a series of listening problems (Unit 1), classification problems (Unit 2), and communication problems in which pupils passed messages through a screen (Unit 3). In the latter, one pupil had to describe, for example, a picture or a place on a map to another pupil, who had to draw the picture or find the place indicated.

To our knowledge only one school foreign language syllabus, that being developed by a team led by Prabhu in the Bangalore Project in South India (Prabhu 1980a and 1980b), has chosen deliberately not to focus on a predetermined language content and to concentrate instead on a graded series of problem-solving tasks, designed to promote language acquisition. There is to be a focus on meaning and on the truth-value of utterances and not on form. The teacher is encouraged to adopt normal caretaker techniques of expansion, rephrasing, meaning verification, and incidental correction.

No attempt is made at any stage to tackle grammar through explanation or illustration, or to set form-focused exercises. Nor is it thought sensible to teach rules of use, which might run to thousands of statements, and would therefore be unlearnable in any explicit manner (D. J. Carroll 1980). Linguistic data are neither to be selected a priori, nor focused upon a posteriori, because this would falsify the nature of communication, through introducing an element of exemplification into the teaching. Even if such a focus might be useful for one learner at one particular time, it would not necessarily help another, since different learners need different data at different times. It is deemed better to insist that pupils be left to acquire grammar in their own way and in their own time.

To the argument that there was a need for teachers to be able to guarantee coverage of the most useful aspects of grammar, Prabhu replied that if a structure was worth covering it would certainly appear in the course of a year's problem-solving work. To the argument that there was a need to ensure coverage of language appropriate to predictable language needs outside the classroom, Prabhu maintained that there was no certain way of knowing these. He insisted, however, that having ensured that language was used naturally inside the classroom, it was reasonable to hope that pupils would be able to use it outside the classroom, whether they had been rehearsed for this or not.

The tasks were to be selected on two principles: that they should represent an appropriate level of challenge (neither too easy nor too difficult) for the pupil, and that they should engage the pupil's mind, so that there would be a genuine preoccupation with understanding, thinking out, doing or saying something. It was believed that the effort made by the pupils to cope with the negotiation of meaning through such tasks would enable them to develop a communicative ability based on a truly generative capacity. Teacher experience over the years would determine which tasks worked well, and might also permit finer judgements to be made about how best to grade them.

Where tasks were found to be too complex for a particular group of learners to tackle all at once, they would be broken down into sub-tasks. There would be teacher to whole-class preparation for each task through dialogue. Each pupil would then do an individual written task, related to, but different from, the spoken interactive one. There would then be an evaluation of success to guide the choice of the next task to be undertaken. The tasks were to be sequenced in such a way that the earlier, easier tasks would lead on to the later ones procedurally, conceptually, or linguistically. There was to be a deliberate reliance on teacher-class interaction, rather than on paired or group interaction between pupils, since the project team feared that the latter might promote pidginization (Prabhu 1982a).

Johnson (1980b and 1982) has argued that in Prabhu's preparation phase, where tasks may be reduced to sub-tasks, these latter become units similar to Wilkins' (1976) semantic ones. Johnson argues that there may be little distinction between a functional-notional approach and a procedural approach at this level. Prabhu, however, rightly points out that where Wilkins would seem to imply a deliberate predetermined focus on particular form-meaning relationships, the focus in the Bangalore project is always on the task to be completed.

He does not seek to deny that the preparation phase results in a good deal of covert repetition of structures, but claims that this repetition is not deliberately staged and is not made explicit to the pupil. One is, I think, justified, nevertheless, in claiming that from the pupil's point of view there is at this time a focus on form, since it is clear from lesson transcripts of the preparation phase (D. J. Carroll 1980) that pupils are sensibly attempting to repeat whatever forms the teacher uses.

Inevitably, as with all curriculum innovations, the Bangalore Project must be judged in the light of classroom reality and of the reactions of teachers and learners. The results of evaluation conducted so far would appear to be extremely positive (Prabhu 1982b).

We turn now to another 'process' approach, which differs from Prabhu's in so far as there is a deliberate a posteriori focus on form. Brumfit (1979b) has called this the 'deep-end' approach, in which the learners first communicate as far as possible with what they can. The teacher then teaches to the weaknesses exposed, before returning to a new communicative activity.

3.3.3   The 'deep-end' approach

Breen and Candlin (1980) proposed just such a version of the 'process' approach, shunning any prespecification of objectives or of content, but permitting conscious observation of language experienced, discovery of rules, and metalingual discussion.

In their curriculum approach the classroom was not to be seen as a place for artificial rehearsal of real-world activities, but rather as a resource for learning in its own right, with its own participants, its own conventions, and its own reality. It was to become a place in which there would be ongoing negotiation about learning, communication-as-learning, and communication about language in use itself. In the latter phase the classroom was to become 'an observatory of communication as everyday human behaviour' (Breen and Candlin 1980).

Breen, Candlin, and Waters (1979) proposed that for learning resources there should be 'content' and 'process' materials on which teachers and learners could draw. 'Content' materials based on authentic foreign language data were to be adapted to the learner's level and chosen through negotiation to be appropriate to the pupils' ongoing needs, interests, and motivations. These would promote acquisition, and be graded in terms of increasing unpredictability. Continuity would be ensured across units and within units on thematic grounds rather than on any linguistic principles. Learners would acquire system in their own way. In reflection and observation phases they would be encouraged to discover rules and regularities and to discuss these with each other.

There would also be 'process' materials designed to involve the learner in productive problem-solving activity. They would enable learners working as individuals, or more often in pairs and groups, to bring different contributions to the resolution of problems, to adopt different routes through the tasks set, and to carry them out at different levels of proficiency. 'Content' and 'process' materials, which in traditional courses had been closely interlinked, were to be seen as separate strands running through the curriculum.

Learners were thus to be involved in learning language, learning through language, and learning about language.

The final 'process' approach to be outlined here is the use of the foreign language as a medium of instruction for another subject in the curriculum.

3.3.4 The medium-of-instruction approach

Widdowson (1978), among others, has argued that for school foreign language learning to be maximally effective, it must become the medium of instruction for one or more subjects in the curriculum. Such a view clearly belongs to a process approach to foreign language learning. It is, however, a more goal-directed approach than that of Prabhu's or Breen and Candlin's, in so far as it has both a language acquisition and an educational objective. It is not simply foreign language acquisition for its own sake. Such an approach enables conceptual, linguistic, and rhetorical development related to a particular area of knowledge to take place in unison. The language and skills to be acquired are those necessary for the fulfilment of the various rhetorical acts associated with the subject matter. There is thus no dislocation between form and function.

Reports from Canada on 'immersion' programmes (Swain 1974, 1978) have indicated that very much higher levels of communicative ability in French are normally reached by speakers of English in medium-of-instruction contexts than in traditional foreign language classrooms, and that there is no fall in the level of competence in the subject-matter being studied.

It would be counter-productive to wish to extend the medium-of-instruction approach to all educational contexts on the basis of the evidence that it works in Canada, however, since the results of such projects in other countries (for example, the use of English or French as the language of instruction in many African countries) are not always crowned with success. It would seem that the success of ventures involving medium-of-instruction approaches depends to a large extent on the attitudes of the learners to the language used as the medium of instruction, on its use outside the classroom, and on whether development of the mother tongue has attained an appropriate level before the L2 medium of instruction takes over.

3.3.5   Responding to individuals and promoting responsibility

Progressivism is above all learner-centred. Before attempting to outline some of the strategies proposed for responding to individual learner characteristics, it seems important to attempt to examine the ways in which learners may vary.

Various writers have attempted to establish lists of individual characteristics which have some bearing on foreign language learning, to which teachers should aim to respond (Altman 1979, Chastain 1975, McDonough 1981, Krashen and Terrell 1983, Stern 1983). In terms of school foreign language learning the most important would seem to be differences in:

- ability or aptitude
- language background and experience
- cognitive, affective, and social maturity
- sex
- personality
- learning styles
- motivation

These are examined briefly below.

Differences in ability and aptitude

There would seem to be a general IQ factor correlated with success in school language learning (Gardner and Lambert 1959, Pimsleur *et al.* 1963, Green 1975), whatever status IQ tests may now be held to have.

There would also seem to be a correlation between general

academic ability, as manifested in an aggregate of school grades, and success in school foreign language learning (von Wittich 1962, Burstall 1975).

Attempts to provide a definitive way of determining aptitude for foreign language learning have been largely unsuccessful, but a number of factors would seem to be relevant to success in the exercise, such as a good ear, a good verbal memory, and above all an ability to perceive pattern (Pimsleur 1968, Carroll and Sapon 1959, and Green 1975). It seems likely that this grammatical ability together with memorizing ability lies behind Oller's (1972) 'grammar of expectancy', which enables the language user to predict from past context what is likely to come next. Oller found that this ability, measured through cloze tests, correlated highly with success in reading comprehension and in listening comprehension.

Language background and experience

A number of studies have found a positive correlation between tests involving L1 ability and L2 success, (for example, von Wittich 1962). It would seem that foreign language development is parasitic on L1 development, and therefore dependent on the quality of language use in the L1 in the home, that is, on such things as frequent and healthy interaction between the child and his/her parents and other adults, story-telling, reading, and opinion-sharing. It would also seem that a growing language awareness, promoted at home and in school by rhyming games, spelling games, syntactic and semantic games, and other forms of playing with sounds, words, and meanings is also important to foreign language learning.

It has also been demonstrated that those who have already learnt a second language will tend to learn a third language more effectively than monolinguals tackling a second language for the first time. If Hawkins (1981 and 1984) is right, and it is the level of language awareness reached that determines to some extent how well a learner will learn a foreign language , then it is entirely understandable that bilinguals do well, since an experience of two languages, and of the different ways that each encodes reality, is likely to lead to greater awareness as to the nature of language, than will monolingual experience.

Cognitive, affective, and social maturity

Maturity is a function of experience and is of course related to age. Children of different ages tend to think somewhat differently, and have different ways of learning. They have different aspirations and interests at different ages, and their ability to co-operate with others and tolerate diversity changes with age.

In the early primary school years, learners will be unable to cope with much abstraction and generalization, and will learn best through concrete operations that promote spontaneous learning through experience. In later primary and early secondary school years learners seem to benefit from a mixture of experiential learning, reflection, deliberate learning, and awareness-raising. Most 11–12-year-olds will not yet have attained Piaget's formal-operational stage, in which they are able to deal confidently with generalizations or with abstract language rules. Most will still be operating at the concrete level, and will require considerable contextual support in deriving and in handling abstract rules.

> The intellectual evaluations of younger adolescents are dominated by circumstantial and descriptive comment limited to the here and now. The capacity to hold more than one hypothesis and discuss a problem in terms of alternative possibilities is a feature of late adolescent or early adult thinking.
>
> (Peel 1971:151)

A few adolescents, however, may be comfortable in formal operations by the time they start language learning and may have become 'rule-gatherers' (Hatch 1974). As Collis and Biggs point out:

> Deliberately choosing to present material at a totally concrete level, requiring no abstraction on the part of the student, may disadvantage those students who are capable of giving extended abstract responses, by masking the generalizations or patterns that they should be searching for.
>
> (Collis and Biggs 1979:203)

Development of social and affective maturity are important features in the successful achievement of both communicative and cultural goals. In communicative activities, students have to learn to decentre from their own viewpoint, in order to achieve understanding with their interlocutors. Group work, peer-monitoring, helping others to learn, and learning from them, all involve the use of social and affective skills. Adolescent learners find it particularly difficult to decentre and be confident in risk-taking activities such as communicating in a foreign language. Adolescence tends to be a time of inward-lookingness, of peer group conformity, of relative inhibition, and of lack of confidence, none of which is conducive to successful foreign language learning. This is why it may well be a considerable advantage to start foreign language learning well before adolescence sets in. Teachers certainly bear witness to the fact that it is easier to get primary-aged children to perform in a foreign language than it is to coax adolescents into risk-taking of this nature.

The development of affective maturity in terms of the learner's attitudes towards another culture is also clearly crucial to the achievement of cultural goals aiming at empathy towards others. The experience that learners have of other cultural groups will vary enormously, and their level of affective maturity in this respect will do so too. Early adolescence is a difficult time in which to inspire interest in cultures which may be outside the norms of the peer group. This is another reason for suggesting that foreign language learning is better started before adolescence sets in. Both young children and young adults are more likely to be open to other cultures than are adolescents, and it is at a young age that empathic goals are most successfully promoted.

Sex

Sex appears to discriminate in favour of girls in secondary school language learning (Burstall *et al.* 1974, Hawkins 1981). That girls do better than boys, and have more positive attitudes towards foreign language learning, would seem to be connected with the fact that in adolescence girls mature earlier and tend to develop self-confidence and outward-looking attitudes earlier than boys. There would appear to be less distinction between boys and girls at early primary school age.

There is also, undoubtedly, a sexual stereotyping effect in favour of language learning for girls. Boys are typically guided towards scientific/technological careers, while girls are directed towards commercial/secretarial ones, where languages are perceived to be more useful. For boys languages may appear to be a 'sissy' subject and one of little immediate vocational relevance. There are more women than men teachers of foreign languages. This too, no doubt, affects the way in which the subject is perceived.

Personality

There are a number of personality variables that are said to affect the way in which people prefer to learn languages and the extent to which they may be successful.

Extroverts are willing to take risks, and may benefit more from an approach that lays stress on experiential learning through communication, while introverts may be more at home with a more form-focused approach that attempts to ensure accuracy before they communicate. Risk-takers may under-monitor their performance, while the more cautious may over-monitor it (Krashen 1981).

Guiora *et al.* (1972) postulate the existence of a 'language ego' built up over time in the L1. This takes the shape of a 'self-representation with physical outlines and firm boundaries'. At the heart of this is pronunciation – 'the way we sound'. Learning a new language means taking on a new 'self-representation' which may appear threatening.

> Individual differences in the ability to approximate native-like pronunciation should reflect individual differences in the flexibility of psychic processes, or, as we have chosen to conceptualise this ability, empathic capacity.
>
> (Guiora *et al.* 1972:113)

It is clearly important to remember that students need to learn how to be themselves in a foreign language. It is easier to teach students to be a stereotypical 'anybody' in a foreign language than it is to help them to be themselves.

Learning styles

Individuals differ in the way they prefer to learn. While the following list of variables does not pretend to be exhaustive, it may indicate some of the major differences in learning styles:

– ear-based learners versus eye-based learners
– field-dependent learners versus field-independent learners
– holist learners versus serialist learners
– learners who need a great deal of support and those who thrive on taking responsibility for their own learning

Some learners prefer to learn through the ear by listening to information and if possible interacting with others. Others prefer to learn by reading and studying in private.

Field-dependent learners are heavily reliant on the context for their learning. Field-independent learners are more able to handle language items out of context, and to transfer them to other situations. They are also more able to cope with ambiguity.

Some learners appear to prefer holist forms of learning, while others prefer serialist ones. The former prefer to learn through tackling an activity as a whole, gradually getting better and better at it, while the latter prefer to have learning tasks broken down into their component parts and to build up towards the whole. Holists are adventurous and need space to experiment in. Serialists are prudent and need guidance and reassurance.

Hosenfeld (1975) divides learners into those who require a great deal of structure ('low conceptual level' students), those who require some structure ('intermediate conceptual level'), and those who work best with less structure ('high conceptual level'). Each requires a different amount of direction from the teacher for cognitive and emotional security.

Traditional formal teaching methods may be said to advantage eye-based, field-independent, serialist, support-dependent learners, but currently more experiential approaches may cater better for the ear-based, holist, field-dependent, more self-directed learners. Clearly we need to cater for them all.

Motivation

Studies looking into the motivational patterns of school learners have established that in school foreign language learning motivation is best generated by a feeling of successful achievement in the classroom (Clark 1967, Burstall 1975, Fairbairn and Pegolo 1983). In English-speaking countries, among monolingual speakers of English, there is often a low level of motivation in society in general towards language learning in school. There is often little integrative motivation to relate to those speaking other languages, other than as a consumer-tourist, and there is little real faith in the extrinsic value of foreign language learning for vocational purposes, though foreign language learning for examination grades sometimes replaces this to a limited extent.

As a result of studying the motivational patterns of 10-year-olds, 14-year-olds, and 18-year-olds who were studying a foreign language in Scotland, Clark (1967) concluded:

Motivation seems to be even more a matter of individual personality and teacher effect than was hypothesized . . . If class and home background . . . are not significantly associated with pupil motivation, then it must be personal attitudes, personal goals, personal feelings of success and failure, and intrinsic interest that is motivating the pupils . . . This survey would suggest . . . that it is therefore up to the teacher to motivate his pupils by making French pleasant, giving pupils reasons for learning it, making them feel successful at it, and providing direct experience of people and things French.

(Clark 1967:212–13)

It is perhaps interesting to note that in Clark's (1967) study, the self-ratings that 10-year-old and 14-year-old pupils made in terms of perceived global success in learning a foreign language and in speaking it, were not closely related to the teachers' estimate of their position in class. This supports the proposition that feelings of success are individually perceived, and are not rigidly determined by teachers, as maintained by Bloom, for example.

Burstall *et al.* in their 10-year study of Primary French learning in England concluded:

In the language learning context nothing succeeds like success.

(Burstall *et al.* 1974)

In Fairbairn and Pegolo's (1983) study of opinions among Year 12 students in Queensland Secondary Schools, the factor most frequently indicated by students as being relevant to their decision to continue with foreign language learning was: 'I did well at the language.' The most common reason given by students for discontinuing their study was 'I thought it was irrelevant to my future studies or career.'

School students seem to prefer a course which has an enriching mixture of focuses on a wide range of communicative skills, formal work, cultural background, and literature. As Fairbairn and Pegolo concluded:

The typical type of foreign language course that foreign language students had at present was one which gave considerable emphasis to writing and grammatical study, moderate emphasis to reading, speaking, listening and translation to and from the foreign language, and little emphasis to history, literature and cultural background studies. The type of course these students desired would give considerable emphasis to reading, speaking and listening, and moderate emphasis to writing, grammatical study, translation to and from the foreign language, history, literature and cultural background.

Many students claimed that foreign language lessons were dominated by grammatical study and writing activities. This claim was not confined to those who had discontinued a foreign language, but was made also by those who were still enrolled in a foreign language. One of the strongest and most consistently made pleas throughout this study was for more speaking and listening activities to occur in the classroom, in ways that ensured that the language was actually used in meaningful interactions by students.

(Fairbairn and Pegolo 1983)

In brief, motivation would seem to be best promoted in classrooms where there is an emphasis on language in use in a wide range of practical activities involving listening, speaking, reading, and, to a lesser extent, writing in the foreign language, and where students are given a sense of successful achievement according to their own perceptions of how well they would like to be able to perform. Thus, worthwhile communication in the classroom, and successful achievement as perceived by the learner, would seem to be the essential ingredients for enhancing pupil motivation.

Classical humanists and reconstructionists tend to concern themselves solely with differences in ability and achievement, ignoring other variables. The classical humanist approach to coping with individual differences was to stream or set pupils in terms of ability or achievement. The reconstructionist strategy was either to adopt mastery learning techniques, in order to work towards an equalization of achievement, or to create a scheme of predetermined graded objectives and graded levels of performance, and mould learners to the one appropriate to their apparent level of ability. Neither the classical humanist nor the reconstructionist approach can be said to have concerned itself with variables such as differences in aspirations, interests, personalities, learning styles, or motivational patterns, though some reconstructionist thinkers have suggested that teachers should train learners to adopt personality and learning-style characteristics found in those judged to be 'good learners'. While this might be feasible in certain study skill areas, it is unlikely that in aspects of personality, for example, the naturally introverted and cautious can be persuaded to become optimal risk-takers, or the relatively carefree to become optimal monitor-users.

Rather than moulding learners to predetermined 'good' habits, progressivist approaches emphasize the need for sensitive teacher response to individual variables of all sorts. Progressivists argue that since it is impossible to provide each learner with an individually tailored set of learning experiences, what is important is to leave a certain amount of space for individuals to learn according to their own particular aspirations, personality, learning style etc., and to encourage them to take responsibility for the management of their own learning.

As Dickinson (1978) points out, there is a notional scale in the promotion of learner responsibility, which runs from fully directed to fully autonomous learning, with an infinite variety of practices involving choices of one sort or another in between. Learners may at times be made responsible for choosing to work alone or to work with others, to accept responsibility for finding appropriate materials or to ask for teacher guidance, to evaluate their own efforts or be evaluated by the teacher, to pursue their own objectives or to follow a common set of goals. How far one wishes to travel along the road towards learner autonomy in any particular area will depend upon all sorts of factors, such as the particular learning context with its possibilities and constraints, the value currently placed in the educational system on pupil responsibility, the age and experience of the learners, the availability of appropriate resources and equipment, the physical layout of the classroom, the willingness of the individual teacher to give up certain aspects of authority, and the willingness of the pupils to accept some measure of responsibility. What is undoubtedly true for most language learners, and for English-speaking learners in particular, is that no one can predict what language learning needs school pupils may have in their future life, if they are to take full advantage of the various social, vocational, and leisure opportunities that come their way. Progressivists therefore argue that it is important that the school foreign language learning experience that pupils undergo equips them with insights and skills as to how to go about further language learning. As Allwright (1979) notes:

> Language teaching that does not cope satisfactorily with the problem of independence training is simply a sad waste of time, no matter what else gets done well in the classroom.

> (Allwright 1979:114)

At school level, it would seem that working towards some level of learner responsibility is dependent upon teachers having an attitude of mind which is sensitive to the educational advantages of promoting responsibility in the classroom, and of responding to individual differences, developing needs, and changing wishes, while still guiding learners in the general direction of externally agreed common goals. Without that attitude of mind it is unlikely that a sense of responsibility can be fostered. McGregor (1961) argues that the teacher's attitude of mind towards the students leads to a self-fulfilling prophecy. Those teachers who see learners as people who dislike study and therefore have to be coerced into it, directed through it, and threatened with punishment should they fail to complete it, produce students who need direction and lots of encouragement, and who seek security rather than take risks. Alternatively those teachers who see learners as responsible people committed to achieving objectives, and capable of taking responsibility and of exercising imagination in the solving of problems, tend to find that their students come to act accordingly.

Progressivists argue for classroom negotiation in which both teachers and learners have something to say. It is the teacher's job to attempt to secure agreement that the broad common goals are worth working towards, and it is the learner's task to ensure that his/her own needs, aspirations, and interests are being catered for. Thus teachers need to make explicit what they wish to attain, and students should be encouraged to make their wishes known.

There are perhaps three levels of negotiation within progressivism – a weak level, an intermediate one, and a strong one. In the weak version the teacher determines what is to be done in advance. Negotiation at this level simply means discussing objectives and activities with learners to ensure that they understand very clearly what is expected of them. Although the learners may have considerable freedom to carry out the tasks in their own way to their own level, they are given little or no choice in the formulation of them. By discussing the tasks and activities to be performed, however, the teacher is taking an important step in orienting the pupils towards what has to be done, and in attempting to engage their interest and their involvement. Without any discussion of this at all, there is a risk that the pupils' idea of what is to be derived from a particular lesson is not the same as the teacher's.

The intermediate level of negotiation is well described by Boomer:

> Here the teacher ... reflects ... to find worthwhile curriculum content and strategies based on past experience, coming to fairly non-negotiable conclusions about the basic content of the unit ... At this stage the teacher talks openly to the children about the topic to be covered, why it is to be included, why it is important and what constraints prevail ...

The next step is for teacher and children to plan the unit, the activities, the goals, the assignments and the negotiable options ... When the products of learning have been written, made, modelled, promoted or dramatised, the teacher and children carry out the crucial process of reflection.

(Boomer 1982:129)

In language classrooms, for example, teachers can determine an activity to be undertaken, such as a simulation involving going to a café to get something to eat and drink. Students can then suggest what sort of communicative activities this is likely to give rise to. They can attempt to work out in groups how the event might develop, and can ask for help from the teacher when required. Gradually a number of different versions of the same basic scenario emerge and are subjected to examination and reflection by all.

In the strong level of negotiation, objectives and activities are determined entirely through negotiation, and the students have a real say in the formulation of their assignments, and of how they are to contribute to them. It is extremely rare but not unknown for school foreign language learning to be based on such a policy. It must be admitted that progressivist values and the process approach to which they give rise are still largely untried in school foreign language learning, although the process approach to curriculum renewal is better documented, and it is to this we now turn.

3.4   Progressivism in curriculum renewal

Progressivism in curriculum renewal is concerned with the individual and group development of teachers, and through this with the renewal of curricula which evolve to suit the specific requirements of individual schools or groups of schools. Progressivist curriculum renewal is both teacher-based and school-based. Whitehead expressed a progressivist view of curriculum renewal, when he wrote:

The first requisite for educational reform is the school as a unit with its approved curriculum based on its own needs, and evolved by its own staff. If we fail to secure that, we simply fall from one formalism into another, from one dung-hill of inert ideas into another.

(Whitehead 1932:21)

In the same way as learners must be considered as individuals with differing learning histories, aspirations, interests, personalities, and learning styles, so teachers must be acknowledged to have differing background experiences, attitudes, and personalities that they bring to the classroom. Just as learners pass through different stages of development in their learning, so teachers can be said to pass through different stages of development in their teaching.

In terms of attitudes, experience of in-service education and of curriculum renewal in various countries leads me to suggest that there are perhaps four easily recognized types of teacher. At the risk of creating caricatures, these might be labelled the 'conservatives', the 'adopters', the 'adaptors', and the 'innovators'.

The 'conservatives' are those who have discovered a style of teaching and who have developed an approach, strategies, and techniques that suit their existing knowledge, skills, and attitudes, and who do not wish to change these. They may not wish to do so through strong faith in the rightness of their attitude, through fear of the unknown, or because their own education has not equipped them with either the desire or the tools for learning how to learn any further. They are often, but not always, teachers with a transmissive teacher-centred approach in the classroom. It is understandable that there are 'conservatives' among older teachers, whose education and teaching experience may have been acquired in less rapidly changing times, but one also finds a number of 'conservatives' among younger teachers too. They sometimes attend INSET courses, but find it difficult to come to terms with ideas or strategies that do not accord with the approach they have developed. They adopt new curricula somewhat reluctantly and, when they do, they often transform them to accord with their existing approach.

The 'adopters' are those who wait for the 'official' stamp of approval on any innovation before making a move. They are very concerned about whether they are doing the 'right' thing, and tend to have a somewhat naïve faith in the notion of the 'official' panacea which will solve their problems. They become rigorous attenders of INSET courses when, for example, the examinations change. Only then do they become keen to come to terms with innovations that they have kept at arms' length up till then.

The 'adaptors' like to tinker with official guidelines and with course materials in order to make them more suitable for their own classroom circumstances. They are sufficiently independent to wish to bring their own personal ideas, attitudes, and practice to bear upon classroom procedures, but may not wish to jettison existing materials and practices entirely, often for very pragmatic reasons. They are usually keen to attend INSET meetings, but only if they are relevant to problems relating to their own classroom reality.

The 'innovators' believe that they can devise curricula which respond to their pupils' needs and aspirations better than any external body. They work best when they are experimenting with new ideas and new techniques. There are 'solo innovators' who work best in isolation from others, either as individuals or as a school department with a fierce loyalty to its work. 'Solo innovators' find it hard to share their ideas and experiences with others or to work with them, and tend through this to cut themselves off from general developments. Like Corneille's Cinna, their aim is to be 'maître de moi comme de l'univers', but they forget that Cinna was a tragic figure, whose aspirations made normal social interaction difficult. 'Interactive innovators', on the other hand, are more open and work more naturally in group mode.

It seems no more reasonable to wish to impose a standard teaching style on teachers, than to wish to impose a standard learning style on pupils. Some teachers succeed in inspiring motivation and learning through a classical humanist approach, others thrive on reconstructionist techniques involving predetermined targets and well-planned lessons, yet others are more at ease with progressivist values, which call for less planning and more room for negotiation and responsive teaching. It seems somewhat arbitrary to impose change on any group. It seems altogether more sensible to seek to get them to widen their conceptual and pragmatic base and thus to extend their potential range of strategies.

An effective classroom process depends upon teacher comfort and self-confidence. The research into mixed-ability teaching, for example, would seem to indicate that where the teacher is doing it reluctantly it is less than effective, but that where it is done with enthusiasm it works (Corbishley 1977).

Viewed in global terms it can be argued that curriculum renewal needs to take into account the particular stage of general development achieved by a particular educational system as a whole. Crucial to this is the level of general education achieved by the teachers, and the quality of teacher training offered them. Beeby (1973) has argued that four stages of educational development can be diagnosed as follows:

– The Dame School stage in which teachers are poorly educated and largely untrained. Schools tend to follow a narrow curriculum

with much rote-learning and little understanding or flexibility.
- The stage of Formalism in which teachers are trained but still poorly educated. Schools follow a rigidly prescribed syllabus with approved materials towards tightly prescribed examinations. Teachers follow textbooks and prescribed methods slavishly.
- The stage of Transition in which teachers are better educated and better trained and where appropriate adaptations to the syllabuses and existing materials are encouraged. Experimentation, however, is usually restricted by the examinations in force.
- The stage of Meaning in which teachers are both well educated and well trained, and are encouraged to participate in the curriculum renewal process. Individual differences are catered for, and teacher responsibility for the curriculum promoted.

Beeby maintains that the four developmental stages are linear in nature, and that one cannot bring about changes that belong in the stage of Meaning, for example, in an educational context still engaged in the stage of Formalism.

It is possible in very general terms to view the progress of teachers as passing ontogenetically through the same sort of phylogenetic stages outlined by Beeby. Thus many teachers in their first years tend somewhat unthinkingly to adopt the practices of those who taught them (the Dame School stage), or need close guidance and tight supportive structures (the Formalistic stage), before they are ready to adapt or innovate (the Transitional and Meaning stages), though individual attitudinal predilections are likely to affect this in various ways.

Given the differences in attitudes and stages of development between individual teachers, the progressivist form of curriculum renewal tends to place its emphasis on the need for teachers to work out their own solutions to their own curricular problems in the context of their own school. Whereas the reconstructionist model of curriculum renewal presents schools with externally devised 'solutions' to their problems, the progressivist model encourages teachers to diagnose their own problems and then offers whatever support seems necessary to assist them to solve them.

There would seem to be two basic ways of accomplishing this. The first is to provide teachers with outside agents with whom they can work in collaboration. The research or developmental expertise is provided by the outside agent, and the teachers are cast in the role of clients seeking a solution to their problems through dialogue with the 'expert'. This has been called the 'problem-solving approach'

(Macdonald and Walker 1976). It has the disadvantage that there are very few researchers to whom classroom teachers can turn, and that researchers tend to be more concerned with academic purity and non-intervention than with the need to assist the teacher to take difficult and often theoretically messy decisions.

The other more common and more generalizable model is to provide teachers with an accessible and permanently available support or advisory service, whose basic task is teacher development. Those in the support service act as consultants providing information or access to it, and as facilitators supplying the organizational requirements for teachers to meet together to analyse problems, discuss alternative solutions, implement them, and evaluate the results in the light of their own classroom reality. Teacher development means enabling teachers to carry out ongoing action-research as part of their normal classroom procedures. In this approach curriculum renewal and teacher development become one and the same thing.

The term 'teacher development' is potentially ambiguous. It can mean both teacher development of curricula, and the professional development of teachers. Where teachers have had adequate pre-service training, development is best effected through involving them directly in the renewal of their own curricula. Involvement in curriculum renewal enables teachers to develop broad curricular skills which it was not possible for them to acquire in pre-service training. Through various task-related activities they become proficient at translating broad aims into pedagogical objectives, developing strategies for classroom negotiation, creating syllabuses, thinking through alternative classroom teaching/learning strategies, creating assessment instruments, producing teaching/learning resources, and working out ways of obtaining evaluative feedback on their classroom endeavours. Equally importantly, however, teacher involvement in curriculum renewal leads to a growth in self-confidence and the building up of a healthy self-image; it provides a sense of professional achievement and personal value that leads to better teacher morale and commitment.

As Cane (1969) has shown, the majority of teachers prefer a participatory task-based form of in-service training. Findings from his large-scale survey of teacher opinion on INSET showed that there was an overwhelming desire among most teachers for a democratic participatory style of workshop, rather than a transmissive form of lecture.

The progressivist case for curriculum renewal through teacher development is powerfully put by a number of writers – Eraut (1972), Hoyle (1973), Rudd (1973), Stenhouse (1975 and 1980), Skilbeck (1982b), and Elliot (1982). Rudd writes:

> I regard it as axiomatic that the teacher who learns from his own experience understands in a way which is just not available to persons who merely try to follow the instructions of others . . . Experience-based innovation not only promotes pedagogical skill; from the manner in which the new skill is accumulated the teacher also learns concurrently the art of mastering new professional skills, and that confidence and sureness of touch which are hallmarks of the full professional. In short, I see the local curriculum development group as a setting within which teachers can become the willing agents of their own continuing professional education.
>
> (Rudd 1973:114)

The aims of this form of professional development are well summarized by Eraut:

- to solve specific problems identified by schools
- to create extra manpower resources in the region, i.e. teachers who can advise other schools and assist in in-service education
- to institutionalize the process of innovation in schools by helping them to develop permanent mechanisms for self-evaluation and problem identification, together with a development programme.

(Eraut 1972)

Recent innovations in school foreign language learning afford a striking example of effective progressivist 'bottom-up' curriculum renewal. The various schemes that have emerged under the broad umbrella of the Graded Objectives in Modern Languages movement (GOML) have been created by groups of Modern Language teachers, who have come together to solve the problems posed by the teaching of foreign languages to the whole ability range (Harding, Page, and Rowell 1980, and Page 1983). These groups have been serviced by regional or local support services in the form of regional advisory teams (for example, Lothian and West Sussex schemes), University Language Teaching (or similar) Centres (for example, York and Leeds schemes), an Examination Board (for example, East Midlands), or a local Modern Languages Advisory Committee with access to local funds and outside expertise (for example, Oxfordshire). Without the mediation of such support services to provide a forum for debate and action, school or classroom-based innovation is often dissipated through lack of appropriate information, lack of funds, and lack of an essential critical climate. As Hoyle writes:

> If problem-solving is seen in terms of the individual school then it is unlikely to be successful, unless the school can draw on external materials, services and other forms of help from outside . . . People's attitudes are changed by other people and this suggests the greater use of group methods in effecting value changes.
>
> (Hoyle 1973:95–6)

It is important not to underestimate the essential role in curriculum renewal played by teacher experiential wisdom gained from classroom practice. This is an essential counter-balance to abstract theoretical speculation. Some have argued that since education is such a complex process, teacher experience is likely to prove of much more value than abstract conceptualizations.

> For centuries . . . skilled craftsmen have been making metals. They have learned to add a little of this substance and a little of that, then heat the batch for a certain length of time until it reaches a certain colour, then let it cool at a certain rate . . . Meanwhile, 'scientific' approaches to metallurgy have not succeeded in fully explaining all that the master craftsman does . . . Isn't it possible that teaching is at least as complex as metallurgy?
>
> (Atkin 1968)

The 'feel' about educational practices that teachers develop unconsciously, or the 'awareness' that they reach consciously as a result of reflection upon experience, can both be harnessed to prevent the formulation of curriculum intentions that are unrealizable, or of instruments that are unworkable, however 'right' in the abstract they may appear to be.

It would, of course, be possible for national curriculum renewal to be organized along progressivist, rather than reconstructionist lines, though this has not often been the practice. It is, perhaps, interesting to note that in England the Schools Council decided, after ten years of the reconstructionist Research, Development, and Diffusion style of 'top-down' curriculum development, to shift the emphasis from the production of ready-made 'top-down' curriculum packages, which despite massive investment had seemed to produce meagre dividends, to the support of local 'bottom-up' curriculum initiatives involving teachers in their own development programmes. This they did in the firm belief, as expressed by Skilbeck, that:

> Externally imposed syllabuses, textbooks and examinations all define educational values and set certain standards which are important from the standpoint of the individual as well as for national and social purposes: however, they make the spontaneity, flexibility and diversity which are an equally important part of education much more difficult to achieve.
>
> (Skilbeck 1982b:20)

3.5 A critique of progressivism

Since the progressivist approach has seldom been applied in any serious way in education in general or in school foreign language learning in particular, it is difficult to criticize it from an experiential viewpoint. It is clear, however, that in an age in which educational systems are under constant pressure to become more accountable to the public, the progressivist open-ended view of education is unlikely to gain much ground, whether or not it is guided by well established principles of procedure. We have but recently moved from a classical humanist era, in which educational systems were controlled by the relatively benevolent dictatorship of the educated élite, into a reconstructionist period in which, owing to a combination of socio-political and economic factors, educational systems are being made more directly accountable to central and local government. The latter are insisting on carefully predetermined goals and explicitly worked out means to achieve them. Little space if any is being left for individual interpretation or for classroom-inspired innovation. In brief the current educational climate is inimical to progressivism.

It can be argued, however, that even if the political climate and the classroom conditions of work enabled teachers and learners to take a large measure of responsibility for their own teaching and learning, many might resist this in favour of a more directive approach. The teacher's habit of relying on the textbook and the external examination system is difficult to overcome, and any attempt to move towards a more progressivist approach would have to be done slowly and with caution.

In terms of curriculum design, progressivism is perhaps at its most vulnerable when, in its extreme form, it argues that foreign language classroom learning should simply aim to reproduce effective natural untutored learning. Teacher experiential wisdom seems to indicate quite clearly that neither the limited level of learner motivation, nor the restricted amount of exposure to the foreign language in normal classroom conditions, would permit the adoption of an extremist progressivist approach to the exclusion of practices from the other two approaches. There is not sufficient exposure to the foreign language in the classroom for the teacher to be able to rely on the spontaneous language learning process alone, with its requirement for lengthy gestation and frequent recycling of input. There is a need for some deliberate intervention in the form of focused instruction, feedback, and deliberate language learning. There is not sufficient learner motivation for deep-processing and effective internalization of fleeting communicative data to be assumed, without the adoption of some deliberate mnemonic techniques to aid the learner to retain something. As Miège put it in 1685, without some concentration on form 'the Language steals away . . . , and, like a Building without a Foundation, it falls insensibly' (Howatt 1984:57). Where there is no focus on system or on the creative springs within a language, learners are thrown back on their very limited ability to memorize whole phrases and chunks of language, and may be unable unconsciously to unpackage them and analyse them into their constituent parts for reassembly in novel ways. It seems relatively clear that learning to communicate involves both the building up of an ability to recognize and call upon a number of ready-made phrases or chunks, and the development of a capacity to interpret and create new ones.

In immersion classrooms, where the foreign language is used as a medium of instruction for one or more subjects in the curriculum, despite the high levels of fluency attained, there is nevertheless a tendency for the interlanguage of learners to fossilize and cease to develop. It is then difficult to eradicate the errors that have set in.

As Hawkins (1981:97) has pointed out, classroom language teaching is somewhat like 'gardening in a gale', where the frail seedlings of the foreign language planted in one lesson are then ripped out by the gale of the L1 and have to be replanted again in the next foreign language lesson. Regression is a common phenomenon, not only among pupils, but also among teachers, who do not always have the opportunity to keep their language resource alive. It would seem that regression occurs particularly rapidly where there has been no deliberate learning to support whatever spontaneous learning may have been achieved.

Krashen's (1981, 1982) claim that acquisition and learning are separate processes feeding separate knowledge stores with no interplay between them would seem to be an exaggerated one, deliberately designed to counteract the excesses of the audio-lingual approach dominant in many foreign language classrooms in the USA. Other theorists adopt a less extreme position and acknowledge that there can be interplay between explicit knowledge and implicit knowledge and vice versa. Thus Bialystok (1978) maintains that it is possible to transfer explicit knowledge to implicit knowledge through communicative practice. She also points out that inferencing permits that which was implicitly known to become explicit conscious knowledge. Bialystok's position would seem more in tune with the experience of generations of classroom foreign language teachers than is Krashen's.

However, the major objection to Krashen's denigration of the value of deliberate learning is that by the time children start learning foreign languages in late primary or early secondary school, they will already have become aware to some extent of language as an object to be talked about or studied, and not simply as an embedded and fleeting feature of the context they happen to be experiencing. They will have had some experience of manipulating sounds and forms in various school and family mother-tongue games involving rhyming or spelling (for example, 'I spy with my little eye'). They will already have some awareness of language. This will have been built upon through the experience of literacy in the mother tongue, in which learners become increasingly aware of language as an object, frozen on a page. They will have begun to notice that the written language has norms, and that they sometimes make errors, things which in speech they may not have paid much attention to. They may have noticed that some of the dialectal variations they use in speech are no longer tolerated in writing. They will have become accustomed to looking consciously for sound-symbol regularities to aid spelling, and to using abstract visual images of 'words' to assist memorization. They will have become aware of language as a symbolic representation of experience, rather than just as an embedded component in the fleeting reality of the moment (Donaldson 1978). Having acquired a level of literacy in L1, and through this a capacity to analyse and learn deliberately, it seems counter-productive to expect learners to will themselves back into a totally preliterate spontaneous acquisition state in their approach towards foreign language learning (Howatt 1979).

Education cannot simply be limited to the encouragement of unconscious acquisition. As Donaldson puts it:

In school pupils learn not just to talk, but to choose what to say, not just to interpret, but to weigh up possible interpretations.

(Donaldson 1978:89)

This seems to indicate a real need for some level of deliberate learning and of conscious awareness-raising.

An extreme version of the progressivist approach applied to foreign language curriculum design, such as the one propounded by Krashen and Prabhu, would seem to misunderstand the purpose of language learning in education, which goes beyond acquisition of a communicative capacity. Both Prabhu's and Krashen's proposals appear to ignore the value of attempting to raise language and cultural awareness. Indeed both of these would seem to be excluded by them in so far as they demand a level of conscious reflection. The educational purposes that might be pursued through foreign language learning are ignored. Prabhu is in fact at pains to assert that the tasks and activities in his procedural syllabus 'are not things in themselves to teach children. Instead they are a weapon to teach English' (Prabhu 1980b). Here he would seem to fail to capitalize on the possibility that there are activities that are inherently educationally valuable, as well as useful for promoting language acquisition.

Krashen's and Prabhu's approach to school foreign language learning would also seem to distort that which can be said to be natural in language learning. By late primary or early secondary it is quite natural to learn deliberately as well as spontaneously. This seems to point to the need for an attenuation of the extreme progressivist approach in favour of some measure of deliberate learning, as represented in reconstructionist values, and greater awareness raising and conscious reflection, as represented in classical humanist approaches. It is therefore to an attempt to integrate aspects of the three value systems that we move in the next chapter.

Note

1 'I have spent three years travelling and forgetting everything I learnt through academic study. This "disinstruction" was slow and difficult, but it was more useful to me than all the various studies imposed on me by others. It was truly the beginning of a real education.'

4 Summary and reconciliation

4.1 Introduction

In the first section of this chapter a brief summary is provided of the three educational value systems, and a table is given in which comparisons can be readily made of their differing effects on curriculum design, the foreign language curriculum, and policies for curriculum renewal. In the second section I attempt to work towards a reconciliation of the various tensions between the three value systems, and to suggest a broader approach which permits both some commonality of purpose and some space for individual variation, and which integrates 'top-down' and 'bottom-up' styles of curriculum renewal.

4.2 Summary of the three educational value systems

In terms of general properties:

- Classical humanism is élitist, concerned with generalizable intellectual capacities and with the transmission of knowledge, culture, and standards from one generation to another.
- Reconstructionism is concerned with bringing about social change through the educational system, with achieving a social consensus on common goals, and with planning rigorously to achieve them.
- Progressivism is concerned with the development of the individual as a whole person, with personal and group responsibility, with promoting natural learning processes through various stages of development, and with fostering a capacity for learning how to learn.

In terms of general curriculum design:

- Classical humanism gives rise to a content-driven curriculum, in which the subject matter is analysed into elements of knowledge which are then sequenced from simple to complex. Classes are set or streamed and moved as a block through units of work. Assessment is norm-referenced and concerned with the selection of an élite for the next stage of education.

- Reconstructionism gives rise to a goal-driven curriculum, in which the content is derived from an analysis of the learner's objective needs in terms of behaviour. Content is sequenced from part-skills to whole skills, and from simple to complex. The methodology lays stress on part-skill practice, the rehearsal of goals, and the mastery of predetermined criteria. Assessment is criterion-referenced and concerned to show what learners have mastered and at what levels.
- Progressivism gives rise to a process-driven curriculum, governed by principles of procedure designed to allow learners to negotiate goals, content, and methods. Learning is experiential. There is an acceptance that learners will impose their own order on what is learnt. Assessment is concerned with both process and product, and is negotiated with individuals.

In terms of strategies for curriculum renewal:

- Classical humanism adopts a policy, in which change is to be brought about slowly, through examination reform authorized by the guardians of the nation's wisdom in universities, and by the spreading of good practices by the guardians of the nation's standards in the inspectorate.
- Reconstructionism leads to a 'top-down' approach, in which a committee of government-appointed experts comes to some consensus on what should be done next, and imposes a new curriculum and various educational packages deriving from it on schools, who are then trained to adopt them.
- Progressivism leads to a 'bottom-up' approach, in which teachers are assisted to observe their own classrooms, to analyse their own problems, and to devise and evaluate strategies for overcoming them in a mutually supportive but critical climate.

Table 1 summarizes the information contained in the three previous chapters in more detail. This will enable the reader to make direct comparisons horizontally between the three value systems and the practices and criticisms to which they give rise. It is also hoped that vertically it will help the reader to perceive the interrelationships that hold between the various features in each value system.

Broad Outline of Value Systems

	Classical humanism	Reconstructionism	Progressivism
Basic features of each value system in education	The promotion of generalizable intellectual capacities The maintenance and transmission of the knowledge, culture and, standards of one generation to another The creation of an élite of guardians	Social change through education planned to lead towards certain agreed goals Egalitarian concern for the equal valuing of all citizens Emphasis on the practical relevance of the curriculum to the social goals of the nation	The development of the individual as a whole person The promotion of learner responsibility and of a capacity for learning how to learn

Curriculum Design

	Classical humanism	Reconstructionism	Progressivism
Syllabus	Subject-centred Content-driven Content derived from an analysis of the subject matter into its constituent elements of knowledge Sequencing of elements of knowledge from what was thought simple to what was thought complex	Goal-centred/Ends-means approach Objectives derived from an analysis of the objective behavioural needs of the learner Sequencing in terms of part-skills leading to global activities	Process approach Process-driven, therefore emphasis on methodology and principles of procedure Principles of procedure derived from a study of the learning process Sequencing of a broad global sort in terms of tasks Learners impose own sequence on what is learnt

Table 1 Broad outline of value systems

Curriculum Design

	Classical humanism	Reconstructionism	Progressivism
Methodology	Transmissive and teacher-directed Concerned to promote conscious understanding of rules behind surface phenomena, and control when reapplying them in new contexts	'Good habit' forming Practice of part-skills Rehearsal of behavioural goals	Learner-centred Experiential learning Promotion of learner responsibility Learning how to learn
Basic strategy for coping with individual differences	Stream or set pupils into homogeneous classes in terms of ability or achievement, and teach whole class as one unit	Mastery learning or predetermined pupil contract schemes	Promotion of individual responsibility so that pupils work at their own level Negotiation of appropriate assignments
Assessment	Norm-referenced i.e. compares one pupil with another in a rank order	Criterion-referenced i.e. compares pupil's performance against a predetermined criterion or against a scale of grade-related criteria	Individual evaluation i.e. provides an individual description of process and products achieved May lead to a statement in which the learner evaluates his/her own achievements
Research and evaluation	Research is determined by universities, and evaluation by the inspectorate – both from outside the classroom	Policy-led research determined by government from outside the classroom External evaluation to determine whether prespecified goals have been achieved or not	Encouragement of teachers to evaluate their own classroom practices, and research their own solutions

Table 1   Broad outline of value systems – continued

The Foreign Language Curriculum

	Classical humanism	Reconstructionism	Progressivism
Broad aims of school language teaching/learning	To promote general intellectual capacities such as memorization, analysis, classification, synthesis, and judgement	To promote social, intra-national and international unity and tolerance, through enabling pupils to communicate with other speech communities	To promote individual development, and enable pupils to create wider networks of personal relationships. To learn how to learn, and how to learn a language
Languages likely to be provided	Languages with cultural prestige	Languages of importance to the communities within a country, and languages of significance to the political and economic concerns of the country	Languages which reflect the personal aspirations and interests of the learners
Syllabus content (Selection)	Derived from an analysis of the structure of the language – phonological, grammatical and vocabulary elements, plus literary texts of value. Predetermined in advance of the course	Derived from an analysis of the learners' objective communicative needs. Set out in terms of e.g. situations, themes, functions and notions, grammar, and vocabulary, often in a framework of the four skills of listening, speaking, reading, and writing. Predetermined in advance of the course	A series of activities and tasks of a realistic communicative nature, selected through negotiation with learners. A bank of possible activities may be set out in advance of the course but much is determined as the course progresses

Table 1 Broad outline of value systems – continued

The Foreign Language Curriculum

	Classical humanism	Reconstructionism	Progressivism
Syllabus content (Grading)	Linear progress through structures sequenced from what is thought to be simple to what is thought to be more complex	Linear progress through situations and appropriate language exponents	Some activities and tasks may be graded in advance on the basis of prior experience in using them
	Order determined in advance of the course	The most useful and generalizable first, and/or the most learnable first	Learner is in control of the order in which the knowledge items are learnt on the basis of what can be internalized
	Gradus ad Parnassum, with little or no planned surrender value along the path for those who opt out	Order determined in advance of the course	Gradualist cyclical approach to learning, reintroducing elements in different contexts
	Linear, cumulative approach to learning	Surrender value at all steps along the path in terms of what the learner can do with what has been learnt	
		Linear, cumulative approach to learning	
Methodological emphasis	Raising conscious understanding of the underlying generalizable rules of sentence formation	Forming good habits through practice and rehearsal of real-life situations in role-play	Providing the conditions in which the mental processes for spontaneous learning are activated through engaging in communicative activity
	Deliberate practice and control of language elements	Errors to be avoided	Transitional errors accepted as a normal and necessary part of learning (interlanguage)
Role of the teacher	Teacher as instructor, explainer, transmitter of knowledge predetermined in advance, and corrector of errors	Teacher as model native speaker to be copied, and as organizer and manager of learning experiences predetermined in advance	Teacher as facilitator of learning, and as negotiator of lesson content and process
			Teacher as responder to learner needs, and as encourager of learner responsibility

Table 1   Broad outline of value systems – continued

The Foreign Language Curriculum

	Classical humanism	Reconstructionism	Progressivism
Common classroom activities	Study and practice of grammar Learning of vocabulary Translation into and out of the language being learnt Study and evaluation of literary texts	Habit-forming drills Deliberate learning and practice of phrases of maximum use Rehearsal of target activities through role-play in the situations set out in the syllabus	Problem-solving activities in which learners are involved in the interpretation, expression, and negotiation of their own meanings
Expected learning from students	Linear cumulative mastery of grammar and vocabulary and application of this knowledge to new contexts Accurate use of written language forms Some knowledge of the literature	Linear cumulative mastery of situationally appropriate language, leading to accurate, appropriate, and fluent use of language in predetermined situations	'Interlanguage' forms with errors, which tend to approximate more and more to native-speaker-like forms as the learner progresses Gradual increase in fluency Confidence to tackle new communicative challenges
Purposes of assessment	To create rank order of merit among the pupils To select an élite for the next stage of education To place pupils into relatively homogeneous groups of high and low achievers	To determine what pupils can and cannot do, and how well they perform against pre-determined criteria (summative assessment) To inform the teaching/learning process (formative assessment)	To assist learners to reflect upon their own learning process and their products, and to learn how to learn To promote a capacity for self-evaluation

Table 1   Broad outline of value systems – continued

The Foreign Language Curriculum

	Classical humanism	Reconstructionism	Progressivism
Content of assessment	Items involving the use of general intellectual capacities, usually covering grammar problems, and translation	Items sampling the predetermined goals and objectives of the syllabus. These usually cover structures and vocabulary, functions, notions, and situational activities, through the dimensions of listening, speaking, reading, and writing	Negotiated assignments in the form of process activities which have an end product
Modes of assessment	Summative end-of-term or end-of-year examinations	Formative diagnostic tests to measure how well unit objectives are being mastered Summative tests to assess more global goals	Students asked to reflect upon and describe the learning process experienced during an assignment Students asked to examine the end product with the teacher, and reflect upon how it might be improved
Result/report of assessment	A total aggregate mark converted into a grade for each pupil on the basis of the normal distribution curve A rank order of pupils	A profile for each pupil indicating the grade awarded for each dimension of the course (e.g. listening, speaking, reading, writing)	An individual statement for each pupil describing the process and product of his/her learning

Table 1   Broad outline of value systems – continued

Curriculum Renewal

	Classical humanism	Reconstructionism	Progressivism
Style of curriculum renewal	Top-down, with the two major agencies for change outside the classroom, i.e. the examination board which is largely dominated by university interests, and the inspectorate who produce reports and policy documents, and organize one-off annual in-service courses	Top-down, Research, Development and Diffusion form of curriculum renewal where the agent for change is outside the classroom, i.e. committees of 'experts' set up by government to develop new policies and curricular packages in accordance with certain guidelines	Bottom-up school-based curriculum renewal. The agent for change is inside the classroom i.e. teachers who come together to renew their curriculum. They may be assisted in this by a local advisory service
Form of innovation	New examination syllabuses, which are then embodied in new course materials published commercially	A new policy and/or curriculum package, usually in the form of a new course book or set of materials embodying a new syllabus. This is handed down for schools to implement	Small scale attempts to improve different parts of the curriculum jigsaw in a never-ending process of renewal
Strategies for teacher development	The production of official syllabuses and guidelines for teachers to implement. Annual in-service course at which good practices are spread	In-service courses designed to assist teachers to 'adopt' a new curriculum package, or to implement a new policy	In-service workshops at which teachers come together to analyse their own problems, search for and discuss possible solutions, and experiment with them in the classroom. Teacher development and curriculum renewal become one and the same thing

Table 1   Broad outline of value systems – continued

4.3 Reconciliation

Criticisms of each of the three value systems have revealed that an adherence to an extreme version of any one of the three would be counterproductive. It would not be sensible to pursue élitism, egalitarian stereotyping, or aimless unco-ordinated individual growth, each of which would represent the worst aspects of each value system. Drawing on the most positive aspects of each, however, it seems altogether reasonable to seek through an educational system to maintain and develop the wisdom and cultural traditions of the past, to attempt to work together in a deliberate way towards a fairer and better future for all, and to foster diversity among individuals in the ways in which they find fulfilment now and in that better future. While shunning institutionalized élitism it is possible to promote excellence, provided that this is done in an atmosphere in which the contributions of all are properly and equally valued. While avoiding stereotyping, it is possible to promote common goals such as happiness, freedom, equality, wealth-creation, self-fulfilment, wisdom, health, fellowship, and self-respect, provided that space is left for individual interpretations as to the appropriate balance to be struck between them. Parents are likely to wish to emphasize vocational fulfilment and individual wealth for their children; governments will wish to promote national wealth, or social unity, or both; teachers will show concern for academic wisdom; pupils are likely to be absorbed in the pursuit of happiness through fellowship and self-fulfilment. Any sensitive educational system needs to cater in some balanced way for the pursuit of all these various aspirations in a variety of different ways according to context.

Kelly (1969) and Howatt (1984) have shown that in the history of language teaching there have been various emphases which have tended to resurface again and again in different contexts at different times, according to the prevailing values of the moment. Kelly diagnosed a social (communicative) emphasis, an artistic-literary (cultural) one, and a philosophical (linguistic analysis) one. According to Kelly:

> The total corpus of ideas accessible to language teachers has not changed basically in 2,000 years. What have been in constant change are the ways of building methods from them; and the part of the corpus that is accepted varies from

generation to generation, as does the form in which the ideas
present themselves.

(Kelly 1969:363)

While the various features prevalent in language teaching under the
influence of the three value systems that I have described do not
coincide exactly with Kelly's analysis, there are obvious similarities.
In terms of the three value systems there would seem to be an
intellectual and artistic-literary or cultural bias promoted by classical
humanism, a practical communicative one embodied in reconstructionism, and an individual and group developmental one fostered by
progressivism. There seems little reason for wishing to exclude any of
these features. On the contrary, it would seem sensible to work
towards a foreign language curriculum model in which it is possible
to integrate them all, and at the same time leave space for individual
interpretation as to the exact balance to be struck between them
according to the context.

The tension between the concentration on social consensus
represented by reconstructionism, and the concern for individual
diversity represented by progressivism, has been neatly reconciled,
rhetorically at least, by the masterly SED report on Secondary
Education of 1947, which stated:

If the end of education is individual excellence, we are at once
led to ask how does the individual life develop, and the answer
immediately brings back all the social reference and claims
that the doctrine of self-realisation seemed for a moment to
banish. For the reply must be that selves can develop only in
accordance with their own nature and that their nature is social.

(SED 1947:10)

The same report offers us some help in attempting to work towards
an integration of the reconstructionist concern for predetermined
ends and the progressivist concern for processes leading to open-
ended outcomes.

Education presents itself as at once a preparation for life and
an irreplaceable part of life itself: hence the good school is to
be assessed by the extent to which it has filled the years of
youth with security, graciousness and ordered freedom, and
has thus been a seed-bed for the flowering in due season of
all that is of good report.

(SED 1947:10)

This makes it clear that the process of education is as important as the product. The classroom is to be seen as a real world and at the same time as a preparation for the real world.

In the realm of classroom methodology it has been frequently shown that different methodological emphases achieve different sorts of results, but that no one method would seem to have an inherent superiority to achieve all the results that may be desired (cf. Scherer and Wertheimer 1964). A global grammar-translation method that emphasizes a conscious understanding and control of grammar and vocabulary will promote an ability to create sentences on the basis of rules, but not an ability to communicate in real time. A global reconstructionist method that emphasizes the practice of part-skills and the rehearsal of particular situations will lead to an ability to operate in those situations, but not in others. A global progressivist method which aims to let language grow naturally in the classroom on the basis of exposure and experience, with little deliberate teacher intervention, will lead to a certain fluency, but to a low level of accuracy. In the absence of any convincing studies proving the overall inherent superiority of any one particular global method over another, it would seem that what we should now work towards in language education is a better understanding of the whole range of methodological strategies available to us, in order to know how each is likely to operate. We should then be able to draw on appropriate strategies for particular tasks in particular contexts, and achieve the sort of balance between the different strategies that is required for particular learners.

It would seem sensible to accept that conscious rule-learning, deliberate form-focused practice, and unsystematized experiential learning are all valid at different times for different purposes with different learners. This is confirmed when we examine what Rubin (1979 and 1981) discovered about the variety of learning experiences that good learners valued. Some 'good learners' preferred inductive strategies, others deductive ones, and most a mixture of both. All in all they were able to draw on a whole variety of learning and communicative strategies covering:

- inductive inferencing ('top-down' processing), through using clues from the linguistic and non-linguistic context when processing information
- deductive reasoning (parts to whole), through conscious awareness of pattern (bottom-up processing)
- practice techniques (for example, experimenting with new

sounds, talking to oneself in the foreign language subvocally or out aloud)
- use of communication strategies when trying to convey meaning (cf. Tarone 1981)
- use of clarification requests relating to communication and system-building
- monitoring of self and others' performance
- use of a variety of mnemonic techniques for making semantic, visual, auditory, and kinesic associations.

A similar picture of varied strategies emerges from studies by Stern (1975) and Bialystok (1981).

It would seem, therefore, that in the classroom the teacher should be able to call upon a wide range of strategies drawn from the various methodologies associated with classical humanism, reconstructionism, and progressivism. Some would be designed to promote spontaneous acquisition, some to bring about communicative use, some to focus on underlying competencies and skills, some to promote awareness of pattern and function, and some to assist the learner to develop control over the creative springs of the foreign language. The 'good teacher' would build upon whatever learning strategies were available to learners at the time, both spontaneous and deliberate, would work out an appropriate balance between them, and leave an appropriate space at times for learners to determine their own preferred way(s) of learning. A number of methodologists have come to the same conclusion, insisting that it is a blend of various strategies that is required in classroom foreign language learning. Thus Dodson (1983) recommends a two-pronged approach, in which there would be both 'medium-oriented' and 'message-oriented' work. He bases this recommendation on the findings in his study of how young bilinguals seem to learn their weaker language. He found that they frequently asked for the meaning in their preferred tongue of words and phrases in their weaker one, and compared and contrasted utterances in both languages. They would also express the same concept consecutively in the two languages out loud to themselves when playing, and rehearse chains of utterances in the weaker language for some possible future use.

The lesson here for us was that if any 'natural' language learning procedure was to be adopted in the classroom, it should be the way a young bilingual learns and reinforces his second language and not the way a child learns and reinforces his first and only language.

(Dodson 1983:6)

Dodson's findings and conclusions accord with the experience of many teachers, who have noted that in classrooms where awareness is encouraged, pupils often ask for 'system' information, as well as for 'communicative' information, especially when they are brought to the conclusion that their implicit grammatical knowledge of the moment is in some way inadequate.

Such a two-pronged approach is also favoured by Johnson (1980a), who calls for an amalgamation of the 'systematic' and 'non-systematic' components in the communicative approach. He argues that a systematic component helps learners to internalize rules and regularities, and an unsystematic component helps them to come to terms with the non-systematizable nature of communication.

> One might well conclude that in the same way the insight that there is an unsystematizable element of communicative knowledge sets limits on the feasibility of systematic teaching, so the existence of system in language sets limits on the necessity for process-type teaching.
>
> (Johnson 1980a)

Brumfit (1979a, 1981b, 1984) has also argued in favour of a two-pronged approach, integrating 'accuracy' and 'fluency' work, and Allen (1983) has called for a focus on grammatical form and on discourse features, combined with a focus on experiential learning through communication.

Several attempts have been made to set out how such an approach might work in practice. The first attempt we might label the 'appendage' approach. This is the one featured in Savignon's (1972) experiment, in which a communicative dimension was simply added to an existing instructional medium-oriented programme, but not in any explicit way integrated into it.

The second approach might be labelled the 'build-up' approach. This has been outlined by, for example, Paulston (1971), and Rivers (1972), who see the learner moving from controlled practice, through guided work, to free communication, with an increasing emphasis on choice of what to say along the way. This might be said to be the approach implicit in the Council of Europe's early work. Littlewood (1981), too, has argued for a mixture of what he calls 'pre-communicative' and 'communicative' activities, moving from the controlled to the free, with a focus on form, function, and social meaning, which teachers would draw upon in order to respond to the learner's needs of the moment. Littlewood (1981) and Carroll (1981) suggest that pre-communicative activities are necessary to train learners in the part-skills of communication, so that lower-level grammatical processes can unfold automatically in response to higher-level semantic plans.

The third approach we might label the 'reversible' approach. This is promulgated by Allen (1983), Dodson (1983), Brumfit (1984), and Clark and Hamilton (1984). In this an instruction syllabus, focusing on formal and rhetorical features of language, is linked to a set of communicative activities, focusing on acquisition and experiential learning. At times the learner progresses from instruction to communication, but at other times, as in the deep-end approach, the learner moves from a communicative experience to a more instructional setting, in which exposed weaknesses are remedied, and deliberate reflection upon form-meaning relationships and discourse structure is encouraged. The problem lies in finding the right balance between the one and the other. Allen's (1983) solution was to suggest that there should be a major focus on formal features of language at the beginner level, a major focus on discourse features at the intermediate level, and a major focus on the experiential use of language at higher levels. All three focuses, however, would be present at all three levels to differing degrees. Brumfit (1984) makes a similar proposal, suggesting that 'accuracy' work should occupy a large proportion of an initial language course, but should gradually decrease in importance in favour of 'fluency' work. Both, however, should be present at all levels and should be judiciously mixed in response to learner needs.

It seems sensible to accept that there are unlikely to be any major differences in broad methodological terms between the learning of a foreign language and the learning of any other subject in the school curriculum. There would seem to be a call in all subjects in the curriculum for a judicial mixture of spontaneous and deliberate learning, of systematic focuses and experiential tasks, of working towards automaticity, and of conscious reflexion, awareness, and control. As Donaldson (1978) suggests, it is necessary to build upon the learners' existing knowledge and experience, and structure tasks that are meaningful and relevant to them, so that the learners are able to bring their existing knowledge to bear upon them, in order to solve new problems posed within them. In addition to solving these, however, she insists that it is important that they reflect upon what has happened, and deliberately tease out rules and regularities to help them in future.

In the design of the curriculum for any particular subject, including foreign language learning, it would seem important to create a model that reconciles the concern for socially agreed objective needs ('*Bedarf*') and individually determined subjective ones (*Bedürfnisse*). It would seem that this can best be done by working towards curriculum guidelines which incorporate broadly agreed principles to guide the teaching/learning process, which in their turn give rise to agreed goals, content, and processes, but which leave space and propose strategies for individual variation within and beyond each of these, to respond to individual aspirations (goals), interests (content), and learning styles (processes).

In the same way as it seems important in curriculum design to attempt to integrate the reconstructionist concern for socially agreed goals, content, and processes with the equally important progressivist emphasis on the need for space for individual interpretation within and beyond these, so it would seem sensible to attempt to integrate 'top-down' and 'bottom-up' initiatives into a coherent framework for curriculum renewal. In most systems it is regional advisory services that are the linchpin for both sorts of curriculum renewal. On the one hand their task is to help schools to interpret 'top-down' initiatives in the light of their own particular context, while on the other hand their task is to ensure that teachers and schools are supported in the 'bottom-up' renewal of their own curricula, through enabling them to evaluate their own practices, to become aware of areas which require improvement, to search for alternative solutions, and to try them out and evaluate them. It is clearly essential to the health of any educational system that there is a framework and a climate which enables willing teachers to innovate beyond existing patterns, since it is from such work that the next generation of 'top-down' initiatives will derive its impetus. If Research, Development, and Diffusion forms of curriculum renewal are not to be irresponsible, then they must be based on classroom reality. The primary concern, therefore, is to discover where the best generalizable classroom practices are being carried out, and to embody these in flexible curriculum guidelines in which there is considerable space for personal interpretation and initiative, rather than to create some politically inspired brave new educational world based on untested directives. Ultimately, therefore, responsible 'top-down' curriculum renewal is dependent upon effectively supported school-based development. This latter must be free, and indeed encouraged, to evolve, since subject knowledge changes so quickly, educational theory and practice advance so rapidly, socio-political attitudes shift so unpredictably, and the experiential wisdom held by teachers is always growing. There is therefore a need for a process of curriculum renewal in which ever-evolving 'bottom-up' initiatives can quickly feed into 'top-down' ones, and 'top-down' ones be adapted to suit whatever contexts they are used in.

Having attempted to analyse various educational value systems and their effects, and to work towards a reconciliation of them in Part One of this book, it is time to move to a description of curriculum renewal in action in Part Two.

PART TWO

Curriculum renewal in action

Introduction

Part Two of this book is an attempt to describe curriculum renewal in school foreign language learning in action through describing two geographically distant but interrelated projects in Scotland and Australia. This is done through the framework of the three educational value systems and the various approaches and practices to which they give rise.

The first project examined is the Graded Levels of Achievement in Foreign Language Learning (henceforth GLAFLL) project. This was launched in 1976 in the schools of Lothian Region in and around Edinburgh in Scotland, in order to improve the provision, take-up, teaching, and learning of French, German, Spanish, Italian, and Russian – the languages taught in the secondary schools of the region.

The second project examined is the Australian Language Levels (henceforth ALL) project. This was launched in 1985 by the federal Curriculum Development Centre in Canberra in co-operation with the South Australian Education Department, in order to create a framework and curriculum guidelines for the renewal of language teaching in Australian Primary and Secondary schools. This project has attempted to embrace all languages other than English (henceforth LOTEs), and has therefore had to address itself to the development of a wide range of mother tongues (Aboriginal languages, Greek for Greek speakers etc.), as well as to the learning of a wide range of second languages.

Despite its geographical distance from Scotland, the ALL project has attempted to build upon the experience gained in the GLAFLL project and to bring this to bear in a different context. Both projects can be said to have emerged from similar problems, and to have worked within many similar socio-political, educational, and applied linguistic parameters. There is therefore a thread linking the two projects.

In Chapter 5 the problems affecting contemporary school foreign language learning are set out. While these are described within the essentially British/Scottish context of the later 70s, there is a remarkable similarity between these and the problems and concerns that were expressed by a wide cross-section of language teachers in Australia. It is possible, then, to see the problems described in

Chapter 5 as in many respects (though not, of course, all) common to the background from which both projects emerged, and to which both projects have been a response.

In Chapter 6 the development of the GLAFLL project is traced and commented upon. In Chapter 7 the initial work of the ALL project is described. This is proposed as a possible model for contemporary curriculum renewal in school foreign language learning, integrating the best features of all three value systems.

5   The problems in Scotland

5.1   Introduction

In this chapter an attempt is made to describe the language teaching
scene in Scotland at the outset of the GLAFLL (Graded Levels of
Achievement in Foreign Language Learning) project, and to
highlight the problems it had to address.

5.2   Social attitudes towards foreign language learning

It has to be admitted that in Britain it is not possible to call upon any
deep social awareness of either the practical or the educational value
of foreign language learning in school. There are several reasons for
the somewhat negative attitudes that many have towards it. These
can, perhaps, best be summarized as follows:

- There is little perceived need among British speakers of English for
  the learning of other languages, since in the vast majority of their
  international contacts, whether in Britain or abroad, they think
  that they can get by in English, and given the high levels attained in
  English learning abroad, they often can.
- There is no perceived need among the majority of British speakers
  of English as a mother tongue to learn any of the languages spoken
  by other communities within Britain, such as Welsh or Gaelic,
  Punjabi, or Italian. Intranational contacts between communities
  are conducted in English. Thus the vast majority of our citizens
  have no experience of bilingualism.
- Britain's imperial past has accustomed us to imposing our
  language and culture on others, rather than attempting to come to
  terms with theirs.
- Britain's island mentality, bolstered by a history of wars, has made
  us deeply suspicious of others.

The ethnocentricity to which the various factors above have given
rise has nurtured a web of myths which seriously undermine school
foreign language learning. These myths find expression in statements
such as:

- There is no need to learn a foreign language. Everyone speaks English.
- Language learning is difficult.
- The British have no gift for language learning, whereas foreigners do.

To these must be added the common sentiment that school foreign language learning has proved a less than successful exercise, seldom leading to any worthwhile level of communicative ability. This has led to a vicious circle of failure feeding negative attitudes, which in their turn predispose learners to expect failure.

Given this sort of social background it is not surprising that time and again doubts have been expressed in official curriculum documents about the feasibility and value of teaching foreign languages in school as a compulsory subject to all (for example, SED 1967:11, SED 1977a:24).

To counteract these negative attitudes a number of socio-economic, political, vocational, and leisure-based reasons have been put forward for the learning of a range of foreign languages in British schools. These lay stress on the practical value of the exercise. The most commonly cited of these justifications are as follows:

- The experience of those in industry and commerce indicates that in order to sell goods it is necessary to be able to use the language of the buyer, and to understand the cultural conventions that oil the commercial wheels in each country (British Overseas Trade Board 1979).
- Professional people require a reading knowledge in certain foreign languages for certain purposes. They also benefit from an ability to cope with a foreign language at international conferences.
- Membership of the European Community and of the Council of Europe implies a political commitment to better communication with other member countries and to better understanding of their cultures.
- Increasing freedom of movement and of labour within the European Community may mean that those who learn a foreign language at school feel more able to take advantage of the range of vocational opportunities available in particular countries.
- The recent massive increase in tourism has led to many adults taking up the learning of a foreign language in an evening class or at home, following radio and television courses. Many of these adults express regret at not having had the opportunity to learn a

foreign language at school, or at not having taken advantage of whatever opportunities were offered.

Those who have negative attitudes towards foreign language learning at school, and who favour instead the notion that language learning should be done as and when it is actually needed, tend to argue that it is difficult, if not impossible, to decide which language to teach to which pupil in Britain, since it is manifestly impossible to predict with any accuracy the future linguistic needs of children and adolescents who have English as a mother tongue.

This and other arguments have been countered by those educationists who adduce broad educational reasons for school foreign language learning, rather than, or in addition to, the more language-specific practical ones. They maintain that:

- The learning of any foreign or community language plays an important role in enabling children to grow beyond the ethnocentric limitations of their own linguistic and cultural group, towards a better appreciation of the multilingual, multicultural nature of the society and of the world in which they live. It can thus encourage an attitude of tolerance and of empathy towards a potentially enriching linguistic and cultural diversity.
- Learning another language plays an essential role in the raising of awareness as to the nature and function of language in human life. It is argued that the experience of learning to communicate in another language permits learners to step outside their unilingual categorization of reality, and see the world in terms of another differently organized linguistic system. This may permit them to focus upon their own language and the system it has evolved for representing their own cultural reality, and to reflect upon its relative nature (Byram 1978, Hawkins 1981, Trim 1981).
- Foreign language learning in school provides pupils with an apprenticeship in a trial language, which, if properly carried out, will equip them with strategies for the future learning of other languages, as and when the need arises (Hawkins 1981). It has been shown that an adult who has been involved in foreign language learning at school is more likely to take up the learning of another language later in life, and is likely to be better at it, than one who has not.

The problem with these broader educational aims is that while they may appeal to educationists, they are as yet less easily perceived by a society which remains deeply ethnocentric, and which increasingly looks to immediate practical surrender value for its educational investment.

5.3   The change to comprehensive schools

It might have seemed that the day of second language learning for all had dawned. If it had, many pupils and teachers were loath to get up and greet it.

(R. J. Hill, Adviser in Modern Languages in Lothian Region,
1976)

It was without doubt the switch in Britain from a classical humanist pattern of schooling, in which foreign language learning was reserved for the élite, to comprehensive schools, in which all pupils were to study a modern language for a certain time, that exposed the weaknesses in the existing school foreign language curriculum.

Before the reconstruction of secondary education along comprehensive lines, local authorities in Scotland had operated the classical humanist bipartite system involving senior secondary schools and junior secondary schools, although there were a large number of rural schools that had always combined both types of schooling. About one third of the total secondary intake had been allocated to senior secondary schools, and had followed courses leading to the Scottish Certificate of Education Ordinary Grade Examination, which was taken by pupils in S4 (that is, the fourth year of Secondary school). The other two thirds of the secondary intake had gone to junior secondary schools and had followed for the most part 'non-certificate courses'. All children in senior secondary schools had studied a foreign language for at least two years, while only a very few in the junior secondary had.

In 1965 the Scottish Education Department recommended that there should be only one sort of secondary school, providing education to children of all levels of ability and achievement from the age of 12 in S1 to the age of 17 in S6 (SED 1965). In order to prevent the emergence of a senior secondary and a junior secondary stream within the same school, the Scottish Education Department also abolished entrance tests to the new comprehensive schools, and established a common course for all which would cover the first two years (SED 1966). All pupils were to learn a foreign language as part of this common course.

After comprehensivization, as before it in the senior secondary schools, pupils were to be permitted to opt out of foreign language learning at the end of S2. Those pupils who were considered able to work towards the O Grade examination were placed in 'certificate' classes in S3. Those who were thought unlikely to succeed at O Grade were usually advised not to pursue the subject beyond S2. A few schools, however, began to experiment with non-certificate classes in S3 and S4 during the late 1960s and early 1970s. More schools were to attempt to do this when in 1972 the school leaving age was raised from 15 to 16, and when pressure was exerted on modern language departments to play their part in providing courses for those who were now to be staying longer in school.

Thus, within a relatively short period of time, from comprehensivization in 1966 to the raising of the school leaving age in 1972, school foreign language learning had changed from being an élitist pursuit for the able to being a compulsory subject for all in S1 and S2, and an option for certificate pupils and for a small but growing number of non-certificate ones in S3 and S4. Not only did teachers suddenly find themselves with a new non-academic clientele for whom they would have to learn to adapt aims, objectives, materials, methods, and assessment, but in S1 and increasingly in S2 they had to learn to cope with pupils of widely differing abilities and achievements in the same class. This called for a policy of differentiation for which they had neither the training nor the experience.

5.4 Problems within the classroom

In order to give some indication of the range of problems within the classroom that had arisen at the time of the start of the GLAFLL project, reference is now made to the findings from three contemporary reports on school foreign language teaching – the Burstall report on primary French (Burstall *et al.* 1974), the HMI report on Modern Languages in comprehensive schools in England (DES 1977), and the observational study of Scottish foreign language classrooms conducted by Mitchell, Parkinson, and Johnstone (1981).

The Burstall report was based on a 10-year research project which took the form of a longitudinal study of 18,000 pupils in three cohorts in 125 primary schools in England. Some of these were followed into secondary schools. The major part of the work was concerned with collecting data relating to the pupils' level of achievement in French, and to their attitudes towards learning the language, in order to determine 'on what conditions it would be feasible to contemplate the general introduction of a Modern Language into the primary school' (Schools Council 1966).

Although the major question to which the research team addressed itself was to determine whether there was any substantial gain in the mastery of a foreign language to be achieved by beginning to teach it at age eight instead of eleven, it was the findings in some of the other areas of research that were to prove extremely relevant to what was about to occur at the secondary level.

From their research the Burstall team concluded that although no unequivocal answer could be given to the question as to whether there were levels of ability below which the teaching of French was of dubious value, 'there were large numbers of children who patently failed to achieve even a modest and impermanent measure of success'. The team came to the conclusion that unless there was a substantial effort to redefine the objectives of teaching French in order to meet differing needs, some children would not realize their full potential, while others would inevitably experience failure. The team highlighted the fact that some children seemed already to have developed a sense of failure during their first year of French. They also observed that an early experience of success affected later achievement and attitudes towards learning languages.

> In the language-learning context nothing succeeds like success.
>
> (Burstall *et al.* 1974)

They found that no one method was universally suitable. High achievers seemed to prefer the more traditional methods, while low achievers seemed to like certain aspects of the audio-visual approach. There was, however, universal dislike of the 'enforced passivity, repetition and incomprehension asssociated with the use of the tape-recorder'.

There were two other important findings:

- The pupils were rarely involved in genuine communication in the classroom.
- In both primary and secondary schools observed, the major teaching problem was that of coping with pupils of widely differing achievements within the framework of a class moving at the same pace through the same materials. There were very few secondary teachers who advocated mixed-ability teaching, and even fewer who organized any sort of group work.

The report concluded:

Now that the results of the evaluation are finally available, however, it is hard to resist the conclusion that the weight of the evidence has combined with the balance of opinion to tip the scales against a possible expansion of the teaching of French in primary schools.

(Burstall *et al.* 1974:246)

This, together with a similar negative report by the Scottish Education Department (SED 1968), was to lead to the abandonment of primary French in Scotland and in most of England. The problems, however, were to reappear in a very similar fashion at the secondary level in the new comprehensive schools, as can be seen in the findings of the HMI report on Modern Languages in comprehensive schools in England described below (DES 1977).

This study of the learning and teaching of foreign languages in a representative sample of comprehensive schools in England was initiated by the Department of Education and Science in 1975, against the background of the changes that had taken place in England, as in Scotland, due to comprehensivization and the raising of the school leaving age.

The report concluded that in all but a few of the 83 schools visited, foreign language learning was characterized by some or all of the following features:

– underperformance in all foreign language skills by the abler pupils
– the setting of pointless or impossible tasks for average and less able pupils, and the abandonment of foreign language learning at the first opportunity by all but the most able
– excessive use of English by teachers and pupils, and an inability among pupils to produce anything other than inadequate or largely unusable statements in the foreign language
– inefficient reading skills
– writing limited to mechanical reproduction, which was often inaccurate

In brief:

In all too many language classes, there was an atmosphere of boredom, disenchantment and restlessness. At times this developed into indiscipline of a kind which made teaching and learning virtually impossible.

(DES 1977:8)

The report highlighted the fact that teachers were not able to cope with the mixed-ability situation. The objectives set were often unsuitable, insufficiently challenging in one or more of the four skills for the abler pupils, and overdemanding for the less able.

In the English equivalent of the Scottish S3/S4 'non-certificate' classes, there was a tendency to use huge amounts of background information material of an unstructured, incoherent, and unenlightening nature. This was normally presented and discussed in English.

Although the report provides little precise information to back up these general impressions, the overall picture given of foreign language learning in English comprehensive schools at this time was bleak indeed. A not dissimilar picture, but one with a great deal more detailed information, was produced by Mitchell *et al.* (1981) in Scotland, and it is to this that we turn next.

Mitchell *et al.* aimed in their study in Scottish schools to provide an in-depth description of classroom practice in a small number of schools using the Longman *Audio-Visual French Course*. This was the one most prevalent in Lothian schools at the time. Data were obtained in 1977/8 from six schools with mixed-ability S1 classes of an average size (25–33 pupils), of which two were in Lothian.

An analysis of the data revealed that the two most common activities in the classroom were drills or exercises and talk in the mother tongue. These comprised 56% of lesson time. Despite the fact that there was a heavily pronounced bias in favour of aural/oral activity, only 1.8% of classroom time was spent in real use of the foreign language, 'in which substantive messages are being transmitted, and the focus of attention is on the meaning of what is being said'. What little there was occurred within the context of classroom management. This indicated clearly that the switch of emphasis from written to spoken language brought about by the audio-visual approach had done nothing to make foreign language classrooms more communicative.

The most common 'topic' was third-party situations arising out of the course material. This led to a great deal of descriptive third-party talk. This was followed by what was described as 'fragmented, non-contextualised' discourse involving no one coherent or substantive topic, but concerned with formal aspects of the language being studied. These two topics accounted for approximately 54% of the time. Only approximately 9% of the total time was spent discussing aspects of the pupils' or teachers' real life or interests, and this was almost entirely embedded within drills and exercises.

The predominant mode of class organization involved teacher-to-whole-class work. This accounted for 88% of lesson time. The textbook was used in more than three quarters of the lessons and was thus the key element around which activity was structured.

The picture that emerges from this study is of a classroom in which teachers and pupils communicate for real in English, and only use the foreign language for various manipulative drills and exercises, or for question and answer routines on texts.

> The communicative use of French to transmit substantive
> messages between participants was almost completely absent
> . . . Children do develop foreign language competence of a sort
> in our classrooms, but if they find it hard to improvise, cope
> with the unexpected, do without a text of what is being said,
> and talk about their personal needs and concerns, perhaps this
> paper suggests some possible reasons.
>
> (Mitchell *et al.* 1981:66)

5.5 Teaching and learning in Lothian schools

Foreign language teachers in Lothian Region as elsewhere in the middle 60s had tended to adopt one of three strategies at the change to comprehensive secondary education.

The first strategy was to take the classical humanist *Gradus ad Parnassum* curriculum of the grammar or senior secondary school, and use it in all classes irrespective of the ability or level of achievement of the pupils. The result of this strategy was that as early as possible, at the end of S2, the vast majority of average achievers and all low achievers abandoned language study, leaving only the top 30–35%, who would earlier have gone to a grammar or senior secondary school, to continue.

The second strategy was to use the grammar school curriculum with the more able, and to water it down for the lower achievers. The objections to the sort of watering down and removing of conceptual challenge that such courses for the lower achievers implied have been put by many educationists, and perhaps most powerfully by Hirst:

> It is all too easy, with the best intentions in the world, to cease
> to teach the subject to the less able in any significant sense at
> all. By not really bothering whether or not they have got hold
> of the concepts and can use them, by being content with
> memorised statements, by allowing pure repetition of
> operations, by omitting anything which demands even the
> briefest unrehearsed argument or justification, we simply evade

all the problems and totally fail to develop any significant understanding. However we accommodate ourselves to the less able, it must not be by losing the essential concepts, by losing genuine operations with them, by being uncritical of invalid reasoning and so on.

(Hirst 1969:155)

The third strategy was to use the grammar school curriculum for the élite, and to provide the rest with a different course centred on background studies, in which the pupils learnt *about* the everyday life of a country in English, together with a smattering of the foreign language. This simply turned what was normally seen to be a linguistic subject into a subsidiary part of social studies.

Those who did grapple with the problem of attempting to teach a foreign language to the whole ability range worked towards an approach in which some classroom practices which derived from the classical humanist approach were retained, to which some of the newer audio-visual techniques associated with reconstructionism were added. Language was seen both in classical humanist terms as an amalgam of forms – an external body of knowledge to be ingested – and in reconstructionist terms as a set of skills to be practised through listening, speaking, reading, and writing, and as a set of speech routines associated with particular physical situations or topic areas, which could be learnt and regurgitated.

The textbooks of the day set out a sequence of points of grammar and vocabulary, embedding them in contrived situational dialogues or texts, whose meaning was mediated through visual aids such as pictures, flash-cards or film-strips, which accompanied the language being presented. The class would study these dialogues or texts as a whole, and the teacher would attempt to ensure comprehension of each part of them through lengthy question-and-answer routines in the foreign language.

After having ensured comprehension, the teacher would turn attention to the practice of the forms to be concentrated upon. In this phase of the lesson teachers tended to adopt an eclectic approach, switching between deductive and inductive methods as the task seemed to indicate. Slot and filler drills and written exercises focusing on form were common, as were grammar explanations and paradigm learning.

In the exploitation part of the lesson guided oral role-plays or written assignments would be done, in which recently learnt forms and situational routines could be reused. Errors were to be avoided.

Pupils were not encouraged to try to express meanings that they had not rehearsed, in case they remembered the errors they or their class friends had made. Thus opportunities for spontaneous communication were not provided.

Each of the four skills was rehearsed separately. Initially the emphasis was on aural/oral skills, based on the notion of the primacy of speech, though teachers no longer felt guilty about introducing reading and writing after two or three months.

Teachers tended to demand immediate oral reuse of elements heard or read in the presentation phase of the lesson. What 'went in' was expected to 'come out'. Indeed if it did not 'come out' it was thought that it would not be memorized. There was no progressivist notion of natural acquisition, nor of the need for a gestation period. It was believed that learners could internalize anything at any time, given sufficient form-focused productive practice.

Pupils were seldom if ever involved in the choice of topic or activity to be pursued. These were dictated by the textbook. Nor were pupils given any sense of responsibility for the management of their own work. Even listening and reading tended to be whole-class activities, with everyone working on the same text, rather than individually organized tasks.

Assessment remained a classical humanist norm-referenced affair, in which each subject department was obliged to set a common test to a whole age group, irrespective of whether all the pupils had covered the same ground, in order to get a wide spread of marks which would permit the allocation of a norm-referenced grade to each pupil. These grades would be reported to parents in six-monthly or annual reports. Classes would be set on the basis of these grades, some in S2, all in S3, in terms of likely examination prospects in S4. The main purpose of such an assessment policy, therefore, was to select pupils for placement in the next year-group.

The teachers' curricular skills tended to be limited to the interpretation and implementation of the particular course book in use, and to the training of pupils in the techniques required for passing the O Grade examination in S4, which cast a long shadow right back into S1 and S2. There were no school-created syllabuses at the time. In response to a survey on this, typical comments were:

'We have no specific syllabus beyond the course book.'
'We base our first year syllabus on the course book, pages 1–40.'
'We expect to reach Unit 18 by the end of S1.'

Teachers therefore had nothing against which to measure the content of any particular textbook in use, other than the examination.

In S3 and S4 certificate classes the classroom became a rehearsal for the O Grade examinations. There was a choice of two alternatives in this, one with a bias towards written language, and the other with an emphasis on aural/oral skills. The content of these two exams is given in Appendix 1 at the end of this chapter. Neither were in any sense communicative. Pupil performance in both exams was assessed negatively in terms of deviance from native-speaker norms.

In non-certificate classes in S3 and S4, teachers began to use the Northern Regional Examination Board's CSE Mode 3 examination. For this, schools were required to prepare their own syllabuses and assessment schemes and to submit them for approval to the board. This practice was to grow in popularity over the years as the GLAFLL project took root, so that by 1982 forty submissions had been made from modern language departments in Lothian schools.

The teachers' classroom management skills were limited to the operation of whole-class activities. There was some paired work, but no group work of any consequence. Differentiation was restricted to the watering down for lower achievers of the more difficult form-focused exercises that were set out in the textbook. The following is a fairly typical teacher comment of the time:

> As we find some of the material and many of the exercises unsuitable for some of our pupils, we make up a series of easier worksheets for them for the different units. They do these, while the better pupils are doing the exercises in the book.

In one Lothian school, however, Wheeldon and Hamilton (1977) were experimenting with a core and extension model for mixed-ability classes. For this they extracted that part of a unit of work deemed essential, and provided core learning experiences on it for all. Extension material on the more advanced parts was added for the higher achievers only.

Most schools, however, expected all pupils in S1 and S2 to do the same work to the same level. Inevitably, in classes with a wide spread of ability, the teacher was forced to tailor the rate of progress to the average learners. This meant that the higher achievers became bored, and the lower achievers fell further and further behind as the course advanced.

It was not surprising, therefore, to find that during the later part of S1, and the whole of S2, many pupils at the top and bottom of the various classes became progressively more and more dissatisfied.

This inevitably led to a lowering of morale among teachers, whose training had not equipped them for the curricular skills they now required.

Teachers' attitudes towards what had happened to their subject as a result of comprehensivization can perhaps best be seen against the background of the Munn and Dunning Reports, which in 1977 proposed changes to Scottish education for the 14–16 age group.

5.6 Foreign language teachers' attitudes

In 1975 the government set up the Munn and Dunning Committees to reform the curriculum and assessment arrangements in Scottish schools in S3 and S4, in order to make them more relevant to the whole ability range. They reported in 1977 (SED 1977a and 1977b).

As ever in Britain, the major foreign language learning issue facing the Munn Committee was to decide whether or not it should be compulsory for all pupils in S3 and S4, or compulsory for some and optional for others, or optional to all, or optional for only the better pupils but not available to the less able. There was a considerable range of opinions on this. This was reflected in the two submissions made by the Scottish Central Committee on Modern Languages (henceforth SCCML), a body selected by the Scottish Education Department to reflect the interests of universities, colleges of education, local authorities, HMIs, and teachers. This body was itself an advisory body to the national Central Committee on the Curriculum (henceforth CCC), which in its turn advises the Scottish Education Department and the Secretary of State for Scotland. The membership of the SCCML changed in between the first submission to the Munn and Dunning Committees, which was made in 1975, and the second submission in 1977, which was sent as a reaction to the two reports. The earlier SCCML advocated to the Munn Committee that a foreign language be 'a compulsory component in the curriculum of abler pupils in S3/S4, including those pupils who do not intend to specialize in languages', but went on to recommend that 'those pupils who show little aptitude for learning a Modern Language in S1 and S2 should be allowed to drop the language at the end of S2'.

The Munn Committee appears to have heeded only part of this advice, excluding foreign language learning from the core on the grounds that:

Pupils of low linguistic ability may see little relevance in foreign language study and may in fact have only a limited degree of competence in English itself.

(SED 1977a:24)

In addition to this, on the advice of the first SCCML, the Munn committee maintained that:

The materials and methodology of language teaching for less able pupils have not yet been developed to a point where effective learning can readily take place.

(SED 1977a:24)

Thus foreign language learning was to remain an optional subject in S3 and S4, whereas English, maths, science, social studies, physical education, creative arts, and religious and moral education were to be compulsory.

The decision not to make modern languages a compulsory subject in S3 and S4 was welcomed by the majority of language teachers, who were under the influence of classical humanist values. Lamond, for example, saw it:

as a return to sanity – a recognition that the involvement of language staff in S3 and S4 non-certificate classes over recent years had been the result of an egalitarian argument and not an educational one.

(Lamond 1978)

Lamond argued that since slow learners lacked conceptualizing ability and recall they should not study a foreign language. There were, however, a small number of teachers who had begun to experiment with group work (Howgego 1971, Johnstone 1972 and 1973), who were by now convinced that it was both feasible and valuable to teach a foreign language to the whole ability range. The later SCCML, formed in 1977, seems to have been composed of a small majority of such teachers, who, when asked to react to the Munn and Dunning recommendations, stated:

that a Modern Language should be placed in the core area, either as an obligatory core subject, such as Maths or English, or as an obligatory subject, which if not taken up in the Munn core would become an 'obligatory' elective.

A close reading of this second submission leaves the impression that the members of the later SCCML were so disturbed by the Munn

Report's apparent downgrading of the prestige of their subject, *vis-à-vis* others in the curriculum, so perturbed at the possible consequences this would have on the numbers coming forward to continue a modern language, and at the reduced time allocated to it, that they felt compelled to plead for modern languages to be made compulsory for all in S3 and S4 (that is, for four years from S1 to S4).

When the SCCML conducted a survey of teacher opinion, inviting reactions to questions relating to Munn and Dunning issues, they found 'a very deep division of opinion within the Modern Language teaching profession on the desirability of teaching a foreign language to all pupils' (SCCML 1978). Of the 1,443 returns only 9% were in favour of the subject being compulsory for all. The majority (over 60%) rejected the idea of compulsion, because they felt that certain pupils could not learn a modern language to a useful level by the end of S4, whatever materials and methods were used. More than half the teachers were opposed to the elaboration of a syllabus and certification scheme for the low achievers at what was to be called 'Foundation Level', and only 49% were even in favour of allowing all the pupils the option of continuing the study of a modern language in S3 and S4 (SCCML 1978).

It was clear that the experiences of foreign language teachers in the new comprehensive schools had been far from positive, and that their attitudes towards foreign language learning for all were on the whole extremely negative. Similar feelings were expressed in England (Hornsey 1972).

A final picture of the state of foreign language learning in schools at the time can be obtained from the statistics relating to the provision and take-up of modern languages in Lothian Region.

5.7   Provision and take-up of foreign language learning in Lothian

Regional statistics show that in 1976/7, 65% of pupils chose or were obliged to opt out of foreign language learning at the earliest possible opportunity, that is, at the end of S2. This left only 35% to continue into S3, of whom the vast majority were certificate pupils. This figure is a fair reflection of what was also occurring nationally in Scotland and in the rest of Britain at the time.

Foreign language learning further up the school was in an equally worrying state. At the national level in Scotland, Dickson (1979) showed that over the years there had been a massive decline in foreign language learning in the post-O Grade sector in favour of other subjects, and in particular science. Using the presentations in English at Higher Grade, an examination taken in S5, as a yardstick against which to measure modern language presentations, Dickson revealed that whereas in 1967 42% of S5 boys were presented in H grade French, by 1978 this had dropped to 18%. With girls 62% in 1967 had dropped to 40% in 1978. What was especially distressing to foreign language teachers about these figures was the fact that the decline seemed to be among the more able pupils.

Although no accurate statistics are available at either national or regional level, it is clear that there had also been a gradual decline in the number of pupils opting to take a *second* foreign language. The rough regional calculation that can be made shows that in 1976 only some 6% of the entire S3 population in Lothian schools chose to study a *second* foreign language.

Regional figures showed that boys tended to drop out much more readily than girls. Thus in 1976/7 among those who had opted in at S3 only 28% of the pupils were boys.

It was also revealed that only one in eight pupils actually achieved an O Grade pass (A, B, or C Grade) in a foreign language. This meant that only 12% of pupils setting out on a foreign language course would have anything to show for it.

These figures give some indication of the parlous state of school foreign language learning in Lothian Region and elsewhere in Britain in 1976/7.

To return to the problems outlined at the start of this chapter, however, it must be realized that the poor take-up of foreign language learning in schools in general, and among boys in particular, cannot simply be ascribed to the inadequate quality of the classroom teaching/learning process. It had as much to do with social attitudes towards foreign language learning as reflected by parents, guidance staff, and the teachers of foreign languages themselves.

5.8 Summary of classroom problems

The classroom problems to be tackled can be summarized as follows:

– poor attitudes among teachers and learners as to the feasibility and value of school foreign language learning, and consequently lack of a sense of purpose

- failure to promote a communicative ability among pupils so that they might feel some sense of practical success
- lack of any coherent policy on differentiation
- failure to promote pupil responsibility
- lack of curricular skills among teachers, leading to blind reliance on textbooks and external examinations.

It seemed that the only way to begin to improve the social attitudes towards foreign language learning in schools was to attempt to improve the feeling of success and relevance that pupils obtained in the classroom teaching/learning process, which in the long run might assist in a gradual change of attitudes. It was above all this that the GLAFLL project set out to achieve.

Appendix 1

1 *The Traditional O Grade* had a bias towards written language. It featured the following:

- A listening comprehension test, comprising a written text to be read aloud by an examiner and heard twice by pupils. Questions were in English, as were answers.
- A passage of prose in the foreign language for translation into English.
- A test of language practice involving a passage in the foreign language with questions related to it to be answered in the foreign language.
- Two written compositions (150–200 words) requiring the expansion of a given short summary, or the telling of a story based on a picture series, or the writing of a letter.
- An oral proficiency test involving reading an unprepared passage aloud, answering five questions on it in the foreign language, and conversing on a topic chosen by the examiner.

2 *The Alternative O Grade* examination had an emphasis on spoken language and featured the following:

- An oral test to be done on tape involving reading a passage, answering ten prerecorded questions, and telling a story from a sequence of pictures.
- A listening comprehension test based on two passages, one of which was a dialogue. These were recorded on tape and heard

twice by pupils. Questions and answers on the content were in English.
- A reading comprehension test consisting of a passage of modern prose with questions and answers in English.
- A written composition in the form of a letter (100–130 words).

6   The GLAFLL project

6.1   Introduction

The GLAFLL project, like other British Graded Objectives in Modern Languages (GOML) schemes, was one in which teachers came together to devise solutions to their own problems, and to experiment with a series of interim artefacts and approaches in the form of syllabuses, assessment schemes, methodological strategies, and pupil materials. It was thus a 'bottom-up' teacher-based progressivist form of curriculum renewal.

In curricular terms, the GLAFLL project began in the mixed classical humanist/reconstructionist period of school foreign language learning described in the previous chapter. It moved in its first phase towards a fairly extreme version of the reconstructionist approach, based on the predetermination of behavioural objectives and on criterion-referenced assessment. In its second phase, GLAFLL began to incorporate more progressivist practices, based on learner responsibility and on a more open-ended experiential approach. For the sake of convenience the description of the project is therefore divided into two distinct phases, although in reality progress was along a continuum, rather than divided into two separate periods.

In this chapter the curriculum renewal process adopted in the GLAFLL project is described, and the various developments in the two phases outlined. Evaluative comments are provided and tentative conclusions drawn, which look towards the curriculum model formulated for the ALL project which is described in the subsequent chapter.

6.2   The process of curriculum renewal in the GLAFLL project

The GLAFLL project arose from the decision of a small number of committed Lothian teachers to come together to work towards an improvement in the classroom teaching/learning process. It was apparent to all that the drop-out rate among pupils was alarmingly high, and that the methods and materials in use were not bringing about communicative ability or a sense of success among pupils.

It is, therefore, not surprising that an analysis of the comments made by teachers in 1980, in response to the question as to why they had taken up GLAFLL, revealed two major reasons:

– to improve pupil motivation particularly among the lower achievers:

I saw GLAFLL as an opportunity of providing motivation to well-intentioned pupils, who would never achieve an O Grade pass, but had learnt some French. I hoped it would provide an incentive for those pupils who intended to give up after two years.

– to provide pupils with a more practical ability to communicate than the traditional course did:

What first attracted me to GLAFLL was its emphasis on communication. The communicative approach seemed then (and still does) to offer our pupils something more worthwhile, something they can readily see a use for.

It is thus crucial to an understanding of what was done in the GLAFLL project to bear in mind that teachers were above all concerned with motivation and communication.

Being a regional project, officially endorsed by the regional authorities, GLAFLL was able to call on the curriculum development structures of the region's advisory service. The geographical area covered by Lothian Region is such as to make it possible for any teacher in a regional school to attend workshops without undue difficulty, since all schools lie within 45 minutes of the regional in-service training centre. It was therefore relatively easy to establish a progressivist form of curriculum renewal, which depends upon being able to bring teachers together. Any notion of time constraint within the project was rejected, since it was believed that this invariably led to the premature pickling of embryonic schemes and packages, which sometimes did more to distort progress than to assist it. It was hoped that the creation of a quite different approach would avoid the anxieties caused by having deadlines to meet, and the need to take unnecessary risks and short cuts to complete some sort of product within a predetermined time scale.

The pace of the project would be determined by how much time and energy teachers would be willing to devote to the necessary work. It is indicative of the commitment of modern language teachers in the region that, after only two years of work, 27 out of 49 schools had become participants, and that after seven years all schools were involved to some extent.

Lothian Region's curriculum policy is co-ordinated by a Regional Consultative Committee on the curriculum.

> This takes a global view of all curricular matters . . . For every specialist area of the curriculum we have Regional Study Groups. These, consisting of specialist teachers and normally chaired by a head teacher, take responsibility for guidance on their specialist area. A Regional Study Group may set up working parties and may conduct surveys for research and development projects. At any time it may seek the Regional Consultative Committee's support for a major change in the Authority's policy. While its status must remain an advisory one, it is nonetheless a potent influence in the region . . .
>
> (Gatherer: Foreword to Clark and Hamilton 1984)

The Regional Study Group in Modern Languages (henceforth RSGML) was thus the natural forum for curriculum renewal in foreign language learning. A framework was created in which there was a co-ordinating committee, with a head teacher as chairperson, which co-ordinated the work of a number of sub-groups, each with a modern language teacher as chairperson, and each with a particular area of responsibility and a particular task to fulfil. The chairperson of each sub-group was a member of the co-ordinating committee, to ensure communication between the various groups. All groups were composed of volunteers, since curriculum development and in-service training did not feature in the statutory conditions of work of teachers.

It may be interesting to note that at first, from tradition, teachers preferred to work along language-specific lines, and there were thus French, German, Spanish, Italian, and Russian sub-groups. It was not long before it became clear to all concerned that this meant that there were five separate groups all doing much the same work and confronting much the same problems, whereas a curricular task-based series of groups might be able to break down artificial language barriers, permit a greater cross-fertilization of ideas, and allow more rapid progress in the five languages simultaneously over a wider area of concerns. It was agreed, therefore, that each group should be given a specific curriculum task, but that each group, wherever possible, should contain representatives from each of the various languages. The groups all met voluntarily in their own time after school hours. Over the years a vast number of teachers have become involved and have participated, returning to their particular schools to act as agents for change in those areas of work in which they have been concerned.

In retrospect it is possible to establish a number of principles of procedure that have governed the curriculum renewal process in the project. These can be summarized as follows:

- to place the teacher and school department at the centre of all curriculum renewal work;
- to uphold the principle that involvement in the project meant that schools had to develop their *own* version of GLAFLL, rather than adopting a predetermined package, thus involving teachers in discussing, planning, creating instruments, experimenting, obtaining feedback, and evaluating. There were to be no designated pilot schools;
- to ensure an adequate means of involving any teacher or department who might wish to participate in the project at any level of commitment;
- to permit would-be participants to start from whatever curricular entry point they wished (in practice often assessment);
- to create a set of guidelines, instruments, and resources flexible enough to fit a variety of patterns of organization in a variety of different school contexts;
- to promote simultaneous developments in all languages taught in regional schools, and through this to work towards redressing the imbalance in favour of French;
- to provide a framework which might be of use in the development of languages hitherto not taught (for example, community languages or other foreign languages of importance).

The project was co-ordinated by myself as Adviser in the regional advisory service. I interpreted my roles as follows:

- as project leader: to establish a framework through which teachers could participate in and give direction to the various developments;
- as counsellor: to listen to the anxieties and problems of teachers and to react to their requests and needs;
- as facilitator: to establish a framework for co-operation among schools and teachers; to organize meetings, courses, and work-shops, in central and divisional centres, and in school, to respond to requirements and to produce minutes and reports;
- as information-seeker and provider: to seek out and present

information in various modes (script, video, tape, etc.) that would assist teachers to resolve the various problems raised, and to ensure a firm theoretical and pragmatic base to the innovations;
- as educator: to assist schools and teachers to develop the knowledge and skills required to conduct their own curriculum renewal, through analysing their own problems, examining solutions, experimenting with them, obtaining feedback, and evaluating them; to enable teachers to take responsibility for curriculum renewal at the regional level; to render myself as Project Leader less and less needed in the planning and promotion of the project;
- as motivator: to encourage teachers to participate in the project and to help them to feel a sense of purpose and of involvement;
- as co-ordinator: to attempt to harness the different strengths and energies of teachers in appropriate ways; to pull the threads of the various developments together into a coherent whole, and to ensure continuity;
- as public spokesman: to secure support from Head Teachers, Regional and Divisional Directors of Education, Chief Adviser, and others in positions of authority; to prepare progress reports for various bodies internal and external to Lothian; to write articles outlining GLAFLL principles and practices; to attempt to secure an appropriate level of regional funding and of personnel on secondment to sustain the project in its early years;
- as communications-network organizer: to establish contact with other regional, national, and international school foreign language learning projects, and to exchange information with them; to ensure GLAFLL participation and involvement in as many courses, conferences, and exchange visits as could be financed; to encourage GLAFLL teachers to write of their experiences for the regional GLAFLL Newsletter and for other journals with wider circulation.

For three years I was assisted in the development of the project by a full-time seconded teacher, Judith Hamilton, who, in addition to assisting in the work outlined above, interpreted her specific role as Development Officer as follows:

- as innovator: to experiment with a number of techniques in a variety of classrooms in co-operation with GLAFLL teachers;
- as diffuser of innovation: to answer requests by classroom teachers to assist them in their classrooms to come to terms with new techniques; to build up a video bank of examples of class-

room innovatory styles and strategies which would provide
material for viewing and for discussion at regional courses;
– as co-ordinator of the GLAFLL swapshop of materials for pupils:
to co-ordinate the various efforts of individual teachers; to obtain
feedback on the new materials in use; to exercise quality control,
and through this to create a range of publishable pupil material
which would be available to Lothian schools at discount prices.

Experience has shown that the two most important factors in
school-focused curriculum renewal are the quality of relationships
between participants and the sharing of responsibility. Education is
about people, whether it be teacher education or pupil education,
and the most valuable contribution that a project leader can make is
to ensure that the diverse strengths, energies, and personalities of
those involved are harnessed and forged together harmoniously. For
this to occur, a democratic framework of shared responsibilities is
essential, rather than a simple hierarchical structure. The sort of
accountability that seems to work best in curriculum renewal is not
managerial (of teachers to some authoritative figure), nor consultative (the pseudo-democratic model employed, for example, by the
Scottish Education Department, which effectively retains power and
carefully selects those with whom it wishes to 'consult'), nor
proletarian (of the managers to their teachers), but rather one of
'mutual responsibility', as outlined in Adelman and Alexander 1982,
in which participants are accountable to each other for the work that
they accept to undertake. This admits of the necessity for some
control and co-ordination, but relies heavily on the sense of
voluntarily shared responsibility, and on the mutual shaping of goals
and of patterns of action to attain them. The health of a project, like
that of education in the classroom, is ultimately determined by
whether or not there is a sense of purpose, a sharing of responsibilities, clear goals, cohesiveness, flexibility to accommodate new theoretical concepts and new findings from practical experience, open
communication, a sense of involvement, and a feeling of success.

The sense of co-operation and of mutual responsibility generated
in the GLAFLL project seems to have been appreciated by teachers,
who found great benefits in working together on tasks which
permitted the mutual sharing of ideas and of curricular artefacts. In
evaluating the GLAFLL project, various teachers have commented
on this as follows:

The classroom has traditionally been too much of a closed
shop and too many teachers have been a slave to a particular

course book. The in-service meetings and group work have
helped me to have a much broader view of things.

The GLAFLL in-service policy has meant that teachers can opt
in to RSGML sub-groups to a greater or lesser degree.
Everyone can benefit from the co-operative work produced.
Nobody can justifiably feel left out.

Working with others has been a positive experience, and the
amount of work achieved has been more than ever I would
have expected.

Verrier (1981) rightly points to the difficulty of having an Adviser
acting as project leader, since in some respects he/she is a hierarchical
figure representing authority, and may therefore not be the best
person to co-ordinate work. This is a danger in those regions where
educational administrators have unwisely succumbed to reconstructionist pressure and require advisers to carry out inspectorial duties,
rather than encouraging them to act as consultants, concerned with
teacher development and the promotion of self-evaluation in
schools. In Lothian, however, the advisory service has managed so
far to retain a relatively healthy balance between the conflicting
concerns of representing management on the one hand, and of doing
what is in the best interests of teachers and pupils and schools on the
other. The two are unfortunately becoming less and less synonym-
ous, as Directorates become more and more obsessed with economic
cuts and quantitative accountability exercises, and less and less
concerned with the quality of education.

In addition to the practical work undertaken in the various groups
of the RSGML, other forms of communication and interaction were
established. These included courses and conferences covering:

- an annual two-day seminar in the first term of every academic year
  with a specific focus on an issue to be highlighted during that year
- short courses on topics of importance
- *ad hoc* meetings and workshops on particular issues
- information-exchange meetings for special groups, at which
  GLAFLL matters would be raised, for example, for Principal
  Teachers or for Probationers.

The above took a variety of forms embracing lectures followed by
discussions, conducted by outside consultants or by project members, demonstrations on video tape of classroom interaction
followed by discussion, simulations involving the participants in

trying out various techniques with each other, group discussions, and above all workshops focusing on a specific activity.

The role of such INSET, as Early and Bolitho put it, was to achieve:

> a change of attitude, a genuine lifting of the spirits such that teachers feel able to reapproach the problems confronting them in a more positive frame of mind and go away personally and professionally refreshed; prepared not so much to implement any hand-me-down solutions . . . but to find their own answers or, perhaps, more modestly, feeling able to cope just a little better.
>
> (Early and Bolitho 1981:115)

Schools also conducted their own INSET on a regular basis, and it is here that most of the school-based developmental work was done.

Over the years some thirty GLAFLL Documents have been produced (Clark 1985 Vol. 2). Each school keeps its own set of these. Most arose as starter papers attempting to examine problems raised. They set out theoretical issues and possible strategies to be adopted. Some, however, represent information sheets in the form of guidelines or decisions taken by various groups on various matters. Others are updates of earlier papers and show the evolution in the thinking that has gone on during the years. Topics covered have included:

- the aims, principles, and planned work of the project
- syllabus design
- a report on a survey of pupil aspirations and wishes
- the framework of Stages and Levels adopted
- assessment guidelines
- the elaboration of pupil progress cards
- methodological experimentation
- communication in the classroom
- the conduct of conversation tests and the evaluation of pupil performance
- differentiation: coping with individual differences

It would be foolish to pretend that in the real world events follow a predetermined sequential path. It is possible, however, to indicate the sort of sequence that some of the GLAFLL work took:

- a problem was diagnosed and discussed by teachers;
- the project leader produced a starter paper attempting to provide information related to the problem to be resolved;

- project members read and discussed this, and prepared and examined alternative strategies for resolving the issue;
- where appropriate an RSGML sub-group of volunteers was set up, or an existing one asked to work on the production of an appropriate set of guidelines or resources;
- project teachers experimented using the guidelines or resources produced, and adapted these to their circumstances;
- feedback was obtained from classroom practitioners through discussion, visits to classrooms, and questionnaires;
- if there was to be an eventual product, the RSGML sub-group was asked to work on a final version of this. If the product was a set of methodological techniques, a video might be made for observation and discussion purposes. This was available for schools to borrow and was shown at courses and conferences.

During the two phases of the project, each year has seen a particular focus of attention introduced at the annual seminar and developed throughout the year in the various courses, workshops, and in-school sessions. Thus in Phase 1:

- the first year was devoted to a study of theory and contemporary practices, and to the establishment of the notion of Stages and Levels
- the second year was the 'year of the syllabus'
- the third year was the 'year of assessment'

and in Phase 2:

- the fourth and fifth years were 'years of methodology'
- the sixth year was the 'year of resources'
- the seventh and eighth years have been 'years of review, consolidation and further development', during which new Syllabus Guidelines have been drawn up, new Stage Tests produced, methodology further developed, a large number of video recordings of classroom interaction made, the bank of pupil resources further extended, and a number of pupil materials prepared for publication. In addition, work was started on a GLAFLL approach beyond O Grade, in which appropriate modules and courses were planned to cater for a range of vocational, leisure-related, professional, and specialist interests. This latter work has fed into the national modern languages modules that feature as part of the Action Plan for post-sixteen education in Scotland (SED 1984).

It must be emphasized that the decision to focus upon one theme per year did not prevent schools from continuing to work on a wide front on those aspects of their foreign language curriculum that they considered to be important at the time. It merely served to provide a common focus of attention on one particular area for a sufficient length of time to ensure effective reflection, some experimentation, and evaluation of possible solutions.

6.3   GLAFLL developments: the first reconstructionist phase

Following the lead of the earlier GOML schemes in Oxfordshire (OMLAC 1978) and York (Clarke 1980), it was decided to break down the existing classical humanist *gradus ad Parnassum* into a series of Stages, each of which would have its own surrender value. Each Stage was to have a syllabus with explicit objectives and a suggested functional-notional and grammatical content to fulfil them. The lowest Stage was to cater for the lowest achievers, but was to represent a manifestly successful level of achievement in basic communication. Later Stages were to build progressively upon this.

A graded series of Levels of performance was also to be established. This was to be based on the norms of pupil performance on end-of-Stage communicative tests.

Schools were encouraged to develop their own internal system of assessment to inform the teaching/learning process, and to monitor pupil progress through each Stage.

The GLAFLL framework was, therefore, a reconstructionist one which attempted to establish:

− a series of graded Stages and a suggested teaching syllabus for each
− an internal assessment scheme designed to inform the teaching-learning progress and to monitor pupil progress through each Stage
− a scale of Levels of performance to which to assign pupils on the basis of their performance on end-of-Stage communicative tests

Using this framework it was hoped that schools would be equipped to cope with differences in pupil achievement, so that all pupils could gain success on an appropriate Stage at an appropriate Level. Through negotiations with the teacher, each pupil was to choose the appropriate Stage and Level to work at.

The scheme was eventually to cover all levels of foreign language learning in school, and to provide a framework for pupils of all abilities. Although ideally each Stage would represent a free-standing unit, to be worked through in whatever time scale was required, it was accepted that the vast majority of schools would be operating in two-year blocks within the same pattern of relatively restricted 'drip-feed' provision. The decision as to how many Stages to have, and the nature of the increments between them, was determined according to these institutional constraints.

It was agreed that there should be three incremental Stages to cover the range of pupil achievement in S1/S2. It was thought appropriate in S3/S4 to reintroduce Stage 3 for those who might only have attained a Stage 1 or 2 in the earlier years, and to add Stages 4 and 5 as further units for those who would go on. It was planned that in S5/S6, Stage 5 would be reintroduced and Stages 6 and 7 added.

It was not envisaged that pupils should have to go through each Stage successively. Pupils would undertake whatever Stage they and their teachers judged most appropriate to them, given their current achievement level, apparent potential, personal commitment, and the amount of time at their disposal. The increments between Stages 1, 2, and 3, for example, would represent conceptualizations of the differences required to cater for the capacities and attainments towards the end of S2 of the very low achievers, the average achievers, and the high achievers, respectively. It was accepted for all Stages that initial conceptualizations could at best be hypotheses, and that they would have to be amended in the light of classroom reality.

Each Stage was to represent an advance, both of a quantitative and a qualitative kind, over the preceding one. Each successive Stage would therefore:

– contain all of the previous Stages plus a bit more
– call for a higher Level of communicative performance as a result of an expected increase in communicative capacity.

Each Stage would overlap with the preceding one and have a number of goals in common, making it possible but not easy for the teacher to cope with a range of pupils in the same class, some of whom might be working towards Stage 1, for example, while others were aiming at Stage 2 or Stage 3.

The notion that at each successive Stage a higher Level of communicative performance was to be expected, led to the proposal that for each Stage an 'average' successful Level of performance might be described, based on the real performances of pupils, so that over the years explicit criteria for each Level could be established. This would avoid the danger associated with criterion-referencing, that criteria might simply be plucked out of the air on the basis of intuition. It would be possible to raise the criteria expected at each Level from year to year, if, as was hoped, the learners appeared to be learning better as time went by. It was also agreed that in reality some pupils would perform above and below the notional 'average' level, and that there should be some way of acknowledging this. It was therefore decided to use a system of accreditation that would indicate the Stage worked at *and* the Level awarded. For those who clearly performed above the average Level for a particular Stage, it seemed reasonable to suggest that they were well on the way towards the next Level of performance, and that they should, therefore, be awarded the next one up. For those clearly below the Level normally required at the Stage in question, but who had nevertheless succeeded in carrying out the tasks set, it was suggested that they should be seen as at a point on the continuum more appropriately associated with the Level below. It was thus possible, for example, for a pupil to be given an award on Stage 2 at Level 2 (indicating an average Level for that Stage), or at Level 3 (indicating a high level for that Stage, more closely associated with Stage 3), or at Level 1 (indicating a low Level for that Stage, more closely associated with Stage 1). Thus an overlapping series of Levels was established in line with the overlapping nature of the Stages. Should the pupil have been judged unable to carry out the tasks set at a particular Stage, then no Level could be awarded at all. Since pupils and teachers had a lengthy period within which to negotiate what was an appropriate Stage to undertake, and since pupils in principle would only take a Stage test when they had shown on the basis of their internal assessment results that they were ready for it, it was hoped to remove or at least minimize failure.

As set out in Clark and Hamilton (1984:4) the framework of Stages and Levels established for the S1–S4 years was as shown in Table 2:

At the start of the project it had to be accepted that only in S1 and S2 were pupils of all abilities likely to work within the GLAFLL framework, since in S3 and S4 the most able ones would be preparing for the very different objectives of the national O Grade examination. Effectively, therefore, Stage 5 was not likely to attract any clientele. Stages 3 and 4, however, would attract both those who were working towards CSE Mode 3 with the Northern Regional Examinations Board, and those who preferred to work towards the

Year	Stage	Level
S1/S2	1	0 1 2
	or	
	2	1 2 3
	or	
	3	2 3 4
S3/S4	3	2 3 4
	or	
	4	3 4 5
	or	
	5	4 5 6

Table 2   GLAFLL Stages and Levels

regional GLAFLL awards. It was agreed that as far as possible work on all five Stages should be pursued in the hope that eventually the proposed new national examination system in Scotland would be able to draw on GLAFLL experience. Agreeably for all those Lothian teachers who worked on the first phase of GLAFLL, events have proved that what was done was in fact useful to others. The new national modern languages examination at Standard Grade (SEB 1985) is explicitly based, in part at least, on first phase GLAFLL work. As such it is an example of 'top-down' curriculum renewal being based on 'bottom-up' initiatives.

One of the important principles of the project was that individual schools and teachers were required to participate actively in the planning of their own particular scheme of work for GLAFLL . Since the various Stages towards which pupils would work were relatively

long-term events, and might in some cases take up to two years to
complete, it was decided that each school should establish its own
series of Waystages leading to a particular Stage. The number of
Waystages that a school might decide to set out would depend on
internal school policies, preferences, and constraints. In practice it
was normal for schools to have between three and four Waystages
during a two-year period. Creating Waystages involved matching
the syllabus agreed for each Stage against the commercial and
home-made resources available. It was then necessary to draw up a
scheme of work relating syllabus content to the resources to be used
or created and to work out an appropriate assessment scheme.

In the first phase of the GLAFLL project the syllabus for each Stage
was based explicitly on the Council of Europe's functional-notional
model as exemplified in *The Threshold Level* (van Ek 1975 and
1977) and in *Un Niveau Seuil* (Coste *et al.* 1976).

In order to get a less adult-oriented view of the sort of
communicative goals that might be appropriate for school foreign
language learning, it was decided to conduct a survey into what
Lothian pupils would themselves like to see included in their foreign
language courses. A questionnaire was devised and distributed to a
representative range of S1 and S2 classes studying French, German,
Spanish, or Russian, and a few S3 pupils studying Italian as a second
language. 1,083 returns were received.

This produced some interesting results, which showed that a
number of the suggestions currently in vogue were not in tune with
pupil wishes (Clark 1979a). It may be useful to highlight one or two
of the major findings here:

— contrary to the content of the Oxfordshire and York GOML
  schemes, pupils wished to go beyond tourist language to embrace
  everyday friend-to-friend communication, and beyond public
  signs, notices, and announcements to more substantial and
  extended forms of listening and reading for information and for
  pleasure. 90% also wanted to learn to write in the foreign
  language;
— contrary to the suggestions made by Salter (1972), the vast
  majority of pupils (86%) said they wished to be able to converse in
  the foreign language, and would not be satisfied with simply being
  able to understand it and answer in English.

In addition to the adult-oriented world of communication, embodied, for example, in the Council of Europe Threshold Level

documents, school learners also wished to see topics and activities that took account of the world of adolescent interests.

In brief, the picture of pupil wishes that emerged was an extremely broad one which looked towards a wide variety of communicative goals. These were incorporated into the first Lothian syllabuses in French, German, Spanish, Russian, and Italian, which were produced by groups of teachers in 1978/9 (Lothian Regional Study Group on Modern Languages 1978/9).

Following the Council of Europe's reconstructionist model of curriculum design, the broad communicative goals set out in these syllabuses were broken down into graded communicative objectives, and the functional and notional content of these was set out in lists with suggested language exponents given for each Stage in each language. A grammar section was also given which was explicitly based on the structures involved in the exponents that had emerged to fit the functional/notional component of the syllabus. Thus the total syllabus included communicative objectives, functional-notional content, and a grammar section.

From these syllabuses schools then created schemes of work sequencing goals and content in Waystages and relating these to existing commercial resources (for example, Wheeldon 1980). This encouraged schools to evaluate their course books against the proposed objectives and content of the syllabus, and led to schools adopting a much more responsible and flexible approach towards available commercial materials. No longer did the textbook dictate what had to be done. As one teacher put it:

> It seems to us to be of relatively minor importance what course-book, if any, is used to accompany the scheme. What is important is the way we use the course-book or materials which we have. That is to say we extract from our materials whatever we feel to be of value in helping our pupils towards attaining their stated objectives (and this in relation to the GLAFLL syllabus) rather than following the course-book rigidly. Looking at material from a GLAFLL viewpoint may result in an exploitation which had never been considered before.

One department actually created its own teaching/learning material for its own scheme of work (Chapman 1980).

All schools were asked to create pupil progress cards on the basis of their Waystages. The pupil progress card was an important feature of the first phase of the GLAFLL project. It represented an attempt to create a syllabus for pupils in which the objectives to be mastered during each Waystage would be set out in language intelligible to them. It seemed to teachers that expressing objectives in the form of functions or notions would enable the pupils to see relevance in what they were being asked to do. It was clearly more meaningful for pupils to be told that they would be learning how to ask for something politely, than to be told that the lesson objective was mastery of the conditional tense of *vouloir*. As one pupil put it when asked to evaluate the use of progress cards:

> Progress cards help a lot . . . They explain what they want you to say.

The prototype progress card had three columns (Clark 1980), to which a fourth has been added. In the first column the learning tasks were to be set out. In the second column a space was left for pupils to tick when they had completed a task to their own satisfaction. In the third column a space was left for the teacher (or a peer if appropriate) to tick, should there be a need for a check to be made. The additional fourth column was for pupil, peer, or teacher to assess performance on the learning activity, according to the scheme of levels of achievement worked out by individual schools for the internal profiling of pupil progress.

In the first phase of the project the first column of the progress card tended to contain lists of discrete functions and notions associated with personal information exchanges and tourist transactions, for example:

- I can say my name.
- I can ask for a railway ticket.
- I can count from 1 to 10.

Gradually, as time went by, it became apparent that this was leading to a methodology in which pupils were learning by heart discrete phrases to accord with the functions and notions on their progress cards, but were not always unpacking them into their component elements of grammar and vocabulary, so that they could reuse parts of them in other contexts. As one pupil said:

> I *hate* how you learn phrases without being taught actual words in the sentence. If you were told all the words in the

sentence then you could expand your vocabulary and phrases by yourself.

This meant also that pupils learnt phrases by heart, remembered them for a short time, and then tended to forget them. One pupil remarked:

I do not like the progress cards and I do not think they help much. We revise and learn all the answers before we are tested, and it's easy then, but after a couple of weeks we begin to forget it all.

It also became clear that the discrete functions and notions on progress cards were being learnt separately, divorced from any communicative context. In one classroom, for example, it was found that pupils were only able to say, '*Je m'appelle Peter*', or whatever name they had, if the questioner referred to their progress card directly. They were unable to answer the question, '*Comment t'appelles-tu?*' because they could not understand it. They had learnt by heart a phrase for telling their name, but had never had it set in a communicative context. In order to combat this, it was recommended that some holistic communicative activity should be indicated on the card first, and that only then should this be broken down into discrete functions and notions where relevant. It was hoped that this would lead to a communicative activity, and not just to the learning of atomistic semantic units. An example of such a progress card is given in Table 3.

The methodology in the classroom in the first phase of the GLAFLL project was also a reconstructionist one. The teacher attempted deliberately to get the pupils to learn correct native-speaker routines and phrases associated with certain predetermined situations involving exchanges of personal information (name, address, family background, likes and dislikes, hobbies etc.) and tourist transactions (buying things, finding the way, getting food and drink etc.). Learners concentrated on memorizing discrete phrases corresponding to particular functional-notional meanings, and then on using them in dialogues. Preparation for these dialogues was normally done on a whole-class basis, whether classes were relatively homogeneous in ability or achievement, or whether they were of mixed ability. Everyone was expected to learn the phrases to be used together, and then pairs of pupils would enact a dialogue embodying

PROGRESS CARD 5	Pupil Column	Teacher Column	LOP
1. DISCUSSING LIKES AND DISLIKES WITH FRIENDS:			
Ask if someone likes doing something.			
Say you like doing something.			
Say you don't like doing something.			
Say you prefer doing something else.			
Say you hate doing something.			
Say which school subjects you like/don't like.			
Say which sports you like/don't like.			
Say which pop groups you like/don't like.			
Say you like something a lot.			
a little.			
not a lot.			
2. ORDERING A MEAL AT A RESTAURANT:			
Ask for a table for X people.			
Ask for the menu.			
Order a meal from the menu.			
Call for the waiter.			
Ask for the bill.			
Say that the meal was good.			
Understand a few common dishes on the menu.			
Understand common menu notices.			
3. COMMUNICATION TASK IN GROUPS:			
Find out what your fellow pupils like and don't like, and build up a class survey opinion.			
Things to get reactions to: Particular sports. Which is the most popular to play? Which is the most popular to watch?			
Favourite subjects at school			
Favourite pop groups			
Favourite foods			

Table 3   Extract from a progress card

them on the basis of cue cards. Cues were normally given in English as in Figure 1.

Situation: Buying a ticket at the station

Cue Card A	**Cue Card B**
(you should begin)	(your partner will begin)
Greet the ticket seller.	Greet the client.
Ask for a return ticket to Paris.	Sell the required ticket.
Pay, say thank you, and leave.	

Figure 1   Role-play cue cards

The teacher would move from pair to pair listening to and commenting on the pupils' performances. At the start, such paired work seemed on the whole quite popular among pupils, who seemed to work harder in pairs and groups than in teacher-to-whole-class mode. One teacher remarked:

> The group and paired activities greatly increased the motivation of most of my pupils and also contributed to the increased social harmony of my classroom, perhaps even increased the social skills of some of my pupils. Certainly the Remedial teachers used to remark on how motivated and hard-working certain pupils were in their Modern Languages classroom compared with elsewhere in the school.

The teaching of listening and reading skills was undertaken much the same way as before, though the texts tended to be selected from authentic sources, and were shorter, more functional and less literary in nature. Pupils would listen to or read a particular text and then answer questions in English designed to see whether they had understood what they had heard or read.

In the search for authenticity and short texts, classrooms were soon flooded with menus, timetables, price lists, advertisements, labels, spoken announcements, instructions, news flashes, weather reports, and the like. However, the authenticity of the text was seldom matched by an equivalent authenticity in the sort of response to it that was asked of the pupil. The tasks relating to the texts were merely comprehension checks in English.

As in most reconstructionist schemes, in the first phase of the GLAFLL project, assessment seemed to dominate much of what was done. There were two particular trends which were influencing assessment in foreign language learning at the time. The first was the general move away from norm-referencing towards some form of criterion-referencing. The second was a subject-specific attempt to move away from tests eliciting language-like behaviour to tests attempting to elicit communicative behaviour.

It was felt that criterion-referencing would improve classroom teaching and learning because:

— It would make teachers re-examine what they wished pupils to know and to do, and assist them to come to realistic conclusions about how well pupils should be expected to perform.
— It would improve pupil motivation, because pupils would be competing against a particular standard rather than against each other.
— It would improve the quality of information that could be provided by an analysis of test results. In formative assessment during Waystages, the pupils' strengths and weaknesses could be diagnosed, and appropriate treatment provided, and in summative assessment at the end of each Stage, there would be a clear statement of what pupils could do and how well they could do it.

It seemed sensible to move towards tests that attempted to elicit communicative rather than just language-like behaviour, in order to assist pupils to see the practical relevance of what they were being asked to do.

Morrow (1977) had indicated a number of features of normal language use not normally present in tests. These were as follows:

— the interaction-based nature of most communication
— unpredictability
— context (extralingual or intralingual)
— purpose
— authenticity
— the behaviour-based nature of interaction

It seemed sensible to attempt to create a range of communicative task types in which such features would be present, and to investigate valid and reliable ways of assessing pupil performance on them.

It seemed important, however, not to lose sight of the fact that the assessment of pupil learning was not just concerned with communicative proficiency, although this was of paramount importance.

It also needed to concern itself with ongoing pupil achievement in the mastery of the functional, notional, and grammatical elements in the syllabus. It seemed important, therefore, to strike an appropriate balance between classroom achievement testing, internally determined on the basis of functional/notional and grammatical syllabus content, and both classroom and external proficiency testing, concerned with the pupil's more global communicative performance at the end of Waystages and Stages. Achievement testing was seen as a matter of assessing the extent to which pupils had or had not mastered what they had been taught. It was syllabus-centred. Proficiency testing was seen as a matter of assessing the extent to which the pupils could carry out real life tasks, with whatever communicative resource they had available to them. It was real-life-oriented.

To the often posed question as to whether tests should be mirrors of reality, or instruments constructed from a theory of what language learning involves, the answer seemed to be to retain classroom achievement tests for the latter, and to attempt to ensure that classroom and external proficiency tests reflected the former. In this way it would be possible to have some parts of the assessment scheme whose basic concern was with face validity and the relationship of the test to real life, and others whose prime motivation sprang from content and construct validity, relating assessment to the syllabus and to the methodology adopted in a particular classroom.

In formative assessment within the classroom, pupils were encouraged to present themselves for testing by the teacher or by peers on chosen parts of their progress card, as and when they were ready. In practice it was discovered that it was necessary to encourage and cajole some pupils to test out their knowledge, since they would insist on being word perfect before attempting anything, while with others it was more a question of persuading them to practise a bit more, since they were often all too willing to be tested before having prepared themselves adequately.

Pupils did not all appreciate progress cards. One wrote:

I don't like progress cards. It's just tests, tests, tests.

Others, however, seemed to like them.

The progress cards helped me so when I took the test I could do most of it.

It helps us to revise.

In order not to discourage pupils from wishing to obtain feedback on the state of their knowledge, it was agreed that assessment on progress cards would remain private. Where a pupil asked to be given a level of achievement, this could be noted down in the fourth column of the card, though no public record would be made of this. This meant that over a period of time the teacher could attempt to negotiate with each individual pupil about the sort of level to be maintained, on the basis of that pupil's apparent potential, normal achievement pattern, and professed aspirations. A three-point scale of assessment was proposed for this, where 1 indicated a 'low but adequate' level of achievement, 2 an 'average to good' one, and 3 a 'high' one relative to the Stage being worked on.

The mastery learning practice of giving a diagnostic test to a whole class, as recommended, for example, in the *Tour de France* course (SCCML 1982), was not approved, since it had been shown to lead to the same small group of pupils failing to master the objectives on each unit and becoming gradually more discouraged. In the GLAFLL approach, no one was to be tested until they felt ready. Such a practice was commonplace in art or craft classes, where pupils worked on the creation of a product – a picture, a design, a model of some sort – until they were ready to submit it. There was no question in such classes, other than perhaps under examination conditions, of making all pupils submit their product for evaluation at the same moment.

A public record of pupil progress had to be kept, however. This was generally done on the basis of periodic summative Waystage tests, which would aim to embrace both syllabus-related achievement testing of functional-notional and grammatical content, and proficiency testing calling on the more global communicative ability attained. Waystage tests were to be taken as and when pupils were ready for them. The results were to be kept in the form of a pupil profile of levels of performance in various dimensions of the subject area. Ideally, this profile was to accompany the pupil throughout the school, so that a cumulative record of achievement was available to each teacher in whose care the pupil was put. It was suggested that the profile should cover the following dimensions:

- conversation skills
- correspondence skills
- listening/viewing for information skills
- listening/viewing for pleasure
- reading for information skills

- reading for pleasure
- language resource development i.e. pronunciation, grammar, and
  vocabulary

This was preferred to the more traditional dimensions of listening, speaking, reading, and writing, which failed to capture the mixed-skill nature of most communicative activities.

Over time, other areas were suggested for the profile covering study skills (for more advanced stages), language awareness, cultural awareness, responsibility for one's own learning, and co-operative skills. In practice, in the first phase, most schools chose to restrict their profile to the more traditional dimensions of conversation, reading, listening, correspondence, and language resource areas.

Some schools were already moving towards a criterion-referenced form of reporting to parents, in which a norm-referenced single grade was to be replaced by a profile in each subject, whose grades were based on verbalistic descriptions such as those in the example in Figure 2.

In schools with a reporting policy of this sort, it was clearly sensible for the modern languages department to harmonize the levels of performance in their profile with those of their reports to parents. When submitting their internally determined profile of grades or levels of performance to the regional assessment group, schools were asked to convert these to conform to the scale of overlapping levels of performance outlined on page 143, so that they could be added to the Levels of performance awarded on the regional end-of-Stage Tests.

Regional end-of-Stage Tests were created by the RSGML assessment group, whose members would discuss what had to be done, divide up the work, meet again to examine the results, and amend the drafts as necessary. The first set of Stage Tests created were based on the first phase syllabus (Lothian Regional Study Group on Modern Languages 1978/9), and were therefore manifestations of the belief that a communicative capacity could be conceptualized as an ability to interpret and express certain language functions and notions within a definable range of contexts. In Appendix 2 at the end of this chapter, a description is given of the various test types used in the first phase GLAFLL Stage Tests. These embraced paper and pencil tests covering listening, reading and, where appropriate, writing skills, and conversation tests between a teacher and a pupil on the one hand, and a pupil with another pupil on the other.

At first, since conversation tests were closely cued, function by function, in advance, there seemed to be every reason for assessing

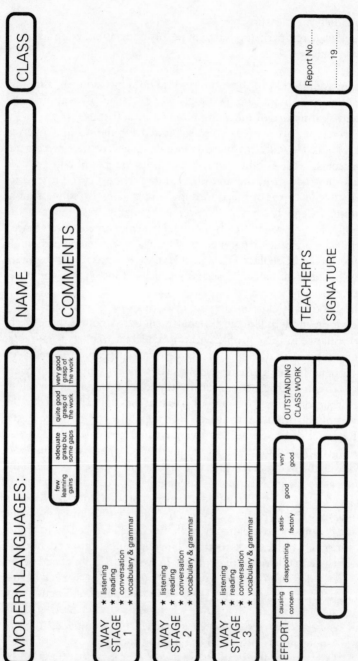

Figure 2   School report in profile form

each utterance individually, and awarding 0 for each unintelligible attempt, 1 for each intelligible attempt with poor pronunciation or grammatical error, and 2 for each intelligible and accurate attempt. It was then relatively easy to determine Levels of performance, according to the total marks obtained in the two conversation tests (pupil-teacher and pupil-pupil). Eventually, however, it was decided to judge pupil performance globally over a whole test, rather than on each discrete utterance, and it became necessary then to determine criteria upon which such global judgements should be made. It was decided to judge conversational performance in two stages by asking two questions:

1 Had the candidate completed the task set? (U/C). If so, some positive Level of performance would be in order. If not, the pupil would have to be given a '0' Level of performance.

In order to determine exactly which Level was to be awarded, a further question was asked:

2 How well has the candidate performed? (LOP)

This system was referred to as 'U/Cing' and 'LOPing', where U/C stood for 'understood and communicated', and LOP for 'level of performance'. In order to judge whether pupils had 'U/Ced' or not, the assessor had to determine whether the pupil had indeed understood and communicated in an intelligible manner, and had also successfully completed the task in an appropriate way. When asked to buy something to drink, if the pupil had asked for a ham sandwich rather than a drink, he/she was considered not to have 'U/Ced', irrespective of the quality of the language used. In coming to decisions as to how well the pupil had performed (how he/she had 'LOPed'), the criteria of accuracy, appropriacy, and fluency were used.

The assessment of written performance was done on the basis that any information had to be conveyed intelligibly in order for the pupil to be awarded a positive level. At Stage 2 intelligibility on set tasks would guarantee a Level 2. When this was combined with a reasonable level of accuracy and of interest value, a Level 3 would be awarded. A Level 1 would be given where on one or two tasks intelligibility was in question. If a great deal of what had been written was of doubtful intelligibility, then Level 0 would be given. While teachers had found it relatively easy to come to terms with the notion of intelligibility in speech, despite formal error, they found it more difficult to accept that this was possible in writing. Indeed, some teachers proposed that writing be removed from the assessment programme altogether, on the grounds that it was both too difficult and an unnecessary skill for the majority of pupils to wish to master. The majority of teachers, however, did not take this view, and held to the principle that one of the main purposes of the Stage Tests was to ensure a healthy teaching/learning process in the classroom. For this, writing was viewed as an essential ingredient since:

- pupils wanted to write (Clark 1979a)
- it was a mnemonic device to aid recall, which most if not all pupils insisted on having fairly early in their course
- it was a tried and trusted method of getting pupils to test out their hypotheses as to how to express meanings in foreign language forms
- it was a better medium through which to practice extended text creation than speech
- it provided necessary teacher and pupil comfort in moments of fatigue or stress

In brief, writing, seen as communication at a distance, as a means of recording personal information, and at later stages as a study skill, was seen to be an essential weapon in the foreign language armoury of literate pupils, whose future communicative needs could not be totally predicted.

Teachers were helped to come to terms with written error by being exposed to the error-ridden pen-friend correspondence of adolescent native speakers, which had been stimulated in GLAFLL classes. In this respect it was also interesting to note that in France the Ministère de l'Education Nationale (1978) had felt obliged to issue a list of *tolérances grammaticales ou orthographiques*, given the existence of so many written errors in the writing of French schoolchildren.

Interesting, too, were the findings of a study by Piazza (1980), who had asked French students to assess the severity of certain frequent anglophone spoken and written errors in French in terms of their incomprehensibility and irritation value. The conclusion drawn from this was that:

Errors were more readily tolerated, that is were both more comprehensible and less irritating, in written than in spoken language samples ... All error types are more comprehensible when presented in written rather than spoken form.

(Piazza 1980:424)

Over the years GLAFLL teachers have come to accept that writing, at the sort of developmental levels we were concerned with at Stages 1, 2, and 3, should not be marked negatively in terms of the amount of errors made, but should be assessed positively, in terms of intelligibility first, and then of other qualities later. On this basis it has been shown that many more children can achieve a worthwhile piece of communicative writing than was earlier believed.

Tests of listening and reading were scored in the traditional manner, on the basis of marks being awarded for correct units of information given. Distinctions between one level of performance and another were determined as a result of examining pupil performance. It was customary for a score of 85% or more to receive the top level of performance available at the Stage in question. 70–84% would be given the middle level available, and below this the bottom level would be awarded, or no level at all.

Teachers were keen to follow the successful schemes in Oxfordshire and York, and to have a form of certificate that would allow pupils of all levels of ability to receive official validation of their achievements. It was hoped that the existence of such accreditations would help to create a more positive climate towards school foreign language learning both among pupils and among parents, and that it might help to get rid of the public view of foreign language learning as a difficult subject, in which failure rather than success was expected.

A few teachers argued for a certificate based solely on internal assessment within the school. The majority, however, wished to have a mixture of internal and external assessment leading to some regional award. For this, Lothian's Regional Consultative Committee on Secondary Education insisted that there should be a regionally set external examination, to ensure comparability of standards between schools. It was therefore agreed that an award on a Regional Record of Achievement would be made on the basis of adding the profile of Levels of performance submitted for each pupil by the classroom teacher, as a result of internal periodic Waystage assessment, to the Levels of performance obtained by the pupils on the various end-of-Stage proficiency tests. Criteria were then set out as to how to achieve aggregate Levels of performance in the various dimensions assessed.

It was decided that the awards on the Record of Achievement should be made as simple as possible for pupil and parent. This led to a system of *Pass* and *Credit* awards at each Stage successfully completed. The regional Record of Achievement explained what was meant by each 'Stage' and by a 'Pass' and a 'Credit' on its reverse side (see GLAFFL Document 21 in Clark 1985 Vol. 2).

In conclusion, the reconstructionist methodology adopted in the first phase of the project meant that there was little experiential learning – little learning through communication – other than in those classrooms where teachers used the foreign language for classroom management. Even in these, while classroom management provided a basis for experiential learning, the rest of the lesson was generally focused upon the practice of part-skills or sub-tasks leading towards the eventual regurgitation of these in paired dialogues. Classroom activity was above all characterized by a determination on the part of teachers to bring about immediate and correct oral performance. Despite the less than adequate theoretical basis to the methodology used in the first phase, the results in terms of improvement in pupil motivation were generally positive.

> Last year it was ded boring but our teacher now gives us exsiteing work which gives us pleasure and exsitement to do.

> I think in the last couple of years it's been getting better. We have started working more with our friends and have been working more orally than written work.

Many pupils seem to have got a great deal of satisfaction out of successfully completing a Stage Test, and being awarded a 'Pass' or a 'Credit' on their Regional Record of Achievement.

> I was amazed, because I had passed by a large amount of marks and I am not bright. I like French now. I am going to take it in third year if I can.

> You feel proud at the end because it says you are able to speak French.

> When you leave school you have a certificate to show to your employer.

The reconstructionist practice of predetermining the goals and the means to achieve them appeared to suit a number of teachers.

> I stopped teaching in a haphazard way, on a 'hand to mouth' basis and started to formulate broad aims and objectives for myself and my pupils. I started to try and teach with an overall plan in mind concerning *what* I expected my pupils to achieve, *how* and *how well* I wanted them to achieve it.
> Instead of teaching 'the Imperfect' on 'a one-off' basis because

they 'needed to know it', I started to try and put it in a wider context.

GLAFLL makes teachers think about what they do and why and how they do it. It is from this change in teacher attitude that the most important results have come.

Some teachers also stated that the reconstructionist emphasis on targets, on mastery, and on tangible proof of success improved motivation among pupils and their parents.

In preparing for a Stage Test, pupils became much more aware of what they could actually do. For example, when asked to give present tense endings or noun genders, most pupils were at best less than confident; being asked questions like: 'How do you say/ask/do ... in German?' evoked a much wider response, particularly among pupils of average ability who were able to show that they were capable of performing some functions in German. Working towards the test has allowed teaching to crystallise around the uses to which various bits of language can be put. Motivation began to rise at a time when it can normally be expected to fall to a low point. Those pupils who received Records of Achievement were delighted with this statement of their prowess. At an S2 parents' evening following the distribution of the 'certificates', several parents remarked how pleased they and their children were to have received tangible recognition of work done.

It seems to have given the pupils more motivation – made the subject much more useful in the pupils' eyes. It is clearer to them what they are supposed to be aiming at.

It seemed important to build on what was proving to be successful, and work towards a more varied methodology in the classroom. This latter was initiated in the second phase of the GLAFLL project to which we now turn.

6.4   GLAFLL developments: the second phase

The second phase in the GLAFLL project began to take shape during 'the years of methodology', when the focus of attention turned away from syllabus blueprints and assessment schemes to the actual teaching/learning process in the classroom. Here it had become apparent that despite the framework of Stages and Levels designed to enable learners to learn at their own pace and to their own level, and despite the intended emphasis on practical communicative work, classes continued to learn as a block all together on the same material, with the vast majority of class time devoted to presentation sequences and to paired dialogue routines as described in the previous section. There was still little or no experiential learning, little or no real communication, and little or no sign of pupils being given responsibility to work on their own at their own level on individual, paired, and group assignments.

Perhaps the two most important factors in the gradual shift towards a more progressivist approach were the decision to experiment in the classroom with the concept of the 'information gap' as outlined by Rixon (1979), and the decision to experiment with a series of techniques designed to promote more learner responsibility (GLAFLL Document 23 in Clark 1985 Vol. 2).

Following the pioneering work of EFL teachers such as Rixon (1979), GLAFLL teachers combined together to produce classroom materials and tasks based on the principle that communication would occur where pupils had to exchange information or opinions in order to complete a particular task.

Teachers began to perceive that this was a quite different form of communication from that associated with the functional-notional approach. As one teacher commented:

> When the first whisper of communicative techniques drifted across Lothian Region to our school, our department was confident that the term referred to a methodological approach we had employed for years. Closer examination, however, brought us to the reluctant conclusion that whatever else we had been doing in our classrooms it was certainly not communicating.

It became clear that listening and reading work could now also be brought into a communicative framework, through setting information gap tasks in which pupils had to search out the information they needed, and then share this with others to complete whatever task was set. In this respect the 'jigsaw' listening and reading activities proposed by Geddes and Sturtridge (1979 and 1982a) proved a particularly rich model to emulate. In addition to this, experiments were conducted with various communication games, in particular with those proposed in Byrne and Rixon (1979), and with imaginative simulations such as those set out by Debyser (1980) and

Maley and Duff (1978). These brought an air of creativity and enjoyment to the foreign language classroom that had been lacking in the more reconstructionist first phase of the project. Pupils seemed to like to have to work out what they would say by themselves.

> The best thing I've done in French was where you and someone else worked out what you would say in a certain situation.

> In our class it (French) is taught in a way which makes you have to think what you mean.

> I like the way we are allowed now to say what we would like to, rather than be told what to say.

Gradually over time a large number of information gap and opinion gap communicative tasks were built up on the basis of resources found or created. A list of suggestions based on these was set out in *Syllabus Guidelines Part 1: Communication* (Clark and Hamilton 1984), which represented the second phase syllabus.

Foreign assistants were asked to create conversations (or occasionally monologues) from semi-scripts along the lines suggested by Geddes and White (1978). These were recorded live on cassettes and on video, and produced with appropriate communicative tasks and suggestions for further work.

A regional 'swapshop' arrangement was set in motion, in which any school which contributed material to the regional bank of resources would have automatic access to all the material available in it. Material based on the second phase syllabus was created, piloted in its school of origin, and when ready submitted to the regional swapshop. It was then subjected to further piloting and evaluation in other schools. One of the tasks of the GLAFLL Development Officer was to assemble and extend such material in a coherent way, and to create packs of self-access or group-access pupil resources and distribute them to schools. It was decided that where such packs warranted it, they should be published, since teachers were tired of being inundated with relatively poorly presented worksheets. They preferred to see a professional publication which would last longer and be more inclined to promote pupil interest. An arrangement was made with Macmillan Publishers Ltd. under which GLAFLL-inspired publications could be produced and sold to Lothian schools at a discount. A number of such publications have now been produced in several of the communication areas outlined in the second phase syllabus, covering the languages most in demand in Lothian schools. These are:

Hamilton, J. (1984a) *Corresponding with a French Pen-Friend.*
Hamilton, J. (1984b) *Corresponding with a German Pen-Friend.*
Hamilton, J. and Cumming, M. (1984) *Corresponding with a Spanish Pen-Friend.*

Hamilton, J., Harris, M., Jardine, K., and Meldrum, D. (1985) *French for Real.*
Hamilton, J., Priester, J., Watkins, S., and Wheeldon, P. (1985) *German for Real.*
Cumming, M. and Mullen, D. (1985) *Spanish for Real.*

Hamilton, J. and Clearie, J. (1985) *Take your partners: French pairwork exercises.*

Hamilton, J. and Wheeldon, P. (1985) *Take your partners: German pairwork exercises.*

Hamilton, J. and Cumming, M. (1985) *Take your partners: Pictorial pairwork exercises.*
Cumming, M. (1986a) *Hear-Say: Listening tasks for French.*
Cumming, M. (1986b) *Hear-Say: Listening tasks for German.*
Cumming, M. (1986c) *Hear-Say: Listening tasks for Spanish.*

Hamilton, J. and Wheeldon, P. (1986a) *The French Writing Folio.*
Hamilton, J. and Wheeldon, P. (1986b) *The German Writing Folio.*

These and other materials have helped schools to build up banks of communicative resources covering various mixed-skill activities and involving various forms of information gap. Materials now cover jigsaw listening and reading, pen-friend correspondence, conversation tasks, games, simulations, and projects. These resources are intended for various Stages in the GLAFLL language learning scheme, and begin to make it possible for pupils to work at their own level on material of their own choice. They form a bank of available options providing learners with a choice of activity along the lines proposed by Geddes (1978), Cross (1980), and Geddes and Sturtridge (1982b). They have made it possible for teachers to devolve responsibility to pupils in the management of their own learning, and have ensured that much of what is done in the classroom is practical and communicative in nature.

Experience has shown, however, that there is still a great need for teacher guidance in pupil choice of activity and of level of work, since, if left to themselves, pupils are all too ready to choose the simpler games options and to play them *ad infinitum*! It is important to ensure that over time they cover a range of different activities. It is also important to ensure that each pupil chooses a task that he/she will be able to tackle, but not without putting some effort into it.

At the time of writing it is perhaps interesting to note that, at the national level in Scotland, a body embracing advisers and curriculum development staff has decided to extend the same swapshop principles and practices as were evolved in the GLAFLL project to the preparation of learning resources for Standard Grade. It is hoped that this will add to the banks of material available to teachers and learners in S3 and S4 (Crispin, in Clark forthcoming).

Innovations have also been made in the provision and layout of equipment in the classroom. Instead of having a language laboratory, which has to be timetabled, and which encourages a lockstep method of use in which all pupils are doing the same thing, classrooms are gradually being equipped with peripheral work stations. These take the form of a continuous work-top along a wall (or walls) to which pupils can quickly draw their chairs. Above these, at an appropriate height, are cassette-recorders placed vertically against the wall on shelves. Individually or in pairs, pupils can work at these on listening material or on speaking activities. The work stations are designed in such a way that video monitors and/or micro-computers can be added. There is little doubt that it is above all the increased availability of such self-access or group-access resources, both software and hardware, that has inspired Lothian teachers to begin to experiment with experiential learning and with the promotion of learner responsibility.

Other techniques which were experimented with to promote more learner responsibility have included progress cards, language resource or 'This is what I know' booklets, and assignments designed to get learners to search out information for themselves, rather than to expect the teacher to provide it for them.

We have discussed the role of progress cards within the more reconstructionist first phase of the project. In the second phase they tended to be used less as predetermined lists of functional and notional content to be mastered within specific activities, than as negotiating instruments, the content of which was to be agreed upon by pupils and teachers together. Gradually pupils are being encouraged to learn how to:

- choose what activity do do
- find the material for themselves
- understand the instructions or cues given
- work through the material by themselves or with others
- know how to get appropriate help
- know how to search out and use information relevant to the task
- evaluate their own or the group's efforts where appropriate

In a number of schools pupils were encouraged to keep a 'Language Resource' or 'This is what I know' booklet, in which they learnt how to record their knowledge in a disciplined and organized way. There were several reasons for this:

- there was a fear that the emphasis on speech might lead to a great deal of material passing by without leaving much trace in the memory;
- pupils of all levels of achievement liked to see things set out systematically, since it helped them to remember them;
- it encouraged pupils to learn how to record useful information in an easily recoverable fashion;
- through the way in which they were encouraged to record the information, pupils could be helped to understand the rule-based nature of language;
- it enabled pupils to revise the knowledge they had learnt, just as the progress card enabled them to rediscover the activities they had performed.

The prototype suggested was a blank booklet in which each page had predetermined headings indicating what would be recorded there. The booklet had a page index and was divided into various sections covering functions, notions, grammar, and phrases and vocabulary related to particular topic areas. Pupils learnt to record information in the appropriate section in a way that helped them to get some feeling for the way in which language could be described and discussed. This seemed a much more purposeful way of recording knowledge than the traditional unsystematized vocabulary jotter. It enabled pupils to build for themselves their own reference systems, adding items as they went along.

Pupils seemed to find satisfaction in keeping their own 'This is what I know' books.

I think this is a good thing, because the things I learn are split up into different sections, i.e., family, school, hotels etc. which is a good help when revising.

It helps me to see how the language works and how it can be used to say things.

Some pupils, however, had mixed feelings about taking responsibility for their own learning:

Learning on your own has some advantages and disadvantages. Some advantages are that you don't get so much forced on you that you can't understand. Some disadvantages are that you might not learn anything if you are to do it on your own.

I found that it was up to me to discover what I needed to know and up to me to settle down and work along with the help of a teacher . . . I am getting more used to it and it is helping to build up my confidence . . . At the beginning I did not like this way of learning because it was so different to how I had been taught before . . . The system was hard to understand at first and I found I was not working as well as I should. This was partly because I did not feel I was learning anything because I couldn't see a set of marks laid down . . . Now I realise that learning this way does help.

Teachers themselves were slow to move towards giving pupils responsibility for the management of their own learning. The following teacher remarks indicate some reasons why this was so:

I am very wary of children of low intelligence becoming disorderly when left to work by themselves.

The pupils like working together and if you can stand the noise it's clearly a good thing. I sometimes wonder, though, how much they are learning in all the hubbub.

I can't really devolve responsibility until there are more ready-made materials at hand to help me to do so.

It doesn't help them to pass their exams.

School administration does not allow for pupil responsibility.

Others began to find advantages:

I found it most encouraging to witness S3 pupils (reared on GLAFLL) who, after finishing a piece of work, would quite happily (and of their own accord!) browse through the reading box I made.

Children would bring out a progress card which they had failed to complete for some reason, absence perhaps, and seek to remedy this. Often they would not even ask me but enlist the help of a neighbour instead.

GLAFLL has changed my attitude to the classroom. I try now to create an atmosphere where pupils tell me what they want to know. It has made teaching and learning a kind of joint enterprise.

The greatest benefit of self-directed learning has been totally unexpected – the pupils enjoy it immensely. They love working at their own pace and recording their own progress. Pair and group-work is undertaken with great enthusiasm. The final seal of approval, and the guarantee of the scheme's survival, came recently when the Headmaster said he had noticed a disturbing trend in his Modern Languages Department – the children were having too much fun.

In order to build on the progressivist practices introduced, it soon became evident that the sort of wholly reconstructionist syllabus and assessment scheme evolved in the first phase of the project would have to be revised. For the syllabus it was decided to adopt a two dimensional approach in line with suggestions made by Dodson (1983), Johnson (1980a), Brumfit (1984), and Allen (1983) outlined on pages 103–5. One dimension was to concern itself with experiential learning and guide the choice of graded classroom communicative tasks and activities, while the other was to focus on aspects of the language resource to be mastered, and on skills and strategies deemed necessary for those communicative tasks that could be predicted as relevant to the learners' objective needs. The former was to be centred on the learners' *Bedürfnisse* (subjective and evolving needs), and to attempt to respond to the sort of aspirations and interests shown by teenage learners. The latter was to be centred on the learners' *Bedarf* (objective needs), and to attempt to incorporate what, by consensus, were agreed to be the broad uses of language, modes of communication, roles and relationships, attitudes, themes and topics, and situational activities likely to be encountered by teenage and potential adult users of a foreign language.

The syllabus guidelines that emerged (Clark and Hamilton 1984) have therefore been set out in two parts – Part 1, Communication, and Part 2, The Language Resource in the various languages covered in the scheme. Part 1 has been referred to as the communication syllabus and Part 2 as the instruction syllabus.

The major problem in the setting out of the communication syllabus was to find a way in which real, simulated, and imaginative communication might be categorized. What finally emerged was a series of communication areas within which to set out various activities. These communication areas are as follows:

- Communication in the classroom and in school
- Communication with speakers of the foreign language:
  - face-to-face communicative activities
  - pen-pal correspondence
  - class-to-class links
- Communicative activities for pleasure:
  - viewing and listening for pleasure
  - reading for pleasure
  - songs
- Communication tasks embracing:
  - conversation and correspondence tasks
  - multi-skill tasks
  - potential tourist transactions
  - foreign visitors in Britain
  - staying in a foreign home
  - projects
- Games:
  - language practice games
  - communication games
- Simulations and plays

In order to help teachers to relate all of the above to the language resource suggestions of the instruction syllabus, each communicative task or activity indicated the probable functional and notional content involved. In addition, the language resource suggestions were set out in both functional/notional and grammatical sections. This permitted the functional/notional components to act as go-betweens or negotiating coins between the two parts of the syllabus guidelines, thus enabling teachers:

- to select communicative activities which appeared to have probable functional/notional content related to that which they wished pupils to work on;
- to check that pupils had a sufficient basis in language appropriate to the carrying out of a particular activity before attempting it;

— to indicate which language exponents might be appropriate to fill gaps in pupil knowledge exposed during 'deep-end' communication phases.

In addition, sections indicating the skills and strategies which might require a deliberate focus of attention were provided under the headings: interaction skills, information-processing and study skills, and communicative strategies — the latter to cope with language deficiencies and communicative breakdowns.

It was made clear that teachers would sometimes wish to work from the instruction syllabus towards a particular task or activity in the communication syllabus. They might wish to focus for example on forms for functions and notions related to getting food in a restaurant, before inviting pupils to simulate eating out at a restaurant. On other occasions teachers would wish to start with a suggested activity from the communication syllabus, as in the 'deep-end' approach, and teach to any exposed weaknesses that were felt to be worth remedying, thus moving from the communication syllabus to the instruction syllabus. Thus the two parts of the syllabus and the methodologies that they implied were to be integrated. It was the teacher alone who could determine how much deliberate learning, based on the instruction syllabus, and how much spontaneous learning, based on the communication syllabus, was to be provided in the light of the particular classroom context.

It was made clear that the second phase syllabus guidelines, like the first phase syllabus, were an interim product rather than a definitive one. They were:

> an attempt to encapsulate a few ideas at a particular moment in the Lothian project's life. They will no doubt have to be revised frequently in the light of fresh insights and further classroom experience.

> (Clark and Hamilton 1984:12)

In creating schemes of work, it was suggested, as in the first phase of the project, that teachers should evaluate their existing course books and materials against both the communication and the instruction syllabus. It was felt that this would reveal a number of gaps to be filled. It was hoped that the GLAFLL swapshop of communicative materials would help considerably to fill these.

Just as the syllabus had required modification, so did the first phase assessment scheme, in order to take account of the more communicative direction that activities in the classroom were taking.

Changes were made to the external Stage Tests in an attempt to move towards a more communicative style of assessment. These Stage Tests are described in Appendix 3 at the end of this chapter.

As in the first phase of the project, it was the evaluation of conversational ability that seemed to provoke the most discussion. The system of U/Cing and LOPing (as described on page 155) was retained, since this appeared to be an appropriate way of rewarding intelligibility, and of counteracting the teacher's over-concern for accuracy. It was useful to find that native speakers judged learner performance primarily on grounds of intelligibility, according to the research findings of Hughes and Lascaratou (1982). In their experiment 32 errors in English, made by Greek learners of English, were judged in terms of seriousness, and marked by three separate groups of judges – ten native speakers of English who were teachers of English as a foreign language (EFL), ten native speakers of English who were non-teachers, and ten Greek teachers of English. Inevitably, perhaps, the Greek teachers of English deducted significantly more marks over the whole range than either of the two native speaker groups. At one end of the spectrum the Greek teachers considered basic rule infringements as the most serious errors, and made the heaviest deductions of marks for these, while at the other end the native speaker non-teachers considered as serious only those errors that gave rise to problems in intelligibility. The native-speaker teachers of EFL fell in between the two positions, torn between their concerns as native speakers with message understanding, and their concerns as teachers with the niceties of the language. Given that the Stage Tests were supposed to be proficiency tests of real-life language use, it seemed sensible to continue to adopt a native-speaker viewpoint and penalize unintelligibility more than any other fault.

Alternative ways of judging how well the pupil had performed (what LOP to give him/her) continued to be explored. Canale and Swain's (1980) components of communicative competence were used as a means of scoring pupils separately in their linguistic competence, socio-linguistic competence, discourse competence, and strategic competence. This was found to be too demanding, since teachers acting as interlocutors as well as assessors did not have the time to analyse the pupil's performance into four categories, while simultaneously conducting a conversation. Nor was it practical, even when recordings had been made of pupil performance, to have to listen to these again and again in order to determine a score on each of the four components. Teachers did not have time to do this.

Brown and Yule's (1981 and 1982) research findings were also examined. They had been asked to develop criteria to judge spoken competence among mother-tongue pupils on a variety of different tasks. They had broken each task down into information units, and pupils were awarded a point for each unit of information successfully conveyed.

> By focusing the teacher's attention in a structured way on one important aspect of speaking (namely the amount of information provided clearly by a speaker) we can give credit to the performance of some of the most competent Foundation (i.e. low achieving) speakers, whereas impressionistic assessment (covering such categories as range of vocabulary, clarity, fluency, confidence etc.) would favour the less detailed but more articulate performances, which are typical of Credit (i.e. high achieving) speakers.

> (Brown and Yule 1981)

Brown and Yule's criteria were tried, but were discovered to apply better to *speaking* tests than to *conversation* tests, since in their tasks the 'hearer' was a silent interlocutor, who was merely asked to register ability or inability to comprehend by non-verbal means. In the task types envisaged for the GLAFLL conversation tests, it was a relatively unpredictable two-way interaction that was looked for. In some of these it was impossible to predetermine informational structure in advance, in order to create a scoring system.

We have come to be sceptical of the benefits of setting out single verbal descriptions for levels of performance on a rising scale, such as those proposed by Wilkins (in Trim 1978), or those set out in the new Standard Grade examination (SEB 1985). These bear little resemblance to the actual performances of pupils, since each description represents a gross averaging out of all sorts of individual differences. At worst they can be said to be distorting, at best a fictional guide. It has therefore seemed better to leave it to the teacher's judgement, on the basis of certain criteria, to determine whether a pupil's performance for a particular Stage was 'good', 'satisfactory', or 'rather weak' (i.e. on a Stage 3 test for example, was it worth Level 4, Level 3, or Level 2). Many different sorts of performance can then be judged 'good', in which excellence in one dimension may compensate for weakness in another. The criteria that teachers are asked to bear in mind have been set out as follows:

– candidate's ability to understand interlocutor, create coherent discourse, and take appropriate turns in conversation;

- quality of language resource displayed (accuracy, range, and appropriacy to context);
- ability to go beyond monosyllabic utterances when required;
- fluency (speed and comfort of decoding and encoding);
- strategic competence (ability to cope with difficulty and avoid embarrassing silences).   (Clark 1984)

In in-service workshops teachers were helped to come to terms with these criteria and gradually to internalize them. Over time reliability has been shown to be very high, as teachers have had to submit a sample of recordings of the tests and assessments that they make to a regional Assessment Monitoring Group, who provide feedback and advice on standards. Those teachers who may have marked too low or too high in their early attempts now seem to mark in a way similar to their more experienced peers. Experiential learning by doing, followed by feedback seems to have been an effective way to promote reliability.

Before leaving the GLAFLL project, an attempt is now made to evaluate what has happened, and to draw some tentative conclusions.

6.5   Interim evaluation and conclusions

In terms of raising the level of take-up for foreign language learning in S3/S4, the GLAFLL project has had some modest success. In 1976/7, at the start of the project, the average regional take-up rate of pupils in Lothian schools was 35%. After eight years of the project, in the two main languages taught in S1 and S2 in 1984/5 the take-up rate was 41% for French and 40% for German.

This improvement is in line with observations made in other GOML schemes (Gordon 1980, Buckby *et al.* 1981, Garside 1982, Sidwell, Smith, and Kavanagh 1983). It was achieved in Lothian against the national trend in other regions, and against the background of the Munn Committee's decision to exclude modern languages from the core of subjects to be studied by all pupils in S3 and S4. It can therefore reasonably be claimed that the increase in take-up represents a modest but positive achievement.

The pupils seem to have appreciated the emphasis on practical communicative work, particularly those who were able to compare this with the more traditional form-focused approach.

Last summer I spent a day in France with my parents. I could hardly speak a word of French. So in actual fact one whole year of French was wasted. This year however, we have been learning through GLAFLL. In my opinion I have learnt more in half of the second year than I could ever have learnt writing boring exercises.

Sometimes my friends and I argue about which class can speak better French, an O Grade class which gets mostly learning verbs, or our GLAFLL class which gets mostly communicating with the teacher in French. I think we're better.

I like German as I can write to my pen-pal in Germany, and when she writes back I am able to read some of it. It is nice being able to read and write a foreign language.

Some, however, found that the emphasis on practical communication meant that there was not enough concentration on grammar.

Through GLAFLL, mistakes happen a lot and are not always detected. We are expected to learn the rules as we go along. I don't like this. I would prefer if the teacher could discuss more with the whole class about cases, articles etc.

Other pupils found it upsetting to change from an approach in which the foreign language was taught and explained largely through the medium of English to an approach in which only the foreign language was used.

The teacher says all the words in German. That means she explains something in German. Therefore we cannot understand what on earth she is going on about.

I think that she should speak in English and teach us German on the blackboard, the same way they do in the other school I was at.

With those starting out on a more communicative approach, however, there seemed to be less resistance to the use of the foreign language for classroom interaction.

Teachers noticed an improved level of motivation, greater confidence among pupils in the second year, and higher take-up rates into S3.

I was surrounded by evidence of pupils' increased enjoyment in learning a language. Other teachers would remark on how they would quite spontaneously talk in German or French in other classes or read their German or French booklet when they were supposed to be doing Maths or History! Parents would remark on the fact that their daughter or son was constantly 'chuntering' away in the foreign language at home.

In terms of 'take-up' there has been a significant improvement since the introduction of the GLAFLL scheme. Nearly 60% of the S2 group in session 79–80 will be continuing with either SCE or CSE courses from June 1980, when the new session begins. This is a three-fold improvement over the situation a year ago.

Apart from actually enjoying teaching the GLAFLL class much more than the O Grade one, it was in fact easier. Even the poorest pupils appeared to be interested a lot of the time. I was not aware of the 'I hate French' feeling that one usually gets from a lot of 2nd year children .... Some of the less able pupils now appear in S3. One pupil has already asked when he'll be able to do the next Stage Tests.

What pleases me more than anything else is the fearlessness with which pupils now approach oral tests and the way one bad result in one test no longer discourages.

Whereas in 1976/7 only 28% of those continuing in S3 were boys, in 1984/5 35% were. It would seem therefore that some of the increase in take-up is occurring where one might least expect it, but where it is particularly welcome, that is, among the boys. The picture that emerges from a study of individual school patterns of take-up over the years in Lothian is that very little is ever achieved very quickly. Contrary to the apparent overnight success of the York and Leeds GOML schemes, described in Buckby *et al.* (1981), the Lothian picture is one of rather slow but gradual improvement in a number of schools, whose staff have devoted an enormous amount of time and energy to bringing this about.

While the records of achievement have been a motivating factor, giving tangible proof of success, they cannot be said to have had an instantaneous effect, all on their own, divorced from the total atmosphere created by the department awarding them. It would seem to be departmental commitment, rather than records of achievement, that maintains a higher level of take-up over a period of time.

Although 60% of pupils continue to drop their study of a foreign language at the end of S2, it seems probable now that the majority no longer do so with feelings of failure and frustration. They would appear to have enjoyed the exercise. Their comments indicate that on the whole:

— they enjoy foreign language learning
— they like the wide range of learning experiences
— they have felt a sense of purpose
— they enjoy working at their own level
— they eventually appreciate being given a sense of responsibility
— they enjoy paired and group-work
— they are deriving some sense of success (which often surprises them)

The improvement in the take-up rate in S3 must be seen as a modest gain, however, in the light of the many areas of concern which remain in the teaching of languages other than English in Lothian and in Britain in general. In S5/S6 the depressing decline in the provision and take-up of languages continues unabated. In Lothian only 14% of the total population in the upper school (S5 and S6) now studies a language. Scottish Examination Board figures reveal that compared with the population being presented for English at Higher Grade, the population being presented for French over the years has continued regularly to dwindle as follows:

1972   40%
1976   33%
1980   30%
1984   25%
1985   23%

The GLAFLL project has as yet been unable to effect any change to foreign language learning in the upper school, since learners at this level study for the national Higher Grade examination, which is still form-focused and ultimately designed in classical humanist style to select an élite for future university work.

In terms of standards, while no comparisons involving control and experimental groups have been made in the GLAFLL project, subjective judgements have indicated that GLAFLL pupils communicate better and are more confident in all skills, including writing, than their counterparts in more form-focused classes.

Teachers have said:

Whereas in the past I had pupils in my classes who could 'do grammar' and were therefore successful in my subject, and pupils who could not 'do grammar' and were therefore not successful, I now have pupils, the vast majority of whom can communicate successfully, but with greater or lesser degrees of linguistic accuracy.

The ability of 1st years to communicate on school trips to France and Germany took me by surprise. I derived enormous pleasure from seeing 12 year olds running all over a strange town, accosting total strangers in French or German, completely confident that they would be understood. And they were never wrong, although they didn't always understand what came back!

I presented my GLAFLL S2 pupils with the same oral situation as my O Grade S4 class. Both sets of pupils produced good conversations, yet the GLAFLL pupils were far more confident and eager to try out their new concoctions of French which might or might not work. Moreover they tended to think things out in terms of what they really wanted to say . . . The O Grade pupils were still obsessed with producing highly accurate French. They thought in English and then tried to translate their ideas into French, which led to difficulties.

As our first real GLAFLL pupils moved up the school into S3 and S4 it was obvious to me that they were proficient in communicative language skills, in all areas, far in excess of anything I had ever encountered with similar classes before. They spoke confidently in the foreign language, communicated well and effectively in numerous, sometimes quite tricky situations, they coped with 'O' Grade listening passages at the beginning of S3, they read for pleasure difficult passages in authentic German (from teenage magazines etc.), understood and listened for pleasure to quite difficult pop songs, and wrote lively, communicative letters in sophisticated, advanced German with evident command of advanced vocabulary and sentence construction. Although their German was in most cases full of minor errors it was always or nearly always comprehensible.

Not everything was a success however. There were constraints common to most classrooms which prevented teachers from doing what they wished to do. The following problems were frequently raised by teachers:

- the problem of coping with large classes when practical work at different levels for different groups has to be arranged;
- the comparative lack of self-access materials that would enable pupils to work by themselves in groups and pairs;
- the immense amount of time that has to be set aside for conversation testing in the GLAFLL Stage Tests;
- the incompatibility between the GLAFLL multi-level assessment arrangements and the insistence in certain schools on norm-referenced grades for all pupils in a particular age group;
- the incompatibility between GLAFLL work and preparation for the existing O Grade examination.

It is hoped that the introduction of the new national examination at Standard Grade in S4 will ease the latter problem, though Standard Grade in modern languages represents a GLAFLL first phase pre-progressivist view of foreign language learning, which many GLAFLL teachers have already left behind.

Of the remaining problems, few have been entirely solved, but:

- teachers now have access to a much wider range of pupil self-access materials, thus easing the problem of managing multi-level work in large classes. The peripheral work stations being supplied also enable individuals and pairs to do various forms of self-directed assignments;
- most Lothian schools have moved to a criterion-referenced form of reporting to parents, which permits multi-level assessment tailored to the achievements of the learners;
- the time required for organizing oral tests in the end-of-Stage Tests has now been halved, since it has been decided that the pupil-to-pupil oral test will no longer form part of the regional external Stage Test. Pupil-to-pupil oral tests will be kept as the main means of assessing conversational ability in internally organized Waystage tests counting towards the internal assessment profile submitted by teachers as their contribution towards determining an award on the Regional Record of Achievement.

In conclusion, it can be stated that schools and teachers in the region have inevitably varied in the extent to which they have involved themselves in the project, and in the choice of strategies and instruments they have selected from the total approach. There are at present, therefore, as many stages and levels of teacher awareness and achievements as there are in pupil language learning. The generalizations that follow should therefore be seen as indications of what has seemed to happen in a number of schools rather than as anything more substantial.

Before teachers were prepared to reconsider their approach and develop new strategies they had to be aware of something being wrong. This was easier in schools where there were large numbers of low-achieving pupils from less privileged homes, whose lack of success in foreign language learning led to demotivation and discipline problems. It was therefore often, but not always, in schools such as these that curriculum renewal through GLAFLL most easily took root. The existing examination system, with its heavy accent on accuracy, and its disregard for communicative activity, successfully masked the extremely low standards of communicative performance actually achieved by O Grade pupils. This prevented some teachers in the more academic schools from taking part in the GLAFLL project, which appeared to them to be out of tune with current examination requirements. A number of these teachers were in any case less than sure that they wanted to encourage a higher opting-in rate in S3. They tended on the whole to be satisfied with the existing system that encouraged the gradual emergence of pupils who could cope with a form-focused academic approach, so that by S3 all non-academic pupils had been eliminated from their care. Other teachers from the more academic schools, like their colleagues in less privileged schools, were dissatisfied with current arrangements, and with the élitist label that was frequently attached to the modern language department in the new comprehensive framework. They were keen to try to come to terms with a new approach which seemed to offer something to pupils of all levels of ability.

The first GLAFLL phase of curriculum renewal seemed to be marked by a determination to bring about visible oral activity in the classroom. It tended to be characterized by a rejection of form-focused drills and exercises and of written work in favour of oral work of a pseudo-communicative nature. Particular techniques favoured were teacher-to-whole-class question-and-answer work on short texts of an authentic nature, and preparation of role-plays related to particular situations, followed by subsequent regurgitation of these role-plays in pairs. With the advent of the functional-notional specification in the first phase syllabus, and the encouragement to be explicit about lesson objectives in progress cards, teachers began to equate communicative ability with the ability to produce a series of fixed exponents for each of the many functional/notional units expressed on the progress cards, and to equate conversational ability with the capacity to create dialogues in pairs on the basis of highly directive cue cards.

This interpretation of what was meant by a communicative approach brought pair work to the classroom. The results, however, were often less than they might have been, since the apparent communicative ability of the pupils was dependent upon the use of a few routines and patterns rather than upon any generative capacity (cf. HMI 1982). There was therefore little or no transfer of knowledge to novel contexts.

During this first phase, teachers also began to come to terms with the use of authentic material. Here, however, the tendency at the beginning was to reject anything other than functional written material produced by native speakers for public or tourist situations. This limited the sort of reading that could be tackled by pupils in the early stages of their language learning to signs, notices, menus, adverts, and other forms of material, in which the skills of extended reading and of discourse processing were simply not exercised.

With the advent in the second phase of the information or opinion gap, a whole new series of techniques became available. These brought reading, listening, and writing into the communicative framework. Authentic or semi-authentic reading and listening material was now incorporated into a variety of multi-skill communicative activities. It was also at this time that games, simulations, projects, and drama techniques were introduced. Teachers found this phase of methodological innovation particularly rewarding. Group work and individualized work were added to class work and to paired work. Pupil responsibility ceased to be a rhetorical aspiration and became a limited reality.

In the early part of the second phase, however, there remained a tendency for teachers to neglect acquisition – promoting activity in favour of more and more productive fluency work dependent upon minimal amounts of input. There was also a tendency to downgrade the role of feedback and of deliberate learning. The pupils' interlanguage, therefore, was seldom as well developed as it might have been. This was lost sight of by teachers in the understandable sense of achievement gained from the fact that the pupils appeared to be much more involved, more fluent, and more confident within the limits of their interlanguage, than they had ever been before.

Meanwhile, through both project phases, teachers have tried to come to terms with the use of the foreign language as medium of classroom management and instruction. It has been shown that if this practice is not started in S1, it may cause initial alienation among older pupils. Teachers vary considerably in the extent to which they now use the foreign language in class, with a distinct trend, however, towards an increase in use.

The picture that emerges is one of a gradual increase in teacher awareness and in curricular skills. There is an ever-widening array of resources, tasks, activities, and interaction patterns. It is clear, however, that there are still several areas of weakness.

Teachers have understandably been more concerned to raise the levels of motivation and of pupil involvement in overt communicative activity, than to investigate ways of promoting better language learning *per se*. Thus the achievement of a sense of 'busyness' in the classroom has been seen as sufficient, with little questioning as to whether the experiences provided have led to increased learning. 'Busyness' has not always guaranteed learning. One teacher sums up the feelings of many at present:

> I don't really know yet how to ensure both use and learning through classroom communication.

Few teachers have managed yet to break through school traditions and administrative constraints towards the development of meaningful negotiation and of pupil responsibility, though a number of teachers have recently begun to do so.

In teacher-based projects, such as GLAFLL, there is a fine balance to be drawn between the encouragement of a positive group feeling and the creation of the necessary critical climate, without which gains may often be illusory.

It is hoped that the framework and style of curriculum renewal adopted for GLAFLL will permit the project to continue so that:

- the gap between the rhetoric of intention and the reality of classroom practice can be further narrowed;
- the teaching/learning process can continue to be improved in the light of further classroom experimentation and experiential learning;
- teachers can continue to be supported by an advisory service which fosters innovation within a critical but co-operative climate.

There seems little doubt that the immediate task to be faced is to work towards a balance between the re-emergence of the concern for language awareness (cf. Hawkins 1984), which derives from classical humanism, the concern for communicative skills fostered by reconstructionism, and the concern for learner responsibility and experiential open-ended learning cherished by progressivism. There is a need for action research into the different effects created when one adopts different constellations of deliberate instruction, acquisition-promoting activity, communicative experiences, and awareness-raising activities, in order to attempt to draw some conclusions about the particular mix that seems best at different stages in the learning process for different pupils in different contexts.

From a wider viewpoint, while it can be maintained that the GLAFLL project has demonstrated that pupils of all levels of ability can learn a language other than English to a successful communicative level, it is nevertheless clear that it requires more than just a project of this nature to bring about an overall improvement in the provision and take-up of languages other than English in Britain. It requires an effective policy on languages in education at national and local government level to build upon the achievements of language teachers, such as those who have been involved in projects like GLAFLL. There is a need now to work towards a much greater participation by pupils in language learning, over a much longer period, than is currently the case. There is a need to work towards greater diversification in the provision of languages in schools, to reflect Britain's political, commercial, and cultural needs, and to respond to the needs and wishes of its own communities, whose indigenous and immigrant languages have been neglected as sources of cultural and economic wealth.

It is to another English-speaking country – one with a greater political commitment to the learning of a whole variety of international, regional, and community languages, that we shall turn in Chapter 7, in order to outline the initial work achieved in the ALL (Australian Language Levels) Project.

Appendix 2

GLAFLL First Phase Stage Tests

Paper and pencil tests

At Stages 1 and 2 there was a sequence of mixed listening and reading items in which pupils were assigned a role (usually that of a tourist), and asked to respond to spoken or written stimuli such as they might encounter on a trip abroad. The items were discrete, but could be linked together into a story, thus providing the pupil with a psychologically coherent context for each item. This form of test had been pioneered successfully by the Oxfordshire group (Oxfordshire Modern Languages Advisory Committee 1978). It permitted the sampling of a number of syllabus items covering the sort of predictable functions and notions associated with fairly well defined tourist situations. Listening items involved the understanding of:

— answers from an imagined interlocutor to questions that the pupil might have put. These might be related to prices, directions, times, distances, food and drink, people, places etc.;
— statements, questions, requests, comments etc. initiated by an imaginary interlocutor;
— information in the form of some simple public announcement related to travel, shopping, directions etc.

Reading items might involve the recognition of:

— signs
— notices
— short messages
— lists of facilities/goods (menus, shopping offers etc.)
— simple adverts

Answers were normally to be written in English, or a grid was to be filled in, or a mark made at an appropriate spot on a map or a plan.

Pupils were able to study the questions before listening to items played twice on tape, or before reading the information given. Their task was to locate and extract information from the sort of everyday speech and writing they might come across in the foreign country.

The test proved popular with the pupils who enjoyed the storyline. It was however limited to language-like behaviour in many respects, since for the listening items, in which there was a conversation with the candidate's contribution missing, there was a lack of discourse coherence and reality.

At Stages 1 and 2 a *letter* from an imaginary pen-pal was given. The pupil was asked to believe that a friend had just received it and needed some help in understanding and answering it. The letter would normally be handwritten and whenever possible would be an authentic one. The pupil was asked to answer his/her friend's questions in English about the content of the letter, and then to write an answer. This was to be in English at Stage 1, and, by popular request from the pupils, in the foreign language (rather than the English suggested in the instructions) at Stage 2. A dictionary was provided. The simulated interactive nature of this test lent some reality to what would otherwise have been a fairly traditional reading comprehension, however well disguised. Whereas the *sequence* sampled the tourist transactional side of the syllabus, the *letter* permitted a sampling of the language of personal social interaction.

At Stages 1, 2, and 3 a separate *listening* test was given. In this, the pupil was given a role as a visitor to the foreign country staying with a pen-pal and family. The rubric indicated in English the context within which a conversation would take place. The foreign family would discuss events and arrangements concerning the pupil, and, therefore, of interest to him/her. It was thus hoped that there was some purpose to the listening. The conversations were scripted and, therefore, idealized, and ran to some three to six exchanges between the participants involved. The pupil was asked to listen for particular bits of information, heard the conversation twice, and then answered questions in English. This test was little more than a traditional listening comprehension test, but it did make an honest attempt to create some psychological reality to the pupil's listening. It became known as 'the involved fly-on-the-wall test'. It permitted the examiner to assess the pupil's ability to pick out relevant information from short stretches of conversation.

At Stages 2, 3, and 4 a separate *reading* test was given. This allowed the examiner to sample a number of the authentic reading materials suggested in the syllabus. A dictionary was provided. Test-types included were:

— material received from a pen-pal or a class-to-class exchange with a foreign school
— adverts
— teenage magazine extracts
— news and other items

Conversation tests

The most important part of the Stage Tests was the conversation element. Pupils were made aware that irrespective of any other achievements in internal assessment, or on the external 'paper and pencil' tests, an award in the regional Record of Achievement could only be made if the pupil 'passed' the conversation tests.

There was a pupil-to-teacher conversation test, in which the pupil played the role of him/herself and the teacher the role of a salesman or other 'sympathetic' foreigner. This permitted the sort of transactional task associated with tourism, as well as the 'getting to know you and your interests' style of test. Ideally a foreign assistant was to play the part of the foreign interlocutor, and the teacher was thus freed to concentrate on assessment. In practice this was often not feasible, and the teacher had to act as both interlocutor and assessor. The tests were cued or partly cued for the pupil as follows:

The examiner is a grocer in a shop. You come in and wish to buy something which you can eat and drink right away.

The teacher will give you some foreign currency. You must do the following:

— Attract the grocer's attention.
— Ask for something particular to eat.
— Ask for something particular to drink.
— Say how much of each you want.
— Answer any questions you are asked.
— Pay the correct amount and get change if necessary.
— Take leave.

(GLAFLL Conversation Test 1978)

There was also a similarly cued pupil-pupil test in which pupils had to imagine that they were speaking to a friend rather than to a foreign stranger. Since a great deal of classroom activity was to involve pupil-to-pupil interaction, it seemed sensible to have pupil-to-pupil conversation in the Stage Test, however unrealistic it might seem to expect pupils to talk to each other in the foreign language in real life. When at the end of the test it was thought that one pupil had not had a reasonable opportunity to participate in the conversation, because of the inability of the other pupil to play the role asked of him/her, the teacher was asked to go through the task again with each pupil in order to make a decision about a level of performance for each.

Appendix 3

GLAFLL Second Phase Stage Tests

Paper and pencil tests

The second phase paper and pencil tests were in many respects more innovative than the first. In the second phase, all the various paper and pencil tests were contextually interlinked, rather than being divided into distinct scenarios. Following Morrow (1977), it was decided to experiment with the use of the same authentic material for adjacent levels, and to vary the level of difficulty of the tasks, to reflect the fact that in real life authentic material is the same for all listeners and readers, irrespective of their stage of learning. The context for the whole test was an exchange of tapes and scripts with a class abroad.

In Stages 1 and 2 pupils were asked to summarize the contents of a letter from the foreign school for a friend who had just joined the class, and who had not yet learnt the foreign language. The pupil was asked to give as much information as possible. This was an attempt to create an open-ended style of question in which the pupil could be rewarded for the amount of correct information extracted.

Stages 1 and 2 pupils also had to listen to a tape sent by the foreign school, in which a number of foreign pupils spoke about themselves. They had to select two with whom they thought they might like to effect a pen-pal exchange, provide information about them, and say why they had chosen them. Again this was an attempt to provide a more selective open-ended style of response.

Stage 2 pupils were asked to write a letter in the foreign language to their first choice of pen-pal telling them about themselves.

Stage 2 pupils were also asked to read written scripts included by the foreign class. These were descriptive and narrative in character and were related to photos of their school and of their classmates. There was also the script of an interview with a member of the foreign class. Stage 2 pupils were asked to explain as much as they could about what was written below each photo. They were also asked to complete a grid giving information about the foreign pupil interviewed.

There was an equivalent but more demanding style of test produced for Stages 3 and 4.

Conversation tests

The conversation tests followed the framework laid down in the first phase of the project and involved pupils in a pupil-teacher conversation and a pupil-pupil one. These were no longer cued in the same manner, however, since the first phase tests with their cues had seemed to lead to two parallel and sometimes unconnected monologues, rather than a conversation. Instead of being told exactly how the conversation would progress, through cues in advance, the pupils were simply placed in a situation and left to solve whatever problems had been set. This gave rise to a more realistic conversation, in which both parties had to listen to what their interlocutor was saying, in order to be able to continue the conversation appropriately. Teachers were asked to act as sympathetic native speakers, but to raise and lower the level of their talk during the pupil-teacher test, to discover the limits of the pupil's comprehension and negotiating ability, without inviting disaster. Where it was possible and felt to be useful, the teacher was to inject a level of unpredictability and invite the pupil to react. Those pupils who merited the highest available level of performance on a particular task were expected to be able to handle this, as well as carrying out the task specified.

7 The ALL Project

I was invited to Australia for six months as Consultant to the ALL project to develop and finalize the ALL project's design, and to initiate work on the first draft of the materials in collaboration with Angela Scarino and Pamela Morley. It is from this initial work that this chapter is drawn.

While I have attempted to reflect the evolution and the thinking behind this initial stage of the project as accurately as I can from the project writing team's viewpoint, it is only fair to point out that the framework of value systems and of curriculum renewal outlined in this book into which I am placing the project remains my personal one.

The project will inevitably evolve and change in certain aspects, as a result of further thinking, evaluative feedback, and unforeseen contextual constraints.

I am extremely grateful to the ALL Project Management Committee for permission to reproduce large parts of the ALL Project Stage 2 Draft Guidelines (Clark, Scarino, Morley 1986) in this chapter.

7.1 Introduction

The ALL (Australian Language Levels) project was conceived and initiated by the South Australian Education Department, which sought and obtained funding from the Curriculum Development Centre in Canberra. A condition of the funding granted was that the Project should be a national one supervised by a Management Committee responsible to the Curriculum Development Centre. It was to be concerned with the development of curricular guidelines and proficiency targets to facilitate the teaching, learning, and assessment of languages other than English (henceforth LOTEs) in both Primary and Secondary schools in Australia, whether as mother tongues or as second languages.

There are approximately thirty LOTEs taught and assessed within the Australian educational system. These embrace international languages such as French and German, regional languages such as Chinese and Indonesian, and Australian community languages such as Greek, Italian, and Vietnamese.

There has recently been a considerable upsurge of interest in LOTEs in Australia, largely inspired by the determination of the various LOTE-speaking communities within the various States that their languages and cultures should be maintained and developed within a multicultural, multilingual Australia. The emergence of papers outlining a possible National Language Policy, which argued strongly for a greater commitment to language learning at all levels in education, was tangible proof of the current climate of concern, though as yet no official National Language policy has emerged.

In this chapter an attempt is made to describe the main features of the initial work of the ALL project as a practical example of curriculum renewal in action, designed to integrate 'top-down' and 'bottom-up' initiatives, and to create a LOTE curriculum model broad enough to integrate the best features of the classical humanist, reconstructionist, and progressivist value systems. The project is still in its early stages of development, and the outline of its early work that follows must be seen as an inevitably limited attempt to capture the principles that underlie it, and to describe what has been achieved.

7.2 Setting the curriculum renewal process in motion

The initial intention behind the setting up of the ALL project was to create a common framework for syllabus creation and for assessment, which would operate across States for the various LOTEs taught in Australian schools (Martin 1984). This framework was to be based on the graded objectives syllabuses and communicative methodology emerging from the various GOML schemes in Britain, and in particular from the work of the GLAFLL project. This was to be allied to the concept of assessing students against a rising scale of predetermined proficiency levels, verbally described in terms of criteria as to what students should be able to do, and how well they should be able to perform at each level. This latter was to be based on work achieved in Australia on the Australian Second Language Proficiency Ratings scale (ASLPR) by Ingram and Wylie (1982), and in the USA by the American Council on the Teaching of Foreign Languages in their ACTFL Proficiency Guidelines (see Higgs 1984: 219–21).

It was initially envisaged that the project team should produce:

– a set of model syllabuses or curriculum guidelines, in English, describing what students should be able to do in a language at

successive stages of learning, together with proficiency criteria for
each stage.
- sample syllabuses in specific languages, providing examples for
the adaptation of the model syllabuses
- a handbook designed to assist syllabus developers, including local
authorities and community and professional groups, in the
adaptation of the model syllabuses to the wide range of languages
taught in Australia
- a handbook for teachers using the ALL syllabuses. This will
contain planning and programming guidelines, learning activities,
information about assessment, procedures and ideas for certification of results.
(Australian Language Levels Project Brochure 1985)

The various curricular products described above were to be created
by a small team guided by a local consultative group of teachers in
the South Australian educational system, and by a national
Reference Group made up of representatives from each State and
from the Curriculum Development Centre in Canberra. When
completed, the various curricular products would be submitted to
the Curriculum Development Centre, and when approved, distributed to the appropriate bodies in each State. In-service training
courses would then be organized so that the users of the products
(in-service educators, curriculum developers, and teachers) could
adopt and implement them. In brief the curriculum renewal process
was to follow the Research, Development, and Diffusion centre-
periphery model favoured by reconstructionists.

As the project developed, however, it became clear to the Project
team:

- that it was not entirely sensible to attempt to create a model
syllabus in English for all LOTEs in Australia, or fixed descriptions
of what learners should be able to do at particular stages in their
learning, since the former (the syllabus) needed to vary considerably across languages to reflect among other things the different
socio-cultural uses of language in different speech communities,
and the latter (the proficiency statements) had to be properly
researched before any descriptions of proficiency to be expected
from students at school could reasonably be made;
- that it was not entirely sensible to adopt a wholly 'top-down'
approach to the creation and dissemination of curricular products,
i.e. to produce something 'fully realized in its essentials prior to its
diffusion', as in the centre-periphery model of innovation outlined

by Schon (1971:81). It was made clear to the Project team by educational administrators, in-service educators, curriculum developers, and teachers in the various States that if they were going to feel commitment to the ALL project's curricular products, then they would have to be involved at some level in the creation of them.

Somehow, a process of curriculum renewal had to be set in motion, which would enable a network of information exchange and of curriculum renewal activity to be set up across States despite geographic and psychological constraints, so that all who wished to could contribute to the project.

Initially the ALL project team would set the curriculum renewal process in motion, co-ordinate and bring together the various state networks, but it was clearly understood, given the limited funding and the likely restricted life-span of the project team's existence, that the curriculum renewal process would need to continue long beyond the life of the central support team, if it was to achieve what it set out to do.

In order to ensure a high level of participation in the production of the various curricular products, it seemed important:

- to ensure that as many people as possible felt part of the initial development process in the formulation of the project;
- to ensure that whatever curricular products emerged would leave space for individual interpretation, and above all for the filling in of large amounts of detail, so that the various products could be closely tailored to the differing requirements of each language group and each individual teaching/learning context within this.

It seemed sensible to work towards a model of curriculum renewal which provided adequate space and opportunity for innovation, and for the involvement of those teachers who were prepared to devote their experiential wisdom, time, and energy, to the creation of ever more appropriate curricula; but which also provided sufficient structure and guidance to teachers working in isolated areas, or lacking the time, ability, energy, or confidence to develop their own solutions to their own problems. It is such a model, involving guidelines on the one hand, and teacher involvement in their completion, adaptation, realization, and ongoing renewal on the other, that the ALL project has proposed.

It seemed that what was initially required was a set of powerful guiding principles for the development of curricula applicable to all LOTEs in education. The principles would derive from educational theory and practice, applied linguistics insights, and the experiential wisdom of administrators, in-service educators, curriculum developers, and classroom teachers.

The project team felt the need to enrich the initial reconstructionist brief with classical humanist features, designed to ensure that a level of professional awareness about education, curriculum renewal, language, and culture was promoted, and with progressivist features, designed to create a process through which those involved in the teaching of the various LOTEs in Australia could participate in a meaningful way.

In order to set the process of curriculum renewal in motion in the State in which the project team were based, a number of Project Advisory Groups were set up within South Australia, to ensure that those involved in LOTEs in that State could participate in the formulation and development of the project, and to ensure that the project team could benefit from the experiential wisdom of a wide range of people. The various groups covered the following areas of concern:

- The teaching of LOTEs in Reception (pupils aged 5) to Year 5 (aged 10). This covered bilingual programmes, the development of mother tongues, and the learning of second languages.
- The teaching of LOTEs in Year 6 (aged 11) to Year 10 (aged 15), covering the same areas as above.
- The teaching of LOTEs in Years 11 and 12 (aged 16 and 17), covering the same areas as above.
- Aboriginal language education.
- Teacher in-service education.

Meetings with in-service educators and with teachers were also set up in other States, at which initial exchanges of information as to how the project was to develop were carried out. The representatives from each State on the Project Reference Group and the national consultants to the project also met with the project team at various times to provide guidance. The Australian Federation of Modern Languages Teachers Associations (AFMLTA) held meetings in various States to ensure an effective flow of information and an involvement of the associations in the work of the project. A Newsletter was also established to act as a forum for an exchange of information on ALL project matters.

When asked to indicate the principal problems that the ALL project should attempt to address, teachers pointed to the following areas of concern:

- It was difficult in many schools, particularly among monolingual speakers, to motivate students towards LOTE learning. Very few students continued LOTE learning for more than one or two years.
- In many schools the school management and staff as a whole placed a low value on LOTE learning, thereby discouraging students from language study.
- The communicative emphasis in some classrooms was missing, and many students saw little relevance in what was being done.
- There was a need for developing teacher language skills to cope with a more communicative style of teaching.
- Teachers were lacking in curriculum development skills, and they did not always have adequate time for working on schemes of work, resources, assessment etc.
- There was not enough in-service education to bring teachers together, so that they could work co-operatively on finding solutions to their common problems.
- There was often little or no continuity of learning in the transfer from primary to secondary or across schools.
- There was often too little time in school devoted to LOTE learning, both in terms of length of time and of intensity, to make the exercise meaningful.
- Teachers were not yet clear as to which methodological strategies they should use in the classroom to promote an effective communicative ability among their students.
- Teachers were as yet unable to cope with classes of mixed ability and mixed achievement, particularly when mother-tongue developers and second language learners came together in the same class. Classes were often too large to permit a great deal of practical work to be done.
- Teachers were not yet clear as to how they should assess students in the classroom, given the move away from norm-referenced grading.
- There were few teaching materials that took the Australian context into account. There were very few teaching resources in languages other than French, German, and to some extent Italian and Greek. Teachers had little time to fill the gaps.
- The examination requirements in some States were not in tune with what teachers wished to do in the classroom.

These concerns were remarkably similar to those diagnosed at the start of the GLAFLL project (see Chapter 5). They seemed to call for:

— a raising of awareness in schools and in the communities which they served, as to the value and purposes of LOTE learning, in order to work towards better social attitudes towards language learning, particularly among English speakers;
— the fostering of a feeling of success among students in their LOTE learning at school;
— the promotion of communicative skills in the classroom to give a sense of practical relevance to the learners;
— a framework for LOTE learning that would provide for continuity of learning, open access, and multiple entry and exit points;
— the promotion of longer periods of study and greater take-up among students;
— better conditions for LOTE learning in school in terms of time, class size, facilities, and resources;
— in-service opportunities for teachers to get together to improve their curricular skills and to co-operate in work designed to find solutions to classroom problems;
— better facilities for teachers to develop their own language skills;
— harmonization between work on the LOTE curriculum and public examinations in each State.

Based on all the above, the ALL project team decided to initiate work in four areas as follows:

— the establishment of a *framework of progressive Stages* for the traditional form of LOTE learning (as a subject in the curriculum), from Reception at age five to Year 12 at age seventeen, with a related framework for bilingual programmes where both English and a LOTE might be used as mediums of instruction;
— the development of *guidelines for schools* aimed at school managers;
— the development of *guidelines for planning and renewing the LOTE curriculum*, aimed at curriculum developers, assessment panels, and classroom teachers;
— the development of *guidelines for in-service educators* aimed at advisers, superintendents, consultants, and other in-service educators.

As in the GLAFLL project, the framework of progressive Stages is intended to provide transitional and terminal targets for students of all ages, abilities, language backgrounds, and achievements, whether mother-tongue developers or second language learners, and to provide a principled means of ensuring continuity of language learning for individual students within and across schools and States. For each Stage, in each language, it is intended that there be a statement of suggested goals, suggested process activities, and when research is completed, some indication of the range of variability in successful performance to be expected at the completion of the various Stages.

The guidelines for schools aim to assist school management teams to build up an effective language teaching policy and programmes. The guidelines for planning and renewing the LOTE curriculum aim to assist all those concerned with curricular work in LOTEs:

- to understand contemporary trends in curriculum design and curriculum renewal;
- to derive principles to guide the language teaching/learning process;
- to create syllabuses;
- to devise strategies to cope with classes of mixed ability, mixed language background, and mixed achievement;
- to elaborate assessment schemes to monitor, record, and report on students' progress;
- to choose, adapt, create, and use appropriate teaching/learning materials and equipment;
- to create schemes of work for particular groups of learners;
- to evaluate classroom practices and improve on them, and thus assist teachers to learn how to renew their own curriculum.

The guidelines for in-service educators aim to assist them:

- to understand the principles behind teacher development and curriculum renewal
- to plan and execute in-service education for LOTE teachers, and create the conditions in which 'bottom-up' curriculum renewal can thrive
- to evaluate their own practices and improve on them

The basic purpose of the initial work and of the documents to be produced is to provide a framework and a set of guiding principles to enable networks of curriculum developers and teachers in each State to create language-specific syllabuses, examinations, resources, and schemes of work within the same framework of reference, so that work achieved in one State or context can be made available to others.

7.3   The ALL project's proposed framework of Stages

The ALL project's proposed framework of Stages is based on the same principle as the GLAFLL Stages (see pages 140–45). The Stages are graded, overlapping and age-related, and designed to offer all students achievable transitional and/or terminal targets towards which to aspire, and to allow multiple entry and exit points into language study. Students should be able to start or continue their LOTE learning at the Stage most appropriate to their age and to their development in the LOTE being learnt. All students should be able to attain some measure of success at performing the goals set out at the Stage which is most appropriate to them.

The framework of Stages must somehow serve three masters. Firstly, it must respond to the realities of student progress, which are not related in any simple or direct way to age or length of study, though the latter is an important aspect of an individual's eventual level of performance. Secondly, it must assist teachers to plan and execute the teaching/learning process for the various groups of learners that they teach. Thirdly, it must be operable within the various administrative frameworks that each State establishes. Each State has to determine for itself how best to apply the framework of Stages proposed. This may well involve the breaking-up of each Stage into smaller Waystages.

It is important to stress that the Stages represent *arbitrary* ways of dividing up a language learning continuum into administratively convenient slices that enable schools, parents, teachers, and students to conceptualize what is being done at different times. Stages cannot be time-related in any neat and tidy way, since faster learners will work through the process activities and attain the goals to an appropriate level more quickly than slower learners. Students must therefore be enabled to progress through the Stages at different speeds and at different levels of performance appropriate to their potential and their aspirations. In addition to the above it must be stated that there is no one obvious moment at which students may be said to be ready to move from being a Stage 1 student to being a Stage 2 one. In principle a student is considered to be ready for Stage 2, when he/she has gone through the process activities that were set out for Stage 1, and has demonstrated success in the attainment of the goals for that Stage at some level of performance appropriate for the student in question.

It is clear that a beginner's Stage for a young primary child will have different goals and different process activities from a beginner's Stage for a student of secondary school age, whose general cognitive and affective maturity will enable him/her to learn more rapidly, more efficiently, and in rather different ways. Thus Stages, as expressions of goals and of the means to attain them, have to be broadly age-related. It is for this reason that the ALL project's proposed framework of interlocking Stages is divided into three broad age groups as follows:

– Reception (K or R) to Year 5
– Year 6 to Year 10
– Years 11 and 12

The proposed framework of Stages is set out in Figure 3.

There are one or two points relating to the proposed framework that need to be made.

The framework does *not* necessarily imply that students should be taught in classes homogeneous in terms of level of achievement (and, therefore, often heterogeneous in terms of age), though there may be contexts in which such an arrangement is appropriate. It is more probable, however, that classes will remain broadly homogeneous in terms of age, and will therefore be heterogeneous in terms of Stage and/or level of achievement in the language being learnt. In such cases it is essential for teachers to have resources and strategies for coping with classes in which students have mixed achievements and different developmental backgrounds.

In K or R, total beginners in a LOTE would start in Stage A. In the Years K or R to 5, they would proceed through Stages A and B. In principle Stage A would be a largely but not entirely pre-literate phase, while B would involve rather more literacy. Those with a good home background in a LOTE would start in Stage C and proceed through to Stage D. The division between total beginners and those with a home background in a LOTE is, of course, deceptive, since learners with home backgrounds in a LOTE may be at very different levels in their development. Some may be able to understand only a few phrases, but have no capacity for speech in the LOTE. Others may already be fluent speakers. Those with a home background in a LOTE may, therefore, fall anywhere within Stage A, or be at some orate but not literate level in Stage B, or be ready to start in Stage C. Diagnostic procedures of some sort will eventually have to be created to situate students roughly within the notional Stages, and thus assist teachers to enable students to develop from where they are.

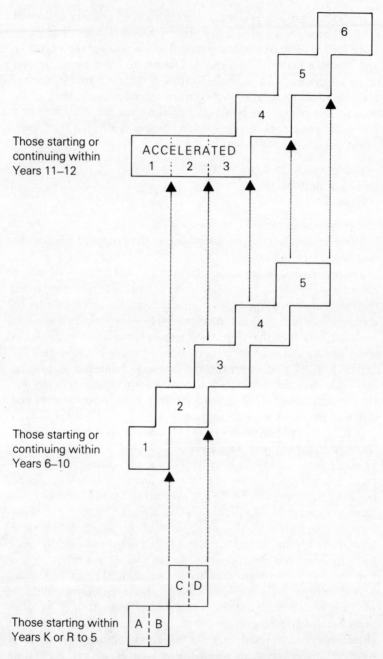

Those starting or continuing within Years 11–12

Those starting or continuing within Years 6–10

Those starting within Years K or R to 5

Figure 3   ALL Project proposed Stages

Stage 1, for Years 6–10, is a beginners' Stage. Given the greater maturity of students undertaking it, the Stage will cover the same sort of ground as Stages A and B in about half the time.

Bilingual students with a home background in the LOTE being learnt, and who are starting in Years 6–10, may start from Stage 2, should their LOTE development warrant this.

In Years 11 and 12, should students wish to take up a new language, an accelerated version of Stages 1, 2, and 3 would be available.

The proposed framework thus envisages several starting points in the learning of languages, whether as first, second, or third languages, and should facilitate a much greater take-up of LOTE learning in Australia at different points than is currently the case.

All students are expected to continue their learning till they have successfully achieved the goals set in the Stage that they are working at. A minimum period of two years of study is foreseen, though it is hoped that schools will work towards LOTE learning as a normal part of the curriculum for all pupils for longer periods of time.

At the top end of the scale it is expected that the highest Stage that will be completed by non-native speakers, starting in K or R, and going through to Year 12, is Stage 5. Stage 6 is likely to be reached only by those with an active home background in a language. It will represent a real challenge and should not be dissimilar in style or content from the equivalent syllabus in Years 11 and 12 for students of English.

7.4 Guidelines for schools

In order to guide school managers in their policy-making and organization for LOTE learning, the ALL project team has produced guidelines which draw on the papers outlining a possible National Languages Policy, and on various State policies and draft policies on languages in education. A rationale for LOTE learning is set out. In essence this proposes that the aims of LOTE teaching and learning, whether of a home language or of a second language, are to promote the students' cognitive, social, and affective development, so that he/she is enabled to live a full and enriching personal life, and to play as full a part as possible in the social, wealth-creating, and leisure-based life of the community.

In terms of cognitive development, the guidelines propose that all language learning involves learning to acquire, encode, and handle concepts, and through this learning how to explore reality, reflect, and act upon the world. Second language learning aims to develop and extend the conceptual knowledge acquired through home language experience and the development of the mother tongue at school. It seeks to enable learners to see that there are other ways of perceiving and encoding reality, of organizing interpersonal relations, and of thinking and behaving. It aims to help learners to understand and value such diversity, and to develop a greater awareness of the nature and role of language and culture in human life. It aims to enable learners to take a growing responsibility in the management of their own learning, so that they can learn how to learn, how to use language in their learning, and how to learn a language in later life should this be wanted.

The guidelines propose that language learning promotes social development through involving learners in learning how to relate to others, and how to move away from their own perspective to achieve mutual comprehension with them. Second language learning aims to build upon the social skills and experience gained through first language development, and to extend these to enable learners to relate to those of other cultures, so that they can participate in the promotion of intercultural understanding and communication.

In terms of affective development, the provision of education in the mother tongue seeks to develop the learner's personality, and his/her means of expressing this, so that a healthy self-identity is fostered. Second language learning aims to build on this, and to enable learners to gain a better understanding of their own linguistic and cultural identity in the wider perspective of a multilingual, multicultural environment. Second language learning aims to assist learners neither to fear nor to denigrate those with other languages and other cultures, but rather to embrace the value of diversity.

Over and above the benefits that language learning affords the individual, the guidelines point to the socio-cultural benefits to be obtained from promoting a better understanding between communities within Australia, through the teaching and learning of community languages, and between Australia and other countries, through the teaching and learning of regional and more global, international languages.

The guidelines also highlight the need for Australians to become proficient in a range of regional and more global, international languages, in order to fulfil the economic (commerce, tourism etc.) and political needs of the country.

The guidelines emphasize that it is the responsibility of the school, through consultation with the community it serves, to determine which language(s) it will offer its students in the light of individual, community, regional, and national needs, and to ensure continuous access to LOTE learning for all students, irrespective of background, according to their needs and aspirations.

The guidelines highlight the advantages to be gained from bilingual programmes, wherever the social attitudes of the community concerned are positive towards this, and wherever a bilingual approach is felt to be more appropriate than the traditional teaching of LOTE-as-a-subject.

The guidelines set out a number of organizational conditions which underlie effective language learning.

7.5 Guidelines for planning and renewing the LOTE curriculum

The intention of the ALL project team is to produce guidelines to cover eight areas as follows:

- a study of contemporary trends in curriculum design and curriculum renewal in LOTE
- a set of principles to guide the teaching/learning process
- syllabus guidelines for the setting of goals, content, and methodology for LOTE learning at different Stages
- suggested strategies for coping with classes of mixed ability, mixed language background, and mixed achievement
- assessment guidelines for the monitoring, recording, and reporting of students' progress
- resource guidelines to assist in the choice, adaptation, creation, and use of learning materials and equipment
- guidelines to assist school departments and teachers to create schemes of work for particular groups of learners
- guidelines to assist teachers to evaluate their own classroom practices and to improve upon them.

Of these, at the time of writing, only the first three have been completed in draft form.

In this chapter, the statement setting out the principles to guide the teaching/learning process, and the syllabus guidelines for the setting of goals, content, and methodology for LOTE learning at different Stages will be outlined. They represent an attempt to integrate the best features of the classical humanist, reconstructionist, and progressivist approaches.

7.5.1　Principles to guide the teaching/learning process

The principles set out here are an attempt to encapsulate the various insights about school language learning that have emerged during the course of this book. They recapitulate a number of the points that have previously been made, in an attempt to draw the threads of the various arguments together into a set of guiding principles. These are designed not as a panacea or recipe for instant success, but as a set of working hypotheses to guide LOTE curriculum renewal. They should be tested against the realities of different classrooms, so that further refining and reshaping of them can be undertaken in the light of experience in the ALL project.

The principles attempt to respond to the objective and subjective needs of learners of LOTE. They reflect a concern with the needs of students:

- as users (or potential users) of the language that is being learnt
- as learners who are learning how to learn a language
- as persons with certain aspirations, an individual personality, a certain communicative background, and a certain level of cognitive, social, and attitudinal maturity

It is a set of principles which will respond to these various needs as a whole that is proposed here.

The principles proposed are as follows:

- The learner needs communicative data in the form of exposure to language in use, which is comprehensible and personally relevant.
- The learner needs to participate in communicative use of the target language in a wide range of tasks.
- The learner needs to focus deliberately on various aspects of what he/she is learning, in order to support the spontaneous learning process.
- The learner needs adequate feedback and an idea of how he/she is progressing.
- The learner needs socio-cultural data, and direct experience of another culture embedded within the language being learnt, or closely associated with it.
- The learner needs to reflect upon and become aware of the role and nature of language and of culture.

- The learner is a person with individual traits and concerns and needs to be treated as such.
- The learner needs to learn how to manage his/her own learning and to learn how to learn.

Each of the above principles is examined in turn.

The learner needs communicative data

All learning is a result of our imposing meaning upon the data to which we are exposed in the environment. Language learning is no exception to this general rule. Evidence from natural untutored learning suggests that learners acquire language from everyday communicative data which are not predetermined structurally or in terms of functional and notional formulae. On the contrary, the untutored learner is exposed to unsystematic language, albeit kept simple in various ways by the native speaker to ease the learner's processing burden. Over time, given motivation and communicative challenge, the learner creates his/her own systematic and ever-evolving communicative resource out of the unsystematic data provided. Gradually the learner's communicative resource improves and expands, and approximates ever more closely to that of a native speaker. Very few learners of an L2 ever achieve a communicative resource equal to that of a native speaker's, but, given appropriate data and tasks, learners can learn to communicate successfully. While some linguistic knowledge and grammar is necessary to all communication, much can be done with a minimal grammar and an adequate vocabulary.

It seems sensible to heed the evidence that we have from untutored learning, and to accept that in order to be able to use language spontaneously, learners require exposure to comprehensible communicative data, that is, language used for a purpose beyond that of merely demonstrating particular grammatical structures, vocabulary, or functional/notional exponents. This is not to say that a deliberate focus at appropriate moments on such things is pointless. Indeed it is argued in the ALL project that in classroom circumstances, where there is limited exposure to data, such deliberate focuses are essential, and respond to the objective learning needs of all learners.

It is important to stress that the communicative data to which learners are exposed need to be relevant and comprehensible to them. They need to be relevant or learners will not attend to them. They need to be comprehensible, because when we are unable to impose meaning on what we hear or read, we cannot process the data and therefore no learning is achieved. We retain only that which we have made meaningful for ourselves. We retain best that which has some immediate personal significance for us, or that which we have worked at deliberately and effectively to impose meaning upon.

Meaning, however, is not derived from spoken or written words alone. We bring a whole set of expectations and experiences to what we hear and read. We often know what is likely to be said or written in certain contexts, and what is likely to happen next in a particular speech event, and we use such knowledge to assist us to predict what we are about to hear and read.

When helping learners to understand communicative data in a target language, it is important to ensure that there is an adequate level of contextual support to assist them, and also to encourage them to transfer to the language learning situation the same strategies that they use to predict and impose meaning on what they hear and read in their L1, rather than simply encouraging them to attend to the words or sentences.

The total attention of beginners in receptive work is likely to be taken up by the difficult exercise of imposing meaning on the data to which they are exposed. There is little extra capacity left for attending to non-meaning-bearing grammatical features, such as concords, case endings, and agreements. It is likely that learners will only start to produce the more redundant grammatical features spontaneously when they have been able to attend to them in the communicative data they meet. It is for this reason that a certain limited amount of deliberate focusing on such grammatical detail may well help in the long run to speed up the learning process.

Most syntactical development in a particular language seems to follow a path common to all learners through various stages of interlanguage. Untutored learners sometimes reach a plateau in their interlanguage development, beyond which they do not seem to progress. On this basis it has been suggested that untutored learners are only motivated to learn the language of the speech community in which they are living to the point at which they can satisfy their communicative needs and their social aspirations towards being accepted as a member of it. They appear to cease to progress when they are able to satisfy these two concerns. Those who have little desire to integrate into a speech community, or who may feel socially or psychologically distant from it, may not develop their communicative resource beyond whatever level permits them to fulfil their limited communicative needs. Their receptive capacity, however, may allow them to understand most, if not all, of what is said by native speakers around them.

It is difficult to compare untutored learners with classroom learners, since it is clear that many of the latter will have little or no motivation to be accepted as members of the speech community whose language they are learning, in the absence of an experience of that community. The motivation to increase the quantity and quality of one's language resource is likely to be provided by the desire to please the teacher and satisfy oneself, or to get a good grade in a test or an exam, rather than by any motivation to integrate into another speech community. Such integrative motivation, however, may well be the essence of some community language learners' motivation.

A receptive capacity is likely to develop earlier than a productive capacity, and to remain ahead of it as learning proceeds. It must not be expected that much of the communicative data understood by the learners will reappear in their talk in the early stages. It seems to take second language classroom learners of secondary school age anything between one and two years to begin to feel comfortable and confident enough in the target language to initiate much in novel ways. It may take primary school learners somewhat longer. That is not to say that opportunities should not be provided in the early stages for students to engage in spontaneous speech. It is merely to point out that expectations of what will be achieved should be realistic and not overambitious.

In brief:

- Learners need communicative data, because these provide the essential input upon which their mental language learning process can operate.
- In order to attend to such data, and to ensure proper processing into the long term memory, such data must be both relevant to them and comprehensible.
- In order to make communicative data comprehensible, an appropriate level of contextual support must be provided, so that learners can use their knowledge of the world and of speech events to assist them to impose meaning on the words.
- Communicative data need to be adapted rhetorically to the learner's level.
- Communicative data do not need to be contrived to contain predetermined structures or vocabulary, or functional/notional exponents. This does not imply that a deliberate focus on how

language forms can be systematized, and on how forms can be related to particular functional and notional meanings, is a waste of time.
- Learners will create their own ever-evolving communicative resource from the communicative data to which they are exposed. They will move gradually through stages of interlanguage development, which contain errors, towards native-speaker norms.
- The learner's mental processes concentrate first and foremost on finding meanings. It is therefore the semantic content words and basic word order that will be internalized first, and it is these features that will appear in production first. The more redundant grammatical features will be attended to and internalized only when sufficient mental capacity is available to permit this. This suggests that some deliberate focus on such matters will assist learners in the long run.
- Syntactical development appears to follow a fairly common path in all learners. The mastery of largely redundant grammatical features, such as concords, endings, and agreements, however, is more idiosyncratic, and depends in untutored circumstances on the extent to which learners wish to integrate into a target language speech community.
- Untutored learners cease to develop their syntactic capacity at the point at which it satisfies their communicative and social requirements, though they may continue to acquire vocabulary from the communicative data to which they are exposed. This would also seem to happen to learners in immersion classes.
- In classroom circumstances it is important for teachers to provide graded communicative data designed at all times to challenge the learners' existing communicative resource, and through this to pressure them gently into expanding and improving it.
- It is likely to take some one or two years for beginners of secondary age in LOTE-as-a-subject classes to gain sufficient input and confidence to initiate much talk in novel ways in the LOTE being learnt. Up till then most of their talk will feature routine unanalysed phrases or chunks.

Communicative data in the classroom should include:

- teacher talk
- other classroom talk
- recordings of talk (audio and video)

- pedagogically-inspired written information
- other classroom written information
- realia and written texts from outside the classroom.

It is suggested that in order to provide a wide range of talk and of written texts in a variety of formats, and in an appropriately expanding range of contexts involving a diversity of registers, it is essential for teachers to build up resource banks of graded written texts and of taped and video recordings. These will bring in the outside world and help to prepare the learner to operate within it.

It is argued that in recent years there has been an enormous emphasis on attempting to provide learners with 'authentic' material, by which is normally meant material created by native speakers for other native speakers for communicative purposes in the world outside the classroom. In this sense, 'authentic' material excludes material produced for language teaching purposes. While this may be one aspect of authenticity, there are others that are equally important, if the term is to mean very much.

For material to be authentic in the outside world, it must have some personal relevance to the listeners/readers. They must see some point in being asked to process the information in it. The information may be intrinsically interesting and enjoyable, or there may be some extrinsic purpose (for example, to find out about something, such as how to make or do something, how to get from one town to another, etc.). If there is no personal relevance to the listener/reader, then he/she will simply cease to process the information. We might call this *authenticity of purpose to the individual listener/reader*.

For material to remain authentic in the real world, the listener/reader must respond to it in an authentic way. We do not normally use poetry to learn about past tenses, or read stories solely to acquire new vocabulary. We read poetry or stories because they stimulate or entertain us. We listen to television documentaries because they entertain and inform us. We listen to announcements in airports or railway stations in order to find out information relevant to our travel plans. What the listener/reader does with material is more important perhaps than where the material comes from. We might call this *authenticity of response*.

For material to be used authentically in the real world, certain conditions are usually present. When reading, we normally have time to consult a dictionary. When listening to others in conversation, we can normally ask our interlocutor to repeat or rephrase something. Thus authenticity in the use of language in the real world implies real world conditions. We might call this *authenticity of conditions*.

It is argued, however, that there is one aspect about authenticity that is being forgotten. Learners are not *communicators* in the outside world at the time when they are receiving classroom communicative data. They are *learners* in a classroom, and the teacher's task is to respond to their objective and subjective needs as *learners*. There is therefore another perspective on authenticity which needs to be taken into consideration. Material needs not only to serve an authentic communicative purpose, but also to serve the purpose of language learning, in order to be authentic to the purposes for which learners find themselves in the classroom. We might call this *authenticity of purpose to the learner as learner*. The way in which this form of authenticity is realized depends, of course, on the particular view that one holds as to how language learning is best promoted. In the ALL project the view is taken that this is best cultivated through an appropriate balance between helping learners to use the LOTE for communicative purposes on the one hand, and deliberately focusing at times on elements of knowledge and skills on the other.

Authenticity is held to be realized through both forms of activity. It is suggested, therefore, that material should be selected or created and treated to serve both ends. For this reason it is suggested that listening and reading material should:

– be focused on meaning, be personally relevant, and serve some genuine communicative purpose;
– be responded to by the learner in an appropriate manner as *communicator* first, *and* as *language learner* subsequently, as learning needs are exposed.

Responding to communicative data is of course merely a subsection of the communicative use of language described in the next section. It has been set out as a separate focus for attention for two reasons:

– It seems important to ensure that in the classroom a sufficient range of suitably graded spoken and written communicative data is made available, upon which the learner's spontaneous learning process can work. There is a serious risk in current perceptions of what a communicative approach to learning in the classroom may mean, that students may spend an excessive amount of time doing role-plays with each other at a relatively poor interlanguage level, and too little time on gaining access to further enriching data that will serve to extend their limited communicative capacity.

– In much current classroom teaching, input in the form of data for
the learner to listen to is viewed as fodder for immediate output,
rather than as potentially feeding an internal growth that can be
capitalized upon later. The active role of the receptive skills in the
building up of a communicative capacity is underestimated, thus
reading has been neglected, and listening is often reduced to an
input-for-output activity. This means that much of what is listened
to and read has been contrived in terms of syntactic control, and
has been trivialized in terms of semantic content, so that it can
immediately be regurgitated.

In order to build up graded banks of varied material, teachers are
advised to choose sources in the outside world and in the commercial
language teaching world, as well as creating home-made material
with the help of native speakers. It must be remembered that much
spoken and written material is ephemeral, and soon loses its
contemporary relevance. There is a constant need, therefore, for
upgrading it. In this area curriculum renewal is an ever-evolving
exercise.

The learner needs to participate in communicative use of the target language

The term 'communicative use' covers not only conversation, but also
listening for information, listening for pleasure, reading for information, reading for pleasure, corresponding for business or for personal
reasons, study skills, and various forms of project work involving
combinations of many skills.

The guidelines suggest that in order to judge whether a particular
classroom activity is communicative or not, it is useful to ask a
number of questions, to which the answer should normally be 'yes':

– Is there a purpose to the activity beyond that of practising
particular forms?
– Are there participants? Is their relationship to one another clear?
or Does the activity involve processing information from a spoken
or written text, and if so, is the text being used for the purpose for
which it was produced?
– Is there an information or opinion gap between the participants
involved, or between the user and the spoken or written text? Is the
speech or writing received or produced unpredictable? Note that a
lot of predetermined role-play may look like communication, but
it is not, since what is said is entirely predictable to the
participants. There is a distinction between 'acting out' and

communicating. In the former the 'subject' is preordained; in the latter it is created by the participants as they proceed.

It often seems easier to say what communication is *not*, rather than what it is. It is not just restricted to conversation. It is not simply using language relating to discrete functions out of context, unstitched into conversation or written text. It is not language practice (the display of language forms for their own sake). It is not skill development (the exercise of an isolated skill such as listening comprehension, as traditionally done in class, with a text and ten comprehension questions on it). The keys to communication are purpose, participants (absent or present), and context.

Students benefit from using language productively themselves, since through this they gain further access to communicative data provided by an interlocutor, as a result of their own contributions. Interactive speech and interpersonal writing can be seen as a means of obtaining further relevant and comprehensible data.

Learners need to use language productively in order to test out hypotheses concerning the way in which the LOTE being learnt can be used to express particular meanings in particular contexts, and get feedback from others as to the success or not of their efforts. Where they are not successful, this motivates them to reconstruct the particular hypotheses used. Language learning involves a continual drawing of hypotheses as to how the underlying formal, semantic, and discourse conventions of the target language work. Many of these hypotheses will be wrong. Some will be so wrong that they lead to communicative breakdown, in which case they must be changed. Others will be wrong but nevertheless successful in communication. The latter are likely to act as working hypotheses until better ones become available.

Learners need communicative experience in producing language, in order to mobilize and integrate the various sub-skills involved in this. They have to learn to get their tongues round utterances, to apply their grammatical, semantic, and discourse knowledge, to use their social skills and knowledge of the conventions of how to behave in speech (for example, how to initiate a conversation, how to participate and take turns, how to interrupt, how to end a conversation etc.). They need practice in executing the various levels of planning, processing, and monitoring that are involved in productive work. They need practice at integrating all of the above in performance, if target language fluency is to be achieved. Gradually they can be helped to work towards more and more automaticity in the execution of the various sub-skills involved in production, so that their attentive capacity can concentrate on what matters – the negotiation of meaning.

Learners need to be provided with the opportunity to develop a range of different rhetorical styles (formal, informal, transactional, private, public, technical, or subject-related etc.). Only if such practice is provided will they be able quickly to adapt their performance to the different contexts in which they may find themselves.

It can also be suggested that communicative experience in production is essential to learners to activate those areas of knowledge of which they have only a conscious control. This may help them to make these more spontaneously available for future use. Teachers have constantly sought to provide opportunities for learners to exploit that which they have just learnt deliberately. While accepting that such tactics have not always led to successful internalization of new material, there is every likelihood that generations of teachers have not been entirely wrong in their actions. It would seem likely that Rubin's 'good learners' (Rubin 1979) are correct in assuming that they benefited from seeking out opportunities to put to communicative use things that they had recently learnt. It can be suggested that it is through engaging in such communicative experience that that which has been learnt deliberately can become more spontaneously available.

Above all, perhaps, learners need to learn to negotiate meanings with others. There is seldom a fixed one-to-one relationship between forms and meanings. Forms take on particular meanings in particular contexts, and it is an amalgam of perceived physical and psychological features that helps learners and speakers to invest forms with the particular meaning desired. We have to work for a reciprocity of perspectives for the conveyance of information and intention (Widdowson 1984). We do this in our L1 largely unconsciously, and must transfer this skill to our use of the target language. The more distant from our own culture the target language and the psychological world of its speakers are, the more difficult it will be to achieve a reciprocity of perspectives. Language intentions will be encoded in ways that differ from the conventions of our own language use. The use of formal and informal codes in interpersonal relations may be very different. The conventions of gesture and other paralinguistic features may not be shared. Situations may be interpreted differently, and the cultural knowledge assumed and referred to may be quite different. In such situations, the negotiation of meaning for mutual understanding becomes crucial. Learning to communicate effectively is thus to a large extent a question of learning to move from one's own perspective to embrace the perspective of one's interlocutor(s). This is a social skill that school LOTE learning can help to foster, and that may have some feedback into L1 development.

Following on from the above it will be clear that in situations where learners are communicating with native speakers of the target language, breakdowns in communication may occur. These may arise from many sources – mismatched cultural knowledge, incompatible interpretations of situations, lack of agreement about the conventions underlying the forms being used, etc. Where these occur, it is essential for the learner to have compensatory or repair strategies to get over the difficulties that may arise. This involves learning to use strategies used in L1 to compensate for lack of knowledge or to repair breakdowns. Helping learners to use these strategies in their target language communication is vital. At the age of school language learning, conceptual and experiential development, obtained through L1 learning and general cognitive development, will far outstrip the learners' capacity to put what they want to say into words in the target language in the early and intermediate stages. There is a frustration involved in having an advanced conceptual system with an infant linguistic capacity in the target language to serve it. It becomes vital to be able to use strategies to compensate for this, if learners are not to remain in alienated silence for much of the time.

In brief, learners benefit from engaging in communicative experience involving the negotiation of meaning in a wide range of different contexts for a wide range of purposes, since this enables them:

- to gain further access to comprehensible communicative data;
- to test out form-meaning hypotheses, and on the basis of feedback to retain or modify them;
- to mobilize and integrate the various sub-skills involved in communication, and to practise the planning, processing, executing, and monitoring skills that are involved;
- to develop a range of different rhetorical styles to promote appropriacy skills and a context-sensitive communicative resource;
- to activate areas of newly learnt knowledge and thus help to make

it more readily available for future use. This may enable learners to shift that which has been deliberately learnt to the more spontaneously available store;
— to negotiate meanings with others, through creating a reciprocity of perspectives on what is said, and thus to develop social skills;
— to transfer the compensatory and repair strategies employed in the L1 to the use of the target language;
— to gain confidence and a feeling of success.

As with listening and reading materials, and frequently related to them, a bank of graded communicative activities is required, some goal-oriented, some of intrinsic value, and some to accord with learners' interests. The first two are part of the activities that all students are likely to engage in, while the latter can be seen as activity options for students to choose from according to their particular aspirations and interests. Activities can be chosen or created on the basis of the many collections of ideas and of material embodying information gap, opinion gap, and jigsaw activities such as those suggested by Ur (1981), Geddes and Sturtridge (1979 and 1982a), Byrne and Rixon (1979), and Clark and Hamilton (1984). Once the principles of how to create such tasks are understood, any number of variations on the themes can be invented.

The learner needs to focus deliberately on various aspects of what he/she is learning

The school LOTE learner, whether mother-tongue developer or second language learner, is unlikely in most circumstances in Australia to have the same level of communicative and social motivation to learn or develop the target language, as to learn or develop English. And, given peer group use of English, the amount of communicative data and experience in the target language are not likely to be as great as in English. It has been clear to generations of teachers that something over and above communicative data and experience must be provided to make up for this inevitably reduced level of motivation and of exposure. That 'something' is deliberate learning, deriving from a deliberate focus on various knowledge, skill, and strategy elements. Deliberate learning is required to act as a mnemonic support to whatever spontaneous learning is occurring, without which it may quickly disappear. In grammar-translation and in audio-lingual methods, however, the emphasis on deliberate learning became distorted to the point at which it completely

replaced any concern with spontaneous learning from communicative data and communicative experience. It is towards a methodology in which deliberate learning is used as a necessary support for
classroom spontaneous learning, and not as a replacement for it, that
the ALL project looks.

In the current climate, in which Krashen and Terrell (1983) and
others are making what appear to be wildly exaggerated claims for
spontaneous learning in the classroom, it seems important not to
rush to a methodological extreme and promote spontaneous
learning to the exclusion of all deliberate focuses on the various
aspects that go to make up a communicative ability. As Wilkins has
pointed out:

> Even a conservative estimate suggests that the amount of
> contact provided by 5 years of classroom-based learning is the
> equivalent of no more than 15–20 weeks of natural language
> contact.

(Wilkins 1983:26)

If we devote five years of classroom learning solely to completely
random communicative data and communicative experiences in the
LOTE, it can be argued that the results cannot realistically be
expected to be much above the extremely meagre ones achieved by
natural learners after 15–20 weeks of natural, unfocused, and
unsystematized exposure to a target language. It is unlikely that such
a poor return for effort expended would be acceptable to the teacher,
learners, parents, or education department. There is a need for a
deliberate focus on certain common communicative goals, on
activities and tasks that realize them, on knowledge and skill areas
that are implied in them, and on the range of compensatory strategies
that will cope with the inevitable lack of knowledge and breakdowns
that will occur, in order to bring about the sort of limited but
effective communicative capacity that is aimed at. In brief, we need
some level of intentional focusing in the syllabus to bring about a
quick communicative ability. This must provide some real surrender
value in a fairly short time to those who choose to opt out early, and
provide effective communicative roots on which further learning can
be grafted for those who wish to continue.

It is useful for learners of a target language to be able to fall back
upon a conscious, deliberately built-up knowledge of a language as a
strategy to compensate for lack of spontaneously available knowledge. If we have time, such conscious knowledge can act both as an

initiator of what we say and write, and as a monitor of what we are about to do or have just done. This conscious initiating and monitoring capacity becomes more and more useful as it becomes increasingly important for us to choose our words carefully, and to lend the appropriate shades of meaning to what we say or write. Human beings are not simple input-output mechanisms. They have complex planning, processing, and monitoring systems to ensure that any deficiencies between intentions and performance, and between intentions and effect are repaired. The development of a self-monitoring capacity is thus an important part of any effective learning. While much of the self-monitoring that we engage in is largely unconscious, it is clearly useful to be able to call upon conscious knowledge to assist us, particularly in those aspects of our life, such as the use of an L2, in which our performance is not as automatically controlled as in other more frequently experienced activities. By calling frequently upon our conscious knowledge we can hope to speed up the time it takes to make it available to us in our performance. In this way not only can we hope to learn to use a target language, but to control our use of it to some extent.

In brief, a deliberate focus on various aspects of the knowledge, skills, and strategies that are required in the building up of a communicative resource is necessary:

- to make up for the reduced level of motivation and exposure in classroom L2 learning, by acting as a mnemonic aid and support to spontaneous learning;
- to assist the learner to develop as quickly as possible a usable communicative resource, focused on a limited but achievable range of activities and contexts;
- to build upon and extend the existing deliberate learning capacity and awareness of language among learners of school age;
- to promote the use of conscious, deliberately learnt knowledge as a compensatory strategy for lack of spontaneously available knowledge, and as a monitor to control what is said or written;
- to reflect learners' needs for system information.

It is perhaps important here to stress that conscious knowledge for its own sake is of little use as an end in itself, and that deliberate learning is only useful if it can be applied. Conscious knowledge through deliberate learning cannot therefore replace communicative experience, but it can support it.

Following Halliday (1978:21), we might suggest that learning a language involves learning:

- how to *act* in accordance with the socio-cultural conventions of the target speech-community;
- how to *mean*, that is, to interpret, express, and negotiate meanings, and stitch them together to create coherent text according to the conventions of the target speech community;
- how to *say*, that is, which lexical and grammatical forms to use to express meanings;
- how to *sound*, that is, which phonological and graphological forms to use in speech and in writing.

Halliday (1973:22–45) sees language performing three functions – the 'ideational', 'interpersonal', and 'textual' functions. Through its 'ideational' aspect language permits us to interpret and express reality in the form of internalized experiences of the world. It permits us to exchange thoughts, feelings, experiences, opinions, and judgements about the world. Through its 'interpersonal' aspect language permits us to participate with others in speech events, to adopt a particular role *vis-à-vis* others, and to assign them roles which they accept or reject. It permits us to relate to each other, to express attitudes to what is said, and to interpret and express our personalities. Through its 'textual' aspect language permits us to relate what we say to what has been said or done before, and to decode and encode new and given information appropriately – in brief, to stitch together our fleeting thoughts and perceptions into relevant and coherent discourse.

All of this suggests that if we are to focus on how meaning is achieved in a target language, we should enable learners:

- to encode their intentions in an appropriate manner to suit the various shades of meaning they wish to convey in the different contexts and with the various people they meet;
- to encode the concepts they wish to refer to in an accurate and appropriate way;
- to encode and distribute new and given information according to the conventions of the language being learnt (for example, use of ellipsis, use of emphasis, use of pronouns for reference backwards and forwards, use of definite articles, word order, intonation features etc.);
- to achieve coherence with what has gone before, and to follow the various conventions of speech initiation and of turn taking in the target language.

Thus, in summary, there should be a series of deliberate and interlinked focuses on:

- phonological and graphological knowledge and skills to be internalized
- grammatical and lexical knowledge and skills to be internalized
- semantic and discourse knowledge and skills to be internalized
- activities and tasks which realize the common activity types, modes of communication, and dimensions of target language use to be aspired towards
- compensatory and repair strategies to cope with ignorance and breakdown

The question inevitably arises as to whether a deliberate focus on grammatical and lexical forms should be made prior to the undertaking of a communicative activity or after it. While some argue that there are reasons why some pre-communicative form-focused exercises should be done (Littlewood 1981), others argue against this (Prabhu 1980a, Breen and Candlin 1980). It seems sensible to accept that, in the early stages of learning, it will often be necessary to focus on the essential structures and vocabulary that realize the functions and notions likely to arise in a particular activity, before engaging in it. Reconstructionist methodology has always advocated the breaking down of global activities into sub-tasks, which are gone through one after the other, before reassembling the components into a global activity. There would seem to be truth in Littlewood's (1981) assertion that sub-tasks, or 'pre-communicative activities' as he calls them, are necessary: 'to give the learners fluent control over linguistic forms, so that lower-level processes will be capable of unfolding automatically in response to higher level decisions based on meanings'.

Alarmingly, that which seems logically to be true may have little psychological reality, for, as Welford (1968:291) pointed out, the division of a global activity into its various sub-components may be counterproductive, and not the best way to approach the teaching of complex skills such as those involved in communication in a target language. It therefore seems sensible to retain an open mind about breaking down global activites into sub-tasks and focusing on each before engaging in them, and the immediate engagement in global activities with no prior preparation. While leaning towards the latter in later stages, it may be sensible to adopt the former strategy more often in earlier ones, where much psychological confidence building and support are required, before the learner can be coaxed into communicative activity.

Where learners are pitched into activities with little or no preparation, it is important for teachers to learn how to structure tasks in such a way as to harness the learner's existing knowledge and experience, and incorporate a challenge which can be coped with, rather than one which will alienate. It is also essential to ensure that there is an adequate opportunity after the event for a deliberate focus on exposed areas of weakness in knowledge or in skills.

It is helpful to encourage learners to reflect deliberately on how forms achieve their meanings and effects, and thus to further their awareness as to the way in which different forms are used to convey different shades of meaning. It is also suggested that learners in intermediate and advanced stages should be encouraged to work together, to derive hypotheses as to how particular structural patterns and stylistic conventions work in the texts to which they are exposed. This encourages learners to become aware of pattern and of rules of appropriacy in the target language. It is a reflection upon the particular instances of perceived language regularity that leads to the general concept of system. It is reflection upon observed language variation that leads to understanding of the context-sensitive nature of language. Given the various findings indicating that awareness of pattern is an enabling factor in language learning, it seems important to help pupils to develop the skills required to perceive rules and regularities for themselves.

To conclude, it would seem, therefore, that in the classroom the teacher should aim to provide a wide range of learning experiences, some designed to promote spontaneous learning, some designed to bring about communicative use, some designed to focus on underlying knowledge, skills, and strategies, some designed to promote awareness of pattern and function, and some designed to assist the learner to develop control in the use of the target language. They will all be effective strategies for different purposes, in different contexts, with different learners, at different stages of development. The balance to be struck between these various strategies at particular points in time with particular students remains a matter for teachers to decide. While certain general statements may be made in advance about the overall methodological balance that seems appropriate for different age groups, it seems important also to stress that the methodology adopted by the teacher at any particular moment should be designed to respond to the particular needs of the student. As in gardening, where plants are growing in odd ways or are ceasing to grow, it is a particular treatment that may be required, so in teaching, where learners are developing bad habits (inhibition from too much deliberate learning, or fossilization from not enough communicative challenge or not enough focus on form), it is a certain methodological treatment that may be required. Methodology, like syllabus content, cannot and should not be so determined in advance that it is unable to respond to the requirements of individual learners or groups of learners, and yet it should have some structure, and be broadly based on what is believed to work best in school language learning, given the sort of goals that have been set for this.

The learner needs to be provided with adequate feedback and with some idea as to how he/she is progressing

The learner needs feedback on performance in order to know whether progress is being made. Awareness of progress is an incentive to further learning. Experience has indicated that nothing is more distressing to many adolescent learners than the extremist style of those who make an ideology of non-intervention. On the other hand experience has also shown that an over-emphasis on correction inhibits. An over-emphasis on positive feedback in the form of verbal encouragement tends to make students dependent upon their teacher. No verbal encouragement tends to be frustrating. It is feedback that is sensitive both to the cognitive and the emotional requirements of learners that we must seek to develop.

It would seem that what is required is a differentiated approach towards handling error, which takes into account the nature of the task being worked upon, the relative seriousness of the error made, the likely effect of correction on the particular learner who made the error, and the realistic expectations of long-term improvement as a result of any correction made. Current practice seems to suggest that in communicative phases it is above all the truth value and comprehensibility of utterances that should be monitored. Thus incomprehensible or ambiguous utterances should be verified, expanded, or reformulated for the learner. It will often be useful for the teacher to make a note of formal errors made in such communicative work, in order to remedy some of them at an appropriate time. In lesson phases when the focus is on particular forms, and where errors occur in the areas being concentrated upon, form-focused correction is necessary. It must be remembered that the accumulation of small errors may make a learner's utterances extremely irritating for native speakers to have to listen to. While errors may not appear to be important in themselves, in quantity they reduce the overall comprehensibility of an utterance. What are small formal errors in one context may give rise to semantic ambiguity in another.

It is important that learners know the criteria upon which their performance is being judged – whether this be communicative success, appropriacy to context, accuracy in formal terms, or a combination of all of these. The feedback provided by the teacher should aim to be relevant to the type of task in which the learner is engaged.

An assessment scheme is required which will assist teacher and learner to monitor progress, both in the process and products of learning. Such a scheme should aim among other things to:

– monitor whether students are learning what they are being taught, and are able to perform communicative activities successfully at a level appropriate to their aspirations, achievements, and apparent potential;
– monitor the outcomes of the students' own self or group-directed assignments;
– monitor students' language development;
– monitor the process by which the learner is learning.

Such an assessment scheme should aim to inform the teaching/learning process, so that appropriate decisions are made as to how best to proceed. If fossilization appears to be occurring, emphasis may need to be placed on further communicative data and/or on a more deliberate focus on form. If deliberate learning appears to be proceeding, but little fluency is occurring, an increase in communicative experience may be required. Students can be encouraged to monitor each other's performances. They can learn a great deal from sessions in which they are encouraged to draw attention to what they think are their friends' mistakes. This motivates, improves their monitoring capacity, and allows them to learn from each other. The ultimate aim of peer monitoring, however, must be to encourage an appropriate level of self-monitoring.

The learner needs socio-cultural data and a direct experience of another culture

There are a variety of ways of fostering understanding of and openness towards others and their ways of life. Perhaps the most used, but the least successful approach, is the direct teaching about 'background information' as subject matter to be learnt and regurgitated. It would seem more sensible to encourage direct experience of target language people and things through fostering contacts in the community, if the LOTE being learnt is a community language, and/or fostering pen-pal correspondence, tape or video exchanges from school to school, school exchange visits and holiday travel, as well as through the provision of authentic documents such as menus, magazines, tourist brochures, songs, poems, books, tapes, visuals, and the like. These will no doubt give rise to discussions of a socio-cultural nature which can then extend into further areas of interest. This is a very different sort of classroom activity from the teacher talk (or textbook script) and student listening (or reading) that characterizes the 'teaching about' approach. Openness towards a foreign culture is probably better fostered by experiencing it, and reflecting upon it, than by hearing about it at second hand.

The learner needs to reflect upon and become aware of the role and nature of language and of culture

Through experience of various languages, and through guided reflection upon this in the classroom, the student can be helped to build up language awareness.

There is much concern at present at the lack of awareness, both in and out of school, as to the nature and function of language. There are several schools of thought as to how to remedy the situation. Some wish to teach directly about language, either in an introductory course before LOTE learning starts (for example, Aplin *et al.* 1981), or as a formal linguistics course at an intermediate or more advanced level. Others wish to foster a school policy around the theme of 'language for learning' or 'language across the curriculum', in which teachers are helped to become aware of the principles underlying language and learning, so that they may reflect upon the way in which they themselves use language in their teaching, and the way they invite their students to use language in their learning. Such a school policy is probably best initiated through an analysis of the sort of language experience students undergo in their various classrooms, which often reveals a number of ills to be remedied. Others see the problem as being largely a question of asking students to reflect upon their own experience of language, language learning, and language use. Through reflection of this sort, insights may be developed which can then be further explored.

There is probably a place for all of these approaches in school. It is hoped that through the ALL project, LOTE departments will feel well placed to assist in the development of a general school language awareness policy. At the very least it will be useful for LOTE teachers to discuss areas of common interest and concern with English teachers, so that insights about the role and nature of language that are imparted to students in school, and the terminology used, are complementary.

Through experience of the various cultures with which the learner has come into contact, and through guided reflection upon this in the classroom, the student can be helped to build up a cultural awareness and sensitivity that may lead to greater understanding and tolerance of diversity.

It is clear that those students developing a home language are likely to wish to learn to operate as a full member of the speech community whose language they are learning. Their aim is acculturation, whereas those students learning an L2 may wish merely to build a bridge between their own communicative and cultural system and that of the target language speech community. This will mean a considerable difference in the emphasis placed on cultural aspects and on appropriacy between L1 developers and L2 learners.

It would seem that only experimentation will enable us to find out how best to integrate awareness-raising into the rest of our concerns, and to discover which strategies to adopt to promote an ever-increasing level of consciousness about language and culture.

The learner is a person with individual traits, and needs to be treated as such

A number of recent language teaching approaches have laid great stress on the need to view the learner as a whole person (Stevick 1976, 1980). This implies that, in addition to appealing to the student's intellect, we need to pay more attention than before to such things as:

- affective growth and the development of confidence
- imagination and creativity
- social relationships in the classroom, and the development of social skills

As well as engaging their intellect in information gap, opinion gap and jigsaw activities, it is important to appeal to the imagination of students, and to harness their creativity through simulations and games, to engage their minds and their imaginations in stories (see

Morgan and Rinvolucri 1983), in drama, in self-created fantasies (Debyser 1980, Caré 1980), or through the use of visuals to which they have to react (Maley, Duff, and Grellet 1980). Children live in their minds as much as in the physical environment, and it is likely to seem every bit as relevant to them to be engaged in stories or fantasies, as to be involved in everyday routines such as shopping or finding the way. It is helpful, too, to provide opportunities for project work of the sort that engages the attention of the learners over a span of time on tasks in which they are prepared to invest personally (Jones 1979, Legutke 1984).

All the above activities encourage the learner to make the necessary links between the deeper processes of their cognitive and affective make-up and the target language, without which they are unlikely to learn how to mould the foreign language to their own ends.

It may occasionally be helpful to involve pupils in the sort of soul-baring exchanges suggested by Moskowitz (1978). It is certainly true that in order to harness the student's interest, we have to create tasks and discussion frameworks that go beyond the relatively banal and unmotivating appeals to personalized language associated with most target language courses (for example, 'When did you get up this morning?' 'Describe the rooms in your house', etc.). It is important, however, to draw a distinction between therapy and education, and to suggest that it is not the role of the teacher to get the students to expose their private inner worlds. Students need to be able to engage that part of themselves that they feel able to in the classroom, but to retain their own privacy.

In order to respond to the affective needs of learners, it is important for teachers to remember that communicative activity in a target language can be particularly stressful.

> Conversations are special because they involve us in taking
> risks to our self-image and our status as members of a
> particular society.
>
> (Di Pietro 1976:50)

Some students will need more help than others in becoming risk takers in conversation. The teacher needs to be particularly careful as to how this is done. An atmosphere of trust where mistakes are expected and not ridiculed is essential.

Adolescents like working together in pairs and groups. It seems sensible to set a variety of tasks which involve co-operative activity. In groups, students discover that it is relatively easy to take risks and to create language that can be understood by others. In communicative activities they learn to work co-operatively, to take turns, to listen to others, to decide on courses of action, and to defend their judgements. In brief, they build up confidence and social skills.

Healthy relationships between teacher and students permit a sharing of minds, mutual empathy, and respect. Where this can be achieved, it is possible for teachers to work towards a classroom where responsibilities can be shared with students. This does not imply that the teacher has to give up the role of teacher and general class manager, in order to take on some sort of spurious equal participant role, but it does mean that he/she should encourage learners to manage their own learning, and through this to learn how to learn.

It can be claimed that classical humanist curricula ignored individual differences, and more recent reconstructionist ones, based on explicit predetermined syllabuses and criterion-referenced assessment (or grade-related criteria), risk doing the same, since they are more concerned with attempting to create a socially desirable stereotype, than with encouraging a range of individually diverse performers.

The various GOML schemes may provide a framework of syllabus content, tests, and levels of performance related to a progressive series of stages, thereby offering pupils alternative targets to reflect their different ability and/or achievement levels, but most schemes have done little or nothing explicit as yet to reflect differences in student aspirations, or differences in student interests due to age, sex, or personality, or differences in learning styles, or in personality. The goals, content, and methodology proposed at the various levels in GOML schemes remain common to all learners, irrespective of whatever differences there may be between them. This is clearly inadequate, and for the ALL project it is suggested that there is a need for a more flexible negotiated style of syllabus creation, which allows teachers to respond to the learners' subjective needs (*Bedürfnisse*), as well as to their commonly agreed objective ones (*Bedarf*). There is a need to ensure that there is adequate space to accommodate individual learner differences in aspirations, interests, and learning styles.

7.5.2 Syllabus guidelines

Unlike adult learners who tend to learn languages for some very specific purpose, school language learning is a more general exercise

which is less specifically targeted. It attempts to provide school
learners with a learning experience of a broad educational nature,
together with a general communicative base in the language being
learnt.

A general communicative base for one particular language,
however, will not necessarily cover the same range of contexts,
activities, and meanings as a communicative base in another
language, since the contexts in which a language is used, the purposes
to which it is put, the language activities engaged in, and the themes
and topics discussed will vary from one culture to another.
Languages reflect particular cultures, since they encode the way in
which reality is perceived and organized by a particular speech
community, and the way interpersonal relations are structured
within it. A general communicative base in an Aboriginal language,
an Asian language, or a language of ex-European origin cannot,
therefore, be exactly the same. In addition to this, in Australia we
have to take into account that a sizeable proportion of LOTE-
learning in school will be done by those developing a home language.
The purposes for which members of a particular LOTE-speaking
community will wish to learn or develop their language will usually
be rather wider than those relevant to non-members. Whereas the
former will normally wish to be fully integrated into the language
and culture of their LOTE-speaking community, the latter is likely
merely to wish to build an effective communicative and cultural
bridge towards a target language group.

In brief, there is a need to ensure that each LOTE syllabus reflects
the differences in the way the various target language speech
communities use language, and to ensure that the goals of various
different categories of learners are adequately provided for. It may
nevertheless be possible for the syllabus for each LOTE taught in
Australia to be derived from the same common syllabus guidelines,
provided that these are broad enough to encompass that which
seems to be common to all languages and all learners, while leaving
space for individual interpretation within and beyond this.

It is proposed that the teaching of all LOTEs-as-a-subject in
Australia should fit into the ALL project's framework of interlocking
age-related Stages. This does not and indeed cannot mean that the
goals and content of a particular Stage in one LOTE have to be
identical to the goals and content of the same Stage in another LOTE.
Not only will the goals and content vary on socio-cultural grounds as
outlined above, but there will also need to be some additional
variation on grounds of comparability of demands made on learners

in each Stage across languages. For example, the written systems associated with languages that do not share the Roman alphabet pose particular problems for many Australian learners, which will make it necessary in these languages to modify the reading and writing demands and expectations in the early Stages.

In brief the ALL project proposes that:

− Stages should pose comparable demands on learners. Content and expectations will therefore differ across languages.
− The goals, content, process activities, and broad methodology for each LOTE at each Stage should derive from common syllabus guidelines.
− The common syllabus guidelines should attempt to embrace that which is common to all languages and all learners, but leave space for teachers of a particular LOTE to include goals and content which reflect learner aspirations, and the socio-cultural uses to which the LOTE being learnt is likely to be put.

The ALL project syllabus guidelines look towards a broad eclectic model of classroom teaching/learning, based on the principle that it is necessary to attempt to find an appropriate balance between the predetermination of goals, content, and methodology, on the basis of what are taken to be common objective needs, and the leaving of space for the negotiation of goals, content, and learning strategies that respond to the more individual and subjective needs, aspirations, and interests of the various individuals involved. This principle operates at two levels:

− At one level the ALL project aims to provide guidelines and a framework of Stages to be adhered to by teachers-as-curriculum-planners, but leaves space for them to interpret these according to their perceptions of the objective socio-cultural and communicative needs of learners in contact with the target speech community concerned.
− At another level the project aims to set out predetermined broad aims and goals and rather more specific objectives, content, and process activities for students, but leaves space for teachers and students together to operate within and beyond these, in response to individual differences.

Just as it is vital to the education of students to be given responsibility in the management of their learning, in order to learn how to learn, so it is important to teachers to be given responsibility in the management of their teaching, in order to learn how to teach and to improve their practices. It is essential to the spirit of the ALL project's proposals to ensure that the planning of any particular classroom scheme of work should not be a once-and-for-all-task, but that teachers should be involved in a constant exercise of fine-tuning an original syllabus concept, filling it out, and reformulating aspects of it in the light of classroom demands and realities.

When selecting syllabus content for a particular Stage, it is helpful to set out:

- the principles underlying the language teaching/learning process
- the broad educational aims to be pursued
- the common goals to be worked towards by all learners. These should represent the objective needs of learners as communicators, learners, and persons
- the content to be covered and converted into process activities

The principles underlying the teaching/learning process have already been set out in 7.5.1. The other three concerns are briefly examined here.

Broad educational aims

The ALL project proposes that along with all other subjects in the school curriculum, school LOTE learning should aim to promote the individual's cognitive, social, and affective development, so that he/she is enabled to live as full and enriching a life, and play as full a part in the life of the community as is possible.

In addition to this, the particular contribution brought to education by LOTE learning is that it sets out:

- to enable students to develop communicative skills in a LOTE, in order that they can widen their networks of interpersonal relations, have direct access to information in the LOTE, and use their LOTE skills for study, vocational, or leisure-based purposes;
- to enable students to develop some understanding of the culture of the target language community, to compare this with their own, and through this to see the validity of other ways of perceiving and encoding experience and of organizing interpersonal relations;
- to enable students to take a growing responsibility in the management of their own learning, so that they learn how to learn, and how to learn a language;

– to enable students to develop an awareness of the role and nature of language and of culture in everyday life.

All of the above broad educational aims seem to be relevant in some form to all Stages of school LOTE learning.

Common goals to be worked towards by all learners

The goals set out below are thought to reflect the objective needs of school language learners. They are therefore presented as common goals towards which all learners should aspire.

The goals derive from the broad educational aims set out above, and attempt to define them in rather more detail. They are set out in four areas as follows:

– communicative goals
– socio-cultural goals
– learning-how-to-learn goals
– language and cultural awareness goals

Communicative goals   The ALL project team have consulted various policy documents and many people as to what communicative goals should be pursued in school LOTE learning. What follows represents an attempt at a distillation of what was said.

It is proposed that there are three basic *dimensions of language use* which seem to be relevant to general school learners of all languages. General learners may be said to need to learn how to:

– establish and maintain interpersonal relations, and through this to exchange information, ideas, opinions, attitudes and feelings, and to get things done;
– acquire information from more or less 'public' sources in the target language, (that is, in books, magazines, newspapers, brochures, documents, signs, notices, films, television, slides, tape, radio, public announcements, lectures, or written reports etc.). They need to learn to process and use this information in some way;
– listen to, read, enjoy, and respond to creative and imaginative uses of the target language (for example, in stories, poems, drama, songs, rhymes, films, or television etc.), and, among certain learners, to create them themselves.

These broad dimensions of use will involve the learners in performing in several *modes of communication* as follows:

- conversation and correspondence (including message writing, telephoning etc.), in order to establish and maintain interpersonal relations;
- listening and reading for information and/or pleasure, when acquiring information from public sources. This may involve subsequent summarizing or other forms of reproducing information, translating into English, or discussing with others in spoken form;
- giving information in speech or writing in the target language in a public form (for example, giving a short talk, or writing a report);
- listening and reading for pleasure and responding in some way to more imaginative uses of the target language;
- creating imaginative texts of one sort or another (for some learners only).

Employing such a rich mixture of modes of communication means that the four skills of listening, speaking, reading, and writing will all be exercised, and will be mobilized appropriately in the sort of activities learners are likely to meet in their future use of the target language.

Going one stage further, it is proposed that the three dimensions of use, and the various modes of communication to which they give rise, can be realized in a basic set of *activity types* that can be established as communicative goals. These are as follows:
To enable learners to:

- solve problems through social interaction with others, for example, participate in conversation related to the pursuit of a common activity with others, obtain goods and services and necessary information through conversation or correspondence, make arrangements and come to decisions with others (convergent tasks);
- establish and maintain relationships and discuss topics of interest through the exchange of information, ideas, opinions, attitudes, feelings, experiences, and plans (divergent tasks);
- search for specific information for some given purpose, process it, and use it in some way (for example, find out the cheapest way to go from A to B);
- listen to or read information, process it, and use it in some way (for example, read a news item and discuss it with someone, read an article and summarize it, listen to a lecture and write notes on it);
- give information in spoken or written form on the basis of personal experience (for example, give a talk, write a report, write

a diary, record a set of instructions on how to do something, or fill in a form);
- listen to or read or view a story, poem, play, feature, etc. and perhaps respond to it personally in some way, (for example, read a story and discuss it);
- create an imaginative text (for some learners only).

Table 4 sets out these common communicative goals into a coherent framework which relates dimensions of use to modes of communication and to activity types.

The activity types are not, of course, always separated the one from the other. They are often combined when a purposeful activity is undertaken. Thus, for example, 'ordering a meal in a restaurant' will be likely to involve:

- establishing relationships with a waiter
- searching for specific information as to what to eat in a menu, perhaps discussing this with others, and making a decision
- obtaining goods and services in the form of a meal

Or, to take another example, 'preparing a visit to the cinema' may involve:

- searching for specific information as to what films are on, and where and when
- making social arrangements with a friend and coming to conclusions as to which film to go to, where to meet, at what time etc.

Thus actual activities in the classroom which draw on these various activity types may well involve a combination of them.

It is suggested that it is important not to confuse communicative goals or objectives with classroom process activities which may help to realize these goals. Communicative goals and objectives are restricted to those activities that learners of LOTEs are expected to need to be able to cope with in real life encounters with the target language or its speech community. While one could not maintain that learning to be a creative writer or story-teller was a common goal for most learners of LOTEs, although it may be for some learners who are developing their ability in a home LOTE, it can be argued that it is an inherently enjoyable and valuable process activity for all.

Socio-cultural goals   The ALL project proposes that classroom

LOTE learning should enable learners to experience the target
language culture through the various communicative activities
undertaken in the classroom, so that at appropriate Stages they:

— have some understanding of how interpersonal relations are
conducted in the target language speech community;
— have some understanding of the everyday life patterns of their
contemporary age group in the target language speech community. This will cover their life at home, at school, and at leisure (pop
world, sport, media entertainment, etc.);
— have some insight into the cultural traditions of the target
language speech community;
— have some knowledge of the historical roots of the target language
speech community and its relationships with the learners'
community;
— have some knowledge of the economy and world of work in the
target language speech community;
— have some knowledge of the cultural achievements of the target
language speech community;
— have some knowledge of current affairs in the target language
speech community.

Through the above it is hoped to enable learners to develop positive
attitudes towards the target language culture.

Learning-how-to-learn goals The ALL project proposes that the
methodology and negotiative strategies adopted should enable
learners to take increasing responsibility for their own learning, so
that they learn:

— to manage the physical environment in which they have to work
(for example, to know how to move about the room purposefully
and quietly, to know how to keep their books and folders, to know
how to work tape recorders, slide projectors, etc.);
— to work individually on assignments;
— to work in groups with others and to determine together how best
to contribute to the common task in hand;
— to negotiate and plan their work over a certain time span, and
learn how to set themselves realistic objectives and how to devise
the means to attain them;
— to search out information for themselves from dictionaries, course
books, grammar books, and commercial or teacher-made self-
instructional material;

Dimensions of language use	Establishing and maintaining interpersonal relations through information exchanges and getting things done.	
Modes of communication	Conversation (listening & speaking)	Correspondence and messages (reading & writing)
Activity types	– Problem solving (e.g. participating in social interaction in the target language related to the solving of a problem, to the pursuit of an activity, to the making of arrangements, to the taking of decisions with others, or participating in transactions for the obtaining of goods and services and public information). [Convergent tasks] – Establishing and maintaining relationships and discussing topics of interest in the foreign language through exchanging information, ideas, opinions, attitudes, feelings, experiences, and plans in informal and more formal settings. [Divergent tasks]	

Table 4   ALL Project communicative goals

Acquiring and using information from more or less public sources through speech, writing, or other medium *and* Giving information in speech or writing or other medium.			Listening to or reading creative and imaginative uses of language *and* Creating them.
Listening & doing*	Reading & doing*	Speaking or writing	Listening or reading
– Searching for specific information in the target language for some given purpose, processing it, and using* it in some way. [Convergent tasks] – Listening to or reading information in the target language, processing it, and using* it in some way. [Divergent tasks] * *Ways of 'Doing', or 'Using' information acquired* – Using the information to make some decision. – Reproducing the information in English or the target language in some form (question and answer, filling in a grid, presenting a report for a project, summarizing). – Translating the information into English for some purpose. – Making notes for one's own purposes in English or the target language (from lectures, instructions, or written information). – Discussing the information with others in English or the target language. – Reacting to the information in speech or in writing in English or the target language.		– Giving information in spoken or written form in the target language on the basis of personal experience (e.g. giving a talk, report, or set of instructions, filling in a form, writing a diary).	– Listening to or reading or viewing a story, poem, play, feature, etc. and responding to it personally in some way in English or the foreign language. – Creating stories, poems, plays, features, etc. through speech or writing in the foreign language.

- to monitor and evaluate their own learning process and styles of work, as well as the products they lead to;
- to record their knowledge for themselves in appropriate ways;
- to elicit rules from language in use, and to discuss their hypotheses with others;
- to build up a folder of completed written work and a personal bank of cassettes of spoken work as testimony to their progress.

Language awareness and cultural awareness goals The ALL project proposes that classroom LOTE learning should enable learners not only to experience another language and culture through engaging in communicative activities, but also to reflect upon this experience, and through this derive a growing awareness about the nature and role of language and of culture in their daily life. LOTE learning should aim to enable the learner:

- to have some understanding of the functions of language in everyday life;
- to have some understanding of the systematic nature of language and the way it works;
- to have some understanding of the way language adapts to context;
- to understand accent, dialect, register, and other forms of language variation;
- to understand how language grows, borrows, changes, falls into disuse, and dies;
- to understand the development and nature of literacy;
- to have some understanding of how language is learnt (both an L1 and L2);
- to understand that language is a manifestation of culture;
- to understand cultural variation and the enriching nature of diversity.

The content to be covered and converted into process activities

Three sorts of syllabus content are envisaged:

- goal-oriented content that is common to all learners of a particular LOTE
- content that is judged to be inherently valuable and enriching in itself, whether or not it seems to lead directly to predetermined goals

– content that reflects the aspirations and interests of particular students or groups of students

It is argued that communicative goal-oriented content for each Stage in each LOTE should be worked out in such a way as to enable learners to learn:

– how to 'act' through the target language
– how to 'mean' in the target language
– how to 'say' in the target language
– how to 'sound' and 'spell' in the target language

This implies that the goal-oriented content can perhaps best be set out in terms of:

– communicative activities
– meanings
– language exponents based on a grammar and a vocabulary
– phonological and graphological features

To which we have to add:

– strategies for compensating for ignorance and repairing break-downs

It is the activities selected that should give rise to the meanings, and it is these latter that should then give rise to the language exponents, to a grammar and a vocabulary, and to the phonological and graphological features, each of which in its turn may become a focus of attention at some point or points during a course.

In order to guide the elaboration of a list of communicative activities as goals deriving from the seven activity types set out earlier, it is suggested that it may be helpful to think through the various categories listed below and establish check-lists of likely content:

– the socio-cultural contexts in which the target language is likely to be used by the learners;
– the roles the learners are likely to have to play through the target language, and the range of relationships they are likely to enter into with members of the target language speech community;
– the themes and topics likely to be embodied in their target language use;
– the modes of communication likely to be encountered or required in the target language;
– the text types likely to be encountered in the target language;

— the skills and sub-skills that are likely to be drawn upon in the use of the target language.

In order to assist a focus on meanings, it is suggested that check-lists, covering common communicative functions, common general notions, and common features of textual coherence, should be set out.

Language exponents, and the grammatical and lexical systems on which they are based, will emerge as a result of prior decisions as to what activities and which meanings are to be included.

It is likely that an almost complete set of phonological features in the target language will be met in the very first Stage of a course, but productive mastery of these is expected to be gradual and to represent a restructuring of L1 habits towards the target language conventions. In nearly all languages there are particular phonological features which will cause trouble to speakers of certain L1s. Similarly, both the formation of letters and characters in languages with non-Roman scripts, and the sound-spelling (or sound-character) relationships in all languages will cause problems in particular places. It may be helpful for syllabus planners to indicate these in advance, so that some focus of attention can be placed upon them at the appropriate moment.

It is also suggested that a check-list of receptive and productive strategies for compensating for ignorance, and for repairing breakdowns, should be set out to assist teachers to focus upon them as and when required.

Principles for grading communicative activities might embody the following criteria:

— That which permits the language user to bring his/her experience of life to bear upon the solution of a problem is easier than that which calls for action that lies outside his/her experience.
— That which permits the language user to refer to concrete things in the context, or to personal experiences, is likely to be easier than that which demands a level of abstraction from the concrete and the personal.
— If the language user can draw support from someone or something in the context in the solution of problems, a task is easier than when he/she cannot (that is, when a sympathetic interlocutor is there to help, or where a dictionary or glossary is available, or where questions are so phrased as to assist learners to find the answers to them etc.).

— Where there is little cognitive demand on the learners a task is likely to be easier than when a high level of thought has to be applied.
— Where the speech or written text to be understood is easy to process linguistically (that is, contains few subordinate clauses or embeddings, and is conceptually easy to follow), then an activity is likely to be easier than when it is not.

Functions cannot really be graded in any very satisfactory way, since it is not the functions themselves that are being learnt, but the forms that realize them, and there is no one-to-one relationship between functions and forms.

It would seem sensible to suggest that for productive purposes functions should be covered in the beginner Stage with simple highly generalizable formulae. They should reappear in more demanding contexts in subsequent Stages, thus helping the learner to build up an ever-expanding, ever more context-sensitive communicative resource to fulfil them.

In order to go beyond goal-oriented work, and to devise other inherently valuable and enriching communicative activities, teachers are asked to consult the GLAFLL project's framework of communication areas (see page 167) or Clark and Hamilton 1984). These will, of course, need to be reviewed in the light of the Australian context.

It is, of course, not possible to predict that part of the syllabus whose content is designed to reflect the aspirations and interests of particular students. This remains a matter for teacher and learner negotiation.

Given the need for communicative data, communicative experiences, and for deliberate focuses on forms, meanings, skills, etc., all duly integrated, there is a need to envisage four sorts of process activities:

— process activities of a communicative goal-oriented nature
— process-activities of a communicative nature that are inherently enriching or that reflect learner aspirations and wishes
— pre-communicative process activities that are form-focused, skill-focused, or that engage particular strategies, related to the communicative activities that they prepare for
— post-communicative process activities that focus on particular forms, skills, or strategies that individual learners have problems with

Each of the above will have its own associated methodological strategies and activity types.

The Syllabus Guidelines conclude by providing a series of suggestions in English for a syllabus in a European language to cover the various Stages in the ALL project's framework.

7.6   Assessment at Year 12

Assessment at Year 12 in Australia is used to determine entrance to higher education and to employment, and is thus a crucial area of concern to students and teachers, and therefore to the ALL project.

Fortunately, the concept of trying to create some common framework for LOTE assessment across the various State examination boards had already found favour among examination administrators and LOTE panels, and a National Consultative Group on Year 12 Language Assessment was in fact set up at the same time as the ALL Project.

Under the existing arrangements each State has to organize syllabus panels and examiners to produce syllabuses and examinations in anything up to 30 different languages, although for some of these there might only be a handful of candidates each year in each State. Given an agreed common framework for assessment at year 12, it was thought that it might be possible to rationalize this system, and have co-ordination across States in the creation of syllabuses and examinations, so that the responsibility for work on each LOTE, (particularly on those with smallish numbers of candidates), might be undertaken by one particular State on behalf of the others. It was thought that this might greatly reduce the costs of administering LOTE examinations in general.

The ALL project was able to co-operate with the National Consultative Group on Year 12 Language Assessment, which brought together representatives from the various State Examination Boards. This collaboration was particularly fruitful, and led to the production of a report outlining a national framework for syllabuses and assessment work at Year 12 (Report of the Third National Consultation on Year 12 Languages: Syllabus and Assessment 1986). The report has embodied the framework of Stages and the principles for syllabus design proposed by the ALL project team. Thus the attempt to work in co-operation across States towards the achievement of a common framework of reference for curriculum renewal is now under way, despite the problems of distance and the strong tradition of State independence in Australia. There seems to be a general climate of willingness among LOTE teachers to pool expertise and to co-ordinate energies across languages, across sectors of education, and across States, and to use the ALL project as one of the means of working together towards the improvement of LOTE teaching and learning in schools.

7.7 Conclusion

The present ALL project team is currently completing the first draft of the materials outlined on page 199. It is to be hoped that an effective level of State participation in the creation of language-specific sylllabuses, of appropriate teaching/learning material, and of year 12 assessments, based on the ALL project guidelines, can now be realized, and that this will involve as many groups as possible. It is now also crucial that an effective level of in-service education in each State is assured to assist all those concerned to undertake the various interrelated tasks, so that rhetoric becomes reality.

I hope that the particular integrative model of curriculum renewal and of curriculum design set out in the ALL project can be put to the test in Australia, so that further insights can be drawn for other similar ventures, and further experience gained as to how best to reconcile the manifest need for structure, planned continuity, and accountability in teaching and learning, with the equally important need for space, flexibility, and innovation along the way.

Bibliography

Adelman, C. 1976. 'On First Hearing.' Mimeo. Reading, Berks: Bulmershe College of Higher Education.
Adelman, C. and **R. J. Alexander.** 1982. *The Self-Evaluation Institution: Practice and Principles in the Management of Educational Change.* London: Methuen.
Allen, J. P. B. 1983. 'A Three-Level Curriculum Model for Second Language Education.' *Canadian Modern Language Review* 40:23–43.
Allwright, R. L. 1979. 'Abdication and responsibility in language teaching.' *Studies in Second Language Acquisition* 2/1:105–21.
Altman, H. B. 1979. 'Foreign language teaching: Focus on the learner.' *AILA Conference Proceedings.* Oxford: Pergamon Press. Reprinted in H. B. Altman and C. V. James (eds.) 1980: *Foreign Language Teaching: Meeting Individual Needs.* Oxford: Pergamon Press.
Aplin, T. R. W., J. W. Crawshaw, E. A. Roselman, and **A. L. Williams.** 1981. *Introduction to Language.* Sevenoaks: Hodder and Stoughton.
Asher, J. J. 1969. 'The total physical response technique of learning.' *Journal of Special Education* 3:253–62.
Asher, J. J., J. Kusudo, and **R. de la Torre.** 1974. 'Learning a second language through commands: the second field test.' *Modern Language Journal* 58:24–32.
Atkin, J. M. 1968. 'Behavioural objectives in curriculum design: a cautionary note.' *The Science Teacher* 35/5:27–30.
Austin, J. L. 1962. *How to Do Things with Words* (Harvard University William James Lecture, 1955). London: Oxford University Press.
Australian Language Levels Project Brochure. 1985. Obtainable from ALL Project, Languages and Multicultural Centre, 139 Grote Street, Adelaide 5000, South Australia.

Bailey, N., C. Madden, and **S. Krashen.** 1974. 'Is there a natural sequence in adult second language learning?' *Language Learning* 24/2:235–43.
Bantock, G. H. 1968. 'The culture of the schools' in T. Horton and P. Raggat (eds.): *Challenge and Change in the Curriculum.* Sevenoaks/Milton Keynes: Hodder and Stoughton/Open University.
Beeby, C. E. 1973, *The Quality of Education in Developing Countries.* Cambridge, Ma and Oxford: Harvard University Press and Oxford University Press.

Bergentoft, R. 1981. 'School education: report on the application of the principles of communicative language learning systems development in schools in Europe' in Council of Europe (1981).

Bialystok, E. 1978. 'A theoretical model of second language learning.' *Language Learning* 28/1:69–83.

Bialystok, E. 1981. 'The role of conscious strategies in second language proficiency.' *Modern Language Journal* 65:24–35.

Birckbichler, D. W. 1977. 'Communication and beyond' in J. K. Phillips (ed.): *The Language Connection: From the Classroom to the World.* Skokie, Illinois: National Textbook Co.

Block, J. H. (ed.) 1971. *Mastery Learning: Theory and Practice.* New York: Holt, Rinehart and Winston.

Bloom, B. S. (ed.) 1956. *Taxonomy of Educational Objectives Handbook 1: Cognitive Domain.* London: Longmans Green.

Bloom, B. S. 1971. 'Mastery learning' in Block (ed.) 1971.

Bloom, B. S. 1976. *Human Characteristics and School Learning.* New York: McGraw Hill.

Bloom, B. S. 1978. 'Educational Leadership: New Views of the Learner.' Paper presented as a General Session address at the ASCD Annual Conference, San Francisco, 1978.

Boomer, G. (ed.) 1982 *Negotiating the Curriculum.* Sydney: Ashton Scholastic.

Boyd, W. 1956. *Emile for Today: The Emile of Jean-Jacques Rousseau* (selected, translated, and interpreted by W. Boyd). London: Heinemann.

Breen, M. P. and **C. N. Candlin.** 1980. 'The essentials of a communicative curriculum in language teaching.' *Applied Linguistics* 1/2:89–112.

Breen, M. P., C. N. Candlin, and **A. Waters.** 1979. 'Communicative materials design: some basic principles.' *RELC Journal* 10/2.

British Overseas Trade Board. 1979. *Foreign Languages for Overseas Trade.* London: BOTB.

Brown, G. and **G. Yule.** 1981 and 1982. 'Assessment of Competence in Spoken English.' Mimeo. University of Edinburgh, Department of Linguistics.

Brown, S., D. McIntyre, E. Drever, and **J. K. Davies.** 1976. *Innovations: Teachers' Views* (Stirling Educational Monographs No. 2). Strathclyde: University of Stirling.

Brumfit, C. J. 1979a. 'Accuracy and fluency as polarities in foreign language teaching materials and methodology.' *Bulletin CILA* 29:89–99.

Brumfit, C. J. 1979b. 'Communicative language teaching: an educational perspective' in C. J. Brumfit and K. Johnson (eds.): *The Communicative Approach to Language Teaching.* Oxford: Oxford University Press.

Brumfit, C. J. 1980. 'From defining to designing: communicative specification versus communicative methodology in foreign language teaching.' *Studies in Language Acquisition* 3/1:1–9.

Brumfit, C. J. 1981a. 'Notional syllabuses revisited: a response.' *Applied Linguistics* 2/1:90–92.

Brumfit, C. J. 1981b. 'Accuracy and fluency – a fundamental distinction for communicative teaching methodology.' *Practical English Teaching* 1/3:6–7.

Brumfit, C. J. 1984. *Communicative Methodology in Language Teaching: The Roles of Fluency and Accuracy.* Cambridge: Cambridge University Press.

Buckby, M. 1976. 'A Unit-Credit Scheme in Modern Languages for York?' Mimeo. University of York, Language Teaching Centre.

Buckby, M., P. Bull, R. Fletcher, P. Green, B. Page, and **D. Roger.** 1981. *Graded Objectives and Tests for Modern Languages: An Evaluation.* University of York, Schools Council.

Burstall, C. 1975. 'Factors affecting foreign language learning: a consideration of some recent research findings.' *Language Teaching and Linguistics Abstracts* 8:5–25.

Burstall, C., M. Jamieson, S. Cohen, and **M. Hargreaves.** 1974. *Primary French in the Balance.* Slough: National Foundation for Educational Research.

Byram, M. 1978. 'New objectives in language teaching.' *Modern Languages* LIX/4:205.

Byrne, D. and **S. Rixon.** 1979. *Communication Games* (ELT Guide 1). London/Slough: The British Council/National Foundation for Educational Research.

Canale, M. 1983. 'From communicative competence to communicative language pedagogy' in J. C. Richards and R. W. Schmidt (eds.): *Language and Communication.* London: Longman (1983).

Canale, M. and **M. Swain.** 1980. 'Theoretical bases of communicative approaches to second-language teaching and testing.' *Applied Linguistics* 1/1:1–47.

Cane, B. 1969. *In-Service Training: A Study of Teachers' Views and Preferences.* Slough: National Foundation for Educational Research.

Caré, J. M. 1980. *Iles.* Paris: BELC.

Carroll, B. J. 1980. *Testing Communicative Performance.* Oxford: Pergamon Press.

Carroll, D. J. 1980. Articles in *New Approaches to Teaching English: Report on Bangalore Project 1979–80.* Regional Institute of English, Bangalore, South India.

Carroll, J. B. 1963. 'A model of school learning.' *Teachers College Record* 64:723–33.

Carroll, J. B. 1971. 'Problems of measurement related to the concept of learning for mastery' in Block (ed.) 1971.

Carroll, J. B. 1981. 'Conscious and automatic processes in language learning.' *Canadian Modern Language Review* 37/3:462–74.

Carroll, J. B. and S. Sapon. 1959. *Modern Language Aptitude Test.* New York: New York Psychological Corporation.

Chapman, D. 1980. 'Graded levels of achievement in foreign language learning.' *Modern Languages in Scotland* 19:62–75.

Chastain, K. 1975. 'An examination of the basic assumptions of individualised instruction.' *Modern Language Journal* LIX/7:334–44.

Cherry, C. (ed.) 1956. *Information Theory.* Sevenoaks: Butterworth.

Clark, J. L. 1967. 'A Psycholinguistic Approach to Motivation and Learning.' Dip. App. Ling. dissertation, University of Edinburgh.

Clark, J. L. 1969. 'Competence and performance: the missing links.' *Audio-Visual Language Journal* 7/1:31–6.

Clark, J. L. 1977. 'Certification – a way forward?' *Modern Languages in Scotland* 13:89–93.

Clark, J. L. 1979a. 'The syllabus: what should the learner learn?' *Audio-Visual Language Journal* 17/2:99–108.

Clark, J. L. 1979b. 'Syllabus design for graded levels of achievement in foreign language learning.' *Modern Languages in Scotland* 18:25–39.

Clark, J. L. 1980. 'Lothian Region's project on graded levels of achievement in foreign language learning.' *Modern Languages in Scotland* 19:61–74.

Clark, J. L. 1984. 'Reflections on Grade-Related Criteria.' Mimeo. Edinburgh: Moray House College of Education.

Clark, J. L. 1985. 'Curriculum Renewal in School Foreign Language Learning: A Project in Context. Volumes 1 and 2.' Ph.D. thesis, University of Edinburgh.

Clark, J. L. (forthcoming). *Change in the Foreign Language Curriculum: The Scottish Experience* (working title). London: Centre for Information on Language Teaching and Research.

Clark, J. L. and J. Hamilton. 1984. *Syllabus Guidelines: Parts 1, 2 and 3: A Graded Communicative Approach Towards School Foreign Language Learning.* London: Centre for Information on Language Teaching and Research.

Clark, J. L., A. Scarino, and P. Morley. 1986. *Australian Language Levels Project. Stage 2: Draft Guidelines (February 1986).* Adelaide, South Australia: Languages and Multicultural Centre.

Clarke, J. (ed.) 1980. *Graded French Tests.* London: Nelson.

Collis, K. F. and J. B. Biggs. 1979. *Classroom Examples of Cognitive Development Phenomena: The SOLO Taxonomy.* University of Tasmania.

Corbishley, P. 1977. 'Research findings on teaching groups in secondary schools' in B. Davies and R. G. Cave: *Mixed Ability in the Secondary School*. London: Ward Lock (1977).

Corder, S. P. 1978. 'Language-learner language' in J. C. Richards (ed.): *Understanding Second and Foreign Language Learning: Issues and Approaches*. Rowley, MA: Newbury House.

Corder, S. P. 1981. *Error Analysis and Interlanguage*. Oxford: Oxford University Press.

Corder, S. P. (undated). 'Some Problems in the Design of a Functional Syllabus.' Mimeo. University of Edinburgh, Department of Applied Linguistics.

Coste, D., J. Courtillon, V. Ferenczi, M. Martins-Baltar, and **E. Papo.** 1976. *Un Niveau Seuil*. Strasbourg: Council of Europe.

Council of Europe. 1973. *Systems Development in Adult Language Learning: A European Unit/Credit System for Modern Language Learning By Adults*. Strasbourg: Council of Europe.

Council of Europe. 1981. *Modern Languages (1971–1981)*. Strasbourg: Council of Europe.

Council of Europe. 1982. *Recommendation No R(82)18 (1982)*. Strasbourg: Council of Europe.

Craik, F. I. M. and **R. S. Lockhart.** 1972. 'Levels of processing; a framework for memory research.' *Journal of Verbal Learning and Verbal behaviour* 11:671–6.

Crispin, A. (forthcoming). 'Co-ordinated resources for modern languages (CORM)' in Clark (ed.) (forthcoming).

Crosland, C. A. R. 1974. 'Comprehensive education' in *Socialism Now and Other Essays*. London: Jonathan Cape.

Cross, D. 1980. 'Personalised language learning' in H. B. Altman and C. V. James (eds.): *Foreign Language Teaching: Meeting Individual Needs*. Oxford: Pergamon Press.

Cumming, M. 1986a. *Hear-Say: Listening Tasks for French*. Basingstoke: Macmillan Education.

Cumming, M. 1986b. *Hear-Say: Listening Tasks for German*. Basingstoke: Macmillan Education.

Cumming, M. 1986c. *Hear-Say: Listening Tasks for Spanish*. Basingstoke: Macmillan Education.

Cumming, M. and **D. Mullen.** 1985. *Spanish for Real*. Basingstoke: Macmillan Education.

Dakin, J. 1973. *The Language Laboratory and Language Learning*. London: Longman.

Daunt, P. 1973. *Comprehensive Values*. London: Heinemann.

Davidson, J. M. C. 1973. 'A common system of examination at 16+: some reactions to the Schools Council Bulletin No. 23.' *Modern Languages* 54/1:14–22.

Dearden, R. F., P. H. Hirst, and R. S. Peters. 1972. *Education and the Development of Reason.* London: Routledge and Kegan Paul.

Debyser, F. 1980. 'L'immeuble.' *Le français dans le monde* 156:19–25.

Department of Education and Science. 1977. *Modern Languages in Comprehensive Schools.* HMI Series: Matters for Discussion 3. London: HMSO.

Dickinson, L. 1978. 'Autonomy, self-directed learning and individualisation' in *ELT Documents 103: Individualisation in Language Learning.* London: The British Council.

Dickson, C. 1979. 'The state of modern languages.' *Centre for Educational Sociology Newsletter 5.* University of Edinburgh, Centre for Educational Sociology.

Di Pietro, R, J. 1976. 'Contrastive patterns of language use: a conversational approach.' *Canadian Modern Language Review* 33/1:49–61.

Di Pietro, R. J. 1978. 'Verbal strategies, script theory and conversational performances in ESL' in C. H. Blatchford and J. Schachter (eds.): *On TESOL 1978.* Washington, D.C.: TESOL.

Dodson, C. J. 1983. 'Bilingualism, language teaching and learning.' *British Journal of Language Teaching* 21/1:3–8.

Donaldson, M. 1978. *Children's Minds.* Glasgow: Fontana/Collins.

Downes, P. J. 1978. 'Graded examinations for elementary language learners: The Oxfordshire Project.' *Modern Languages* LIX/3:153–6.

Dunning Report: see Scottish Education Department (1977b).

Early, P. and R. Bolitho. 1981. 'Reasons to be cheerful, or helping teachers to get problems into perspective: A group counselling approach to the in-service teacher training of foreign language teachers of English. *System* 9/2:113–24.

Elliott, J. 1976. *Developing Hypotheses about Classrooms from Teachers' Practical Constructs.* University of North Dakota Press.

Elliott, J. 1982. 'Implications of classroom research for professional development' in V. Lee and D. Zeldin (eds.): *Planning in the Curriculum.* Sevenoaks: Hodder and Stoughton.

Ellis, R. 1981. 'The role of input in language acquisition: some implications for second language training.' *Applied Linguistics* 2/1:70–82.

Ellis, R. 1983. 'The origins of interlanguage.' *Applied Linguistics* 3/3:207–23.

Eraut, M. 1972. *In-Service Education for Innovation.* Occasional Paper 4. National Council for Educational Technology.

Ervin-Tripp, S. 1978. 'Is second language learning like the first?' in E. M. Hatch: *Second Language Acquisition: A Book of Readings.* Rowley, MA: Newbury House.

244 *Bibliography*

Eysenck, H. J. 1972. 'Comments on Arthur R. Jensen's "Do schools cheat minority children?" ' *Educational Research* 14/2:95–7.

Fairbairn, K. and **C. Pegolo.** 1983. *Foreign Languages in Secondary Schools, Report No. 3: Opinions of Year 12 Students on Foreign Languages in Queensland Secondary Schools.* Queensland, Australia: Queensland Department of Education, Research Branch.

Gardner, R. C. and **W. E. Lambert.** 1959. 'Motivational variables in second language acquisition.' *Canadian Journal of Psychology* 13/4:266–72.

Garner, E. 1981. 'Background studies and graded examinations.' *NALA (Journal of the National Association of Language Advisers)* 12:9–10.

Garside, T. 1982. 'What graded objectives has meant to us.' *GOML Newsletter* 6, April 1982. London: Centre for Information on Language Teaching and Research.

Gary, J. O. and **N. Gary.** 1981. 'Caution: talking may be dangerous to your linguistic health.' *International Review of Applied Linguistics* 19:1–14.

Geddes, M. and **J. McAlpin.** 1978. 'Activity options in language courses.' ELT Documents 103: *Individualisation in Language Learning.* London: The British Council.

Geddes, M. and **G. Sturtridge.** 1979. *Listening Links.* London: Heinemann.

Geddes, M. and **G. Sturtridge.** 1982a. *Reading Links.* London: Heinemann.

Geddes, M. and **G. Sturtridge** (eds.) 1982b. *Individualisation.* Oxford: Modern English Publications.

Geddes, M. and **R. White.** 1978. 'The use of semi-scripted simulated authentic speech and listening comprehension.' *Audio-Visual Language Journal* 16/3:137–45.

Gide, A. 1897. *Les Nourritures Terrestres.* Paris: Gallimard (1947).

Glaser, R. 1963. 'Instructional technology and the measurement of learning outcomes: some questions.' *American Psychologist* 18:519–21.

Gordon, K. L. 1980. 'Oxfordshire Modern Languages Achievement Certificate.' *Modern Languages in Scotland* 19:99–114.

Green, P. S. (ed.) 1975. *The Language Laboratory in School: Performance and Prediction. The York Study.* Edinburgh: Oliver and Boyd.

Grice, H. P. 1975. 'Logic and conversation' in P. Cole and J. Morgan (eds.): *Syntax and Semantics 3: Speech Acts.* New York: Academic Press.

Grittner, F. M. 1975. 'Individualised instruction: an historical perspective.' *Modern Language Journal* 59/7:323–33.

Bibliography 245

Gronlund, N. E. 1973. *Preparing Criterion-Referenced Tests for Classroom Instruction*. New York: Macmillan.
Groot, P. and A. Harrison. 1982. *A Specimen Test of Threshold Level Proficiency in English*. Strasbourg: Council of Europe.
Guiora, A. Z., C. L. Brannon, and C. Y. Dull. 1972. 'Empathy and second language learning.' *Language Learning* 22/1:111–30.

Halliday, M. A. K. 1973. *Explorations in the Functions of Language*. London: Edward Arnold.
Halliday, M. A. K. 1978. *Language as Social Semiotic*. London: Edward Arnold.
Halliday, M. A. K., A. McIntosh, and P. Strevens. 1964. *The Linguistic Sciences and Language Teaching*. London: Longman.
Hamilton, D., D . Jenkins, C. King, B. Macdonald, and M. Parlett. 1977. *Beyond the Numbers Game*. Basingstoke: Macmillan Education.
Hamilton, J. 1984a. *Corresponding with a French Pen-Friend*. Basingstoke: Macmillan Education.
Hamilton, J. 1984b. *Corresponding with a German Pen-Friend*. Basingstoke: Macmillan Education.
Hamilton J. and J. Clearie. 1985. *Take Your Partners: French Pairwork Exercises*. Basingstoke: Macmillan Education.
Hamilton J. and M. Cumming. 1984. *Corresponding with a Spanish Pen-Friend*. Basingstoke: Macmillan Education.
Hamilton J. and M. Cumming. 1985. *Take Your Partners: Pictorial Pairwork Exercises*. Basingstoke: Macmillan Education.
Hamilton J. and P. Wheeldon. 1985. *Take Your Partners: German Pairwork Exercises*. Basingstoke: Macmillan Education.
Hamilton J. and P. Wheeldon. 1986a. *The French Writing Folio*. Basingstoke: Macmillan Education.
Hamilton J. and P. Wheeldon. 1986b. *The German Writing Folio*. Basingstoke: Macmillan Education.
Hamilton, J., M. Harris, K. Jardine, and D. Meldrum. 1985. *French for Real*. Basingstoke: Macmillan Education.
Hamilton, J., J. Priester, S. Watkins, and P. Wheeldon. 1985. *German for Real*. Basingstoke: Macmillan Education.
Hanley, J. P., D. K. Whitelaw, E. W. Moo, and A. S. Walter. 1970. *Curiosity, Competence, Community, Man: A Course of Study, an Evaluation*. Cambridge, MA: Educational Development Center.
Harding, A. 1983. 'The grading of modern language learning objectives in the United Kingdom' in Council of Europe: *Contributions to a Renewal of Language Learning and Teaching: Some Current Work in Europe*. Strasbourg: Council of Europe.
Harding, A. and S. Honnor. 1974. 'Defined syllabuses in modern languages.' *Audio-Visual Language Journal* 12/3:157–64.
Harding, A. and J. A. Naylor. 1979. 'Graded objectives in second

language learning: a way ahead.' *Audio-Visual Language Journal* 17/3:169–74.

Harding, A. and **B. Page.** 1974. 'An alternative model for Modern Language examinations.' *Audio-Visual Language Journal* 12/3:237–41.

Harding, A., B. Page, and **S. Rowell.** 1980. *Graded Objectives in Modern Languages.* London: Centre for Information on Language Teaching and Research.

Hatch, E. M. 1974. 'Second language acquisition – universals?' *Working Papers on Bilingualism* 3:1–17.

Havelock, R. G. *et al.* 1973. *Planning for Innovation Through Dissemination and Utilisation of Knowledge.* Ann Arbor, Michigan: Centre for Research on Utilisation of Scientific Knowledge.

Hawkins, E. W. 1981. *Modern Languages in the Curriculum.* Cambridge: Cambridge University Press.

Hawkins, E. W. 1984. *Awareness of Language: An Introduction.* Cambridge: Cambridge University Press.

Her Majesty's Inspectorate. 1982. *A Survey of the Use of Graded Tests, of Defined Objectives, and Their Effect on the Teaching and Learning of Modern Languages in the County of Oxfordshire.* London: Department of Education and Science.

Higgs, T. V. (ed.) 1984. *Teaching for Proficiency: The Organising Principle.* Lincolnwood, Illinois: National Textbook Company/American Council on the Teaching of Foreign Languages.

Hill, C. P. 1977. Review of van Ek: *The Threshold Level. ELT Journal* 31/4:334–5.

Hirst, P. H. 1969. 'The logic of the curriculum.' *Journal of Curriculum Studies* 1/2:142–58.

Holec, H. 1980. 'Learner-centred communicative language teaching: needs analysis revisited.' *Studies in Second Language Acquisition* 3/1:26–33.

Hornsey, A. W. 1972. 'A foreign language for all?' *CILT Papers and Reports 8: Teaching Modern Languages Across the Ability Range.* London: Centre for Information on Language Teaching and Research.

Horton, T. and **P. Raggatt** (eds.) 1982. *Challenge and Change in the Curriculum.* Sevenoaks: Hodder and Stoughton.

Hosenfeld, C. 1975. 'The new student role: individual differences and implications for instruction.' *ACTFL Review of Foreign Language Instruction.* Lincolnwood, Illinois: National Textbook Co.

Howatt, A. P. R. 1979. 'Deliberate semantics: an interventionist approach to second language teaching methodology.' *CILA Bulletin* 29:5–22.

Howatt, A. P. R. 1984. *A History of English Language Teaching.* Oxford: Oxford University Press.

Howgego, J. 1971. 'Experiment in group teaching in modern languages.' *National Steering Committee for Modern Languages Bulletin* 3:11–16. Scottish Education Department.

Hoyle, E. 1973. 'Strategies of curriculum change' in R. Watkins (ed.): *In-Service Training: Structure and Content.* London: Ward Lock.

Hughes, A. and **C. Lascaratou.** 1982. 'Competing criteria for error gravity.' *ELT Journal* 36/3:175–82.

Hyltenstam, K. 1977. 'Implicational patterns in interlanguage syntax variation.' *Language Learning* 27/2:383–411.

Hymes, D. H. 1971. 'On communicative competence' in J. B. Pride and J. Holmes (eds.): *Sociolinguistics: Selected Readings.* Harmondsworth: Penguin Education, 1972.

Ingram, D. E. and **E. Wylie.** 1982. *Australian Second Language Proficiency Ratings (ASLPR).* Darwin, Australia: Darwin Community College.

Johnson, K. 1980a. 'Systematic and Non-Systematic Components in a Communicative Approach to Language Teaching.' Paper delivered at Berne Colloquium on Applied Linguistics.

Johnson, K. 1980b. 'Reactions to the seminar, South India, Bangalore' in Regional Institute of English: *New Approaches to Teaching English.* Bangalore, South India: Regional Institute of English.

Johnson, K. 1982. *Communicative Syllabus Design and Methodology.* Oxford: Pergamon Press.

Johnstone, R. M. 1972. 'Teaching modern languages to mixed-ability classes.' *Scottish Central Committee on Modern Languages Bulletin* 6:7–13. Scottish Education Department.

Johnstone, R. M. 1973. 'Should a foreign language be taught in mixed-ability or setted classes in S1 and S2 of a comprehensive school?' *Modern Languages in Scotland* 1:47–52.

Jones, B. 1979. 'Le jeu des colis.' *Audio-Visual Language Journal* 17/3:159–67.

Kelly, L. G. 1969. *25 Centuries of Language Teaching.* Rowley, MA: Newbury House.

Krashen, S. D. 1981. *Second Language Acquisition and Second Language Learning.* Oxford: Pergamon Press.

Krashen, S. D. 1982. *Principles and Practice in Second Language Acquisition.* Oxford: Pergamon Press.

Krashen, S. D. and **T. D. Terrell.** 1983. *The Natural Approach: Language Acquisition in the Classroom.* Oxford/New York: Pergamon/Alemany.

Krathwohl, D. R., B. S. Bloom, and **B. B. Masia.** 1964. *Taxonomy of*

Educational Objectives, Handbook II: Affective Domain. London: Longman.

Lamond, C. M. 1978. 'The Munn Report and Modern Languages.' Scottish Association for Language Teaching Newsletter 1.

Legutke, M. 1984. 'Project Airport, Part 1 and Part 2.' *Modern English Teacher* 11/4 and 12/1.

Littlewood, W. 1981. *Communicative Language Teaching: An Introduction.* Cambridge: Cambridge University Press.

Lothian Regional Study Group on Modern Languages. 1978/79. *Draft French, German, Spanish, Italian and Russian Syllabuses for S1 and S2.* Edinburgh: Lothian Region Education Department.

Lozanov, G. 1978. *Outlines of Suggestology and Suggestopedy.* New York: Gordon and Breach.

Macdonald, B. and **R. Walker.** 1976. *Changing the Curriculum.* London: Open Books.

MacMurray, J. (no date). 'Learning To Be Human.' Mimeo. Moray House Annual Public Lecture.

Mager, R. 1962. *Preparing Objectives for Programmed Instruction.* Palo Alto, CA: Fearon.

Maley, A. and **A. Duff.** 1978. *Drama Techniques in Language Learning.* Cambridge: Cambridge University Press.

Maley, A., A. Duff, and **F. Grellet,** 1980. *The Mind's Eye.* Cambridge: Cambridge University Press.

Martin, A. L. 1984. 'Scenarios for the Future of Graded Levels in Australia.' Paper delivered at AFMLTA Conference, Hobart, Tasmania, 1984.

McDonough, S. H. 1981. *Psychology in Foreign Language Teaching.* London: Allen and Unwin.

McGregor, D. M. 1961. 'The human side of enterprise' in W. G. Bennis, K. D. Benne, and R. Chin: *The Planning of Change.* New York and London: Holt, Rinehart and Winston.

McGregor, I. 1982. Talk on the use of the foreign language in the classroom. Given at the Scottish National Conference on Modern Languages, Jordanhill College of Education, Glasgow.

Miller, G. A. 1956. 'The magical number seven plus or minus two: some limits on our capacity for processing information.' *Psychological Review* 63:81–97.

Miller, G. A., E. Galanter, and **K. Pribram.** 1960. *Plans and the Structure of Behaviour.* London: Holt, Rinehart and Winston.

Ministère de l'Education Nationale. 1978. 'Arrêté du 28 décembre 1976: tolérances grammaticales ou orthographiques.' *Audio-Visual Language Journal* 16/1:19–24.

Mitchell, R., B. Parkinson, and **R. Johnstone.** 1981. 'The Foreign Language Classroom: An Observational Study.' *Stirling Educational Monographs* 9. University of Stirling.

Monippally, M. M. 1983. 'A Holistic Learning Model for Developing School Curricula in Foreign Languages.' Ph.D. thesis, University of Manchester.

Moore, S. and **A. L. Antrobus.** 1973. *Longman Audio Visual French.* London: Longman.

Morgan, J. and **M. Rinvolucri.** 1983. *Once Upon A Time.* Cambridge: Cambridge University Press.

Morrison, D. M. and **G. Low.** 1983. 'Monitoring and the second language learner' in J. C. Richards and R. W. Schmidt (eds.): *Language and Communication.* London: Longman.

Morrow, K. 1977. *Techniques of Evaluation for a Notional Syllabus.* Study commissioned by the Royal Society of Arts. RSA, John Adam Street, Adelphi, London WC2N 6EZ.

Moskowitz, G. 1978. *Caring and Sharing in the Foreign Language Class.* Rowley, MA: Newbury House.

Munn Report: see Scottish Education Department: (1977a).

Newmark, L. and **P. Reibel.** 1968. 'Necessity and sufficiency in language learning.' *International Review of Applied Linguistics* VI:145–61.

Nord, J. R. 1980. 'Developing listening fluency before speaking: an alternative paradigm.' *System* 8/1:1–22.

Norman, D. A. 1976. *Memory and Attention* (second edition). New York: John Wiley.

Ognyov, N. 1928. *The Diary of a Communist Schoolboy.* Quoted in Grittner (1975).

Oller, J. W. 1972. 'Cloze tests of second language proficiency and what they measure.' *Proceedings of the AILA Congress 1972.* Heidelberg: Julius Groos.

Olmsted-Gary, J. 1975. 'Delayed oral practice at the beginning of second language learning' in M. K. Burt and H. Dulay (eds.): *New Directions in Second Language Learning, Teaching and Bilingual Education.* Washington, D.C.: TESOL.

Oxfordshire Modern Languages Advisory Committee (OMLAC). 1978. *New Objectives in Modern Language Teaching: Defined Syllabuses and Tests in French and German.* Sevenoaks: Hodder and Stoughton.

Page, B. 1973. 'Another look at examinations.' *Audio-Visual Language Journal* 11/2:127–30.

Page, B. 1983. 'Graded objectives in modern language teaching.' *Language Teaching* 16/4:292–308.

Palmer, H. E. 1921. *The Principles of Language Study.* Republished 1964, ed. by R. Mackin. London: Oxford University Press.

Parkinson, B., R. Mitchell, and **R. Johnstone.** 1981. *Mastery Learning in Foreign Languages: A Case Study.* Stirling Educational Monographs No. 8. Department of Education, University of Stirling.

Parlett, M. and **D. Hamilton.** 1972. 'Evaluation as illumination: a new approach to the study of innovatory programmes' in Hamilton *et al.* (eds.) 1977.

Paulston, C. B. 1971. 'The sequencing of structural pattern drills.' *TESOL Quarterly* 5/3:197–208.

Paulston, C. B. 1981. 'Notional syllabuses revisited: some comments.' *Applied Linguistics* 2/1:93–5.

Peck, A. J. 1969. 'Talking to some purpose (Choosing the language-teaching points of the Nuffield/Schools Council German course)' in G. E. Perren and J. L. M. Trim (eds.): *Applications of Linguistics.* Cambridge: Cambridge University Press.

Peel, E. A. 1971. *The Nature of Adolescent Judgement.* London: Staples Press.

Perren, G. E. 1972. Introductory paper, *CILT Reports and Papers 8: Teaching Modern Languages Across the Ability Range.* London: Centre for Information on Language Teaching and Research.

Peters, R. S. 1966. *Ethics and Education.* London: George Allen and Unwin.

Piazza, L. G. 1980. 'French tolerance for grammatical errors made by Americans.' *Modern Language Journal* 64/4:422–7.

Pimsleur, P. 1968. 'Language aptitude testing' in A. Davies (ed.): *Language Testing Symposium.* London: Oxford University Press.

Pimsleur, P., D. M. Sunderland, and **R. D. McIntyre.** 1963. 'Underachievement in foreign language learning.' *International Review of Applied Linguistics* II:113–50.

Plato. *The Republic.* Translated by H. D. P. Lee, 1955. Harmondsworth: Penguin.

Popham, W. J. 1983. Public lecture delivered at Moray House College of Education, Edinburgh.

Porcher, L. 1980. *Interrogations sur les besoins langagiers en contextes scolaires.* Strasbourg: Council of Europe.

Postovsky, V. A. 1974. 'Effect of delay in oral practice at the beginning of second language learning.' *Modern Language Journal* 85/5–6:229–39.

Prabhu, N. S. 1980a. 'Teaching English as communication. Proposals for syllabus design, methodology and evaluation.' *Newsletter* 1/4. Regional Institute of English, South India, Bangalore.

Prabhu, N. S. 1980b. 'Theoretical background to the Bangalore Project' and 'Methodological foundations of the Bangalore Project' in *New Approaches to Teaching English.* Regional Institute of English, South India, Bangalore.

Prabhu, N. S. 1982a. 'The Communicative Teaching Project, South India: Outline.' Mimeo. Regional Institute of English, South India, Bangalore.

Prabhu, N. S. 1982b. *Communicational Teaching Project Madras: Some Lesson Reports*. Regional Institute of English, South India, Bangalore.

Raths, J. D. 1971. 'Teaching without specific objectives.' *Educational Leadership*, April 1971: 714–20.

Richards, J. C. 1983. 'Communicative needs in foreign language teaching.' *ELT Journal* 37/2:111–20.

Richterich, R. 1973a. 'Comment définir des besoins de communication.' Paper given at AILA/BAAL seminar, Lancaster March/April 1973.

Richterich, R. 1973b. 'Definition of language needs and types of adults' in Trim, Richterich, van Ek, and Wilkins (eds.) 1973.

Richterich, R. 1978. 'The analysis of language needs: illusion—pretext—necessity' in Council of Europe: *A European Unit/Credit System for Modern Language Learning by Adults*. Strasbourg: Council of Europe.

Rinvolucri, M. 1982. 'Awareness activities for teaching structures' in *ELT Documents* 113. London: The British Council.

Rivers, W. M. 1972. *Speaking With Many Tongues*. Rowley, MA: Newbury House.

Rixon, S. 1979. 'The information gap and the opinion gap: ensuring that communicative games are communicative.' *ELT Journal* 33/2:104–6.

Rogers, C. R. 1969. *Freedom to Learn*. Columbus, Ohio: Merrill.

Rubin, J. 1979. 'What the good language learner can teach us' in J. B. Pride (ed.): *Sociolinguistic Aspects of Language Learning and Teaching*. Oxford: Oxford University Press.

Rubin, J. 1981. 'Study of cognitive processes in second language learning.' *Applied Linguistics* 2/2:117–31.

Rudd, A. 1973. 'Local curriculum development' in R. Watkins (ed.): *In-Service Training: Structure and Content*. London: Ward Lock Educational.

Salter, M. V. 1972. 'A plea for realism in teaching slow learners.' *CILT Reports and Papers 8: Teaching Modern Language Across the Ability Range*. London: Centre for Information on Language Teaching and Research.

Savignon, S. J. 1972. *Communicative Competence: An Experiment in Foreign Language Teaching*. Philadelphia: The Center for Curriculum Development.

Savignon, S. J. 1981. 'Three Americans in Paris: a look at "natural" second language acquisition.' *The Modern Language Journal* 65/3:241–7.

Scherer, G. A. C. and **M. Wertheimer.** 1964. *A Psycholinguistic Experiment in Foreign Language Teaching*. New York: McGraw Hill.

252   Bibliography

Schon, D. A. 1971. *Beyond the Stable State: Public and Private Learning in a Changing Society*. Harmondsworth: Penguin.

Schools Council. 1966. *Working Paper No. 8: French in the Primary School*. London: HMSO.

Schools Council. 1974. *Vorwärts Stufe 1–5: Nachschlagewerk und Vokabeln*. Leeds: E. J. Arnold/Schools Council.

Schwab, J. J. 1964. 'Structure of the disciplines: meanings and significances' in G. W. Ford and L. Pugno (eds.): *The Structure of Knowledge and the Curriculum*. Chicago: Rand McNally.

Scottish Central Committee on Modern Languages. 1978. 'Survey of Scottish teacher opinion on the Munn and Denning Reports.' *Modern Languages in Scotland* 16:22–33.

Scottish Central Committee on Modern Languages. 1982. *Tour de France*. London: Heinemann.

Scottish Education Department. 1947. *Secondary Education: A Report of the Advisory Council in Education in Scotland*. Edinburgh: HMSO.

Scottish Education Department. 1965. *Circular No. 600: Reorganisation of Secondary Education on Comprehensive Lines*.

Scottish Education Department. 1966. *Circular No. 614*.

Scottish Education Department. 1967. *The Ruthven Report: Organisation of Courses Leading to the Scottish Certificate of Education*. Edinburgh: HMSO.

Scottish Education Department. 1968. *French in the Primary School: A Report of a Survey Carried Out by HMIs, between January and September 1968*. Edinburgh: HMSO.

Scottish Education Department (Consultative Committee on the Curriculum: Sub-committee chaired by J. Munn). 1977a. *The Structure of the Curriculum in the Third and Fourth Years of the Scottish Secondary School*. Edinburgh: HMSO.

Scottish Education Department (Committee chaired by J. Dunning). 1977b. *Assessment for All: Report of the Committee to Review Assessment in the Third and Fourth Years of Secondary Education in Scotland*. Edinburgh: HMSO.

Scottish Education Department. 1984. *16s–18s in Scotland: An Action Plan*. Edinburgh: Scottish Education Department.

Scottish Examination Board. 1985. *Arrangements for Standard Grade French*. Dalkeith, Midlothian: Scottish Examination Board.

Scriven, M. 1967. 'The methodology of evaluation' in R. W. Tyler, R. M. Gagné, and M. Scriven (eds.): *Perspectives of Curriculum Evaluation*. AERA Monograph Series on Curriculum Evaluation No. 1. Chicago: Rand McNally.

Searle, J. R. 1975. 'Indirect speech acts' in P. Cole and J. Morgan: *Syntax and Semantics Vol. 3: Speech Acts*. New York: Academic Press.

Senior Secondary Assessment Board of South Australia. 1986. Report of the Third National Consultation on Year 12 Languages: 'Syllabus and Assessment 1986: A National Framework for Syllabus and Assessment at Year 12 in Languages.' Obtainable from Mrs W. Sarre, SSABSA, 134 Fullarton Road, Rose Park, South Australia 5067.

Sidwell, D., D. Smith, and **B. Kavanagh.** 1983. 'Graded assessment and in-service education' in R. Dunning (ed.): *French for Communication.* The East Midlands Graded Assessment Feasibility Study. University of Leicester, School of Education.

Skilbeck, M. 1982a. 'Three educational ideologies' in T. Horton and P. Raggat (eds.) *Challenge and Change in the Curriculum.* Sevenoaks: Hodder and Stoughton.

Skilbeck, M. 1982b. 'School-based curriculum development' in V. Lee and D. Zeldin (eds.): *Planning in the Curriculum.* Sevenoaks: Hodder and Stoughton/Open University.

Stenhouse, L. 1970. 'Some limitations on the use of objectives in curriculum research and planning.' *Paedagogica Europaea* 6:73–83.

Stenhouse, L. 1975. *An Introduction to Curriculum Research and Development.* London: Heinemann Educational.

Stenhouse, L. 1980. *Curriculum Research and Development in Action.* London: Heinemann Educational.

Stern, H. H. 1975. 'What we can learn from the good language learner.' *Canadian Modern Language Review* 31:304–18.

Stern, H. H. 1983. *Fundamental Concepts of Language Teaching.* Oxford: Oxford University Press.

Stevick, E. 1976. *Memory, Meaning and Method.* Rowley, MA: Newbury House.

Stevick, E. 1980. *Teaching Languages; A Way and Ways.* Rowley, MA: Newbury House.

Swain, M. 1974. 'French immersion programs across Canada: research findings.' *Canadian Modern Language Review* 31:117–29.

Swain, M. 1978. 'French immersion: early, late or partial.' *Canadian Modern Language Review* 34:577–88.

Taba, H. 1962. *Curriculum Development: Theory and Practice.* New York: Harcourt, Brace and World.

Terrell, T. D. 1977. 'A natural approach to second language learning and acquisition.' *Modern Languages Journal* 61/7:325–37.

Terrell, T. D. 1980. 'The Natural Approach to Language Teaching: An Update.' Mimeo. University of California.

Tour de France: see Scottish Central Committee on Modern Languages, 1982.

Trim, J. L. M. 1973. 'Draft outline of a European unit-credit system for modern language learning by adults' in J. L. M. Trim *et al.* (1973).

Trim, J. L. M. 1978. *Some Possible Lines of Development of an Overall Structure for a European Unit-Credit Scheme for Foreign Language Learning by Adults.* Strasbourg: Council of Europe.

Trim, J. L. M. 1979. 'The Place of Needs Analysis in the Council of Europe Modern Languages Project.' Paper given at Pergamon Specialist Conference, April 1979, Oxford. Also in H. B. Altman and C. V. James (eds.): *Foreign Language Teaching: Meeting Individual Needs.* Oxford; Pergamon Press (1980).

Trim, J. L. M. 1981. 'What place should modern language learning have in the curriculum if it is to contribute to a soundly based secondary education?' in J. M. C. Davidson: *Issues in Language Education.* NCLE Papers and Reports 3. London: Centre for Information on Language Teaching and Research.

Trim, J. L. M., R. Richterich, J. A. van Ek, and D. A. Wilkins. 1973. *Systems Development in Adult Language Learning.* Strasbourg: Council of Europe.

Tyler, R. W. 1949. *Basic Principles of Curriculum and Instruction.* Chicago: University of Chicago Press.

Ur, P. 1981. *Discussions that Work: Task-Centred Fluency Practice.* Cambridge: Cambridge University Press.

Valdman, A. 1980. 'Communicative ability and syllabus design for global foreign language courses.' *Studies in Language Acquisition* 3/1:81–96.

van Ek, J. A. 1973. 'The "Threshold Level" in a unit-credit system' in Council of Europe 1973.

van Ek, J. A. 1975. *The Threshold Level.* Strasbourg: Council of Europe.

van Ek, J. A. 1978. *The Threshold Level for Modern Language Learning in Schools.* London: Longman.

Verrier, R. 1981. 'A case for consultancy' in J. Nixon (ed.): *A Teacher's Guide to Action Research, Evaluation, Enquiry, and Development in the Classroom.* London: Grant McIntyre.

Von Wittich, B. 1962. 'Prediction of success in foreign language study.' *Modern Language Journal* 46/5:208–12.

Welford, A. T. 1968. *Fundamentals of Skill.* London: Methuen.

Wheeldon, P. J. 1980. *German Waystage 1 and Spanish Waystage 1.* Edinburgh: Portobello High School.

Wheeldon, P. J. and J. Hamilton. 1977. 'Teaching Modern Languages in a Large City Comprehensive School.' Mimeo. Portobello High School, Edinburgh.

Whitehead, A. N. 1932. *The Aims of Education.* London: Ernest Benn. (Second edition 1950.)

Widdowson, H. G. 1978. *Teaching Language As Communication*. Oxford: Oxford University Press.

Widdowson, H. G. 1983. *Learning Purpose and Language Use*. Oxford: Oxford University Press.

Widdowson, H. G. 1984. 'Procedures for discourse processing' in Council of Europe: *Towards a More Comprehensive Framework for the Definition of Language Learning Objectives II*. Strasbourg: Council of Europe.

Wight, J., R. A. Norris, and **F. J. Worsley.** 1972. *Concept 7–9: Teachers' Manuals for Units 1, 2 and 3*. Leeds: E. J. Arnold/ Schools Council.

Wilds, C. P. 1975. 'The oral interview' in R. L. Jones and B. Spolsky (eds.): *Testing Language Proficiency*. Arlington, VA: Center for Applied Linguistics.

Wilkins, D. A. 1973. 'The linguistic and situational content of the common core in a unit/credit system' in Council of Europe 1973.

Wilkins, D. A. 1974a. 'Notional syllabuses and the concept of a minimum adequate grammar' in S. P. Corder and E. Roulet (eds.): *Linguistic Insights in Applied Linguistics*. Brussels: AIMAV/ Paris: Didier.

Wilkins, D. A. 1974b. *Second Language Learning and Teaching*. London: Edward Arnold.

Wilkins, D. A. 1976. *Notional Syllabuses*. London: Oxford University Press.

Wilkins, D. A. 1981. 'Notional syllabuses revisited: a further reply.' *Applied Linguistics* 2/1:96–100.

Wilkins, D. A. 1983. 'Some issues in communicative language teaching and their relevance to the teaching of languages in secondary schools' in K. Johnson and D. Porter (eds.): *Perspectives in Communicative Language Teaching*. London: Academic Press.

Index